THE
NEGOTIATOR
HANDBOOK

THE NEGOTIATOR'S HANDBOOK

GEORGE FULLER

PRENTICE HALL
Englewood Cliffs, New Jersey 07632

Prentice-Hall International (UK) Limited, *London*
Prentice-Hall of Australia Pty. Limited, *Sydney*
Prentice-Hall Canada, Inc., *Toronto*
Prentice-Hall Hispanoamericana, S.A. *Mexico*
Prentice-Hall of India Private Limited, *New Delhi*
Prentice-Hall of Japan, Inc., *Tokyo*
Simon & Schuster Asia Pte. Ltd., *Singapore*
Editora Prentice-Hall do Brasil, Ltda., *Rio de Janeiro*

© 1991 *by*

George Fuller

10 9 8 7 6 5 4 3 2

Library of Congress-in-Publication Data

Fuller, George.
Negotiator's handbook / by George Fuller.
p.   cm.

Includes index.
ISBN 0-13-612672-3. — ISBN 0-13-612664-2 (pbk.)
1. Negotiation in business—Handbooks, manuals, etc. I. Title.
HD58.6.F85   1991
658—dc20

90-23181
CIP

ISBN 0-13-612672-3

ISBN 0-13-612664-2 (PBK)

PRENTICE HALL
BUSINESS & PROFESSIONAL DIVISION
A division of Simon & Schuster
Englewood Cliffs, New Jersey 07632

PRINTED IN THE UNITED STATES OF AMERICA

INTRODUCTION

For those whose business and professional careers depend upon success in bargaining, negotiation knowledge is more than a nicety—it's a crucial necessity. And the list of jobs that require a mastery of negotiation skills encompass far more than labor negotiators, lawyers, and headline-making deal makers. In fact, the ability to negotiate a wide range of transactions is a vital element for success at any level of business management.

For example, corporate executives must make deals that can have a profound effect on the future course of a company. Meanwhile, middle managers are constantly engaged in activities which on a cumulative basis are equally important in meeting business objectives. Even people in supervisory and staff positions that don't appear to require negotiation expertise must wrestle on a daily basis with workplace issues such as salary demands, promotion requests, and union matters. Then, of course, there are those employed in purchasing, sales, and other professions where negotiation is a primary duty of their position.

In fact, wherever you work, and whatever you do, it's almost impossible to avoid the need to negotiate, at least on occasion. But unfortunately, negotiation is an area where many hidden traps lie waiting for the unwary. Sure, seat-of-the-pants techniques can be used to negotiate, but doing it that way comes with a golden guarantee that you'll end-up with the bad end of the bargain. Therefore, when you go up against a savvy negotiator, it pays to be prepared to protect your interests.

Knowing how to negotiate from "A" to "Z" has another benefit—and that's peace of mind. Frequently, people not well-versed in negotiation techniques conclude a deal and walk away thinking that they got a pretty good bargain, when in reality they didn't do very well at all. Sometimes, they live in bliss, never realizing they could have done much better.

More often, reality comes home to roost when subsequent events prove that what seemed like a good deal was instead a foolish mistake. However, those familiar with negotiation techniques can always bargain with confidence, knowing that they have the necessary skills to do the best job possible.

Unfortunately, negotiation hasn't always been given the recognition that it deserves as a fundamental skill that's essential for business success. This knowledge void has been partly filled by seminars and books on the subject. However, to some extent this has added to the confusion, since many of these books advocate different negotiation methods and techniques. That in itself is valuable, but it can foster the impression that there's one "right way" to negotiate, when the tactics and methods you use should vary to reflect the facts of any particular negotiation situation.

In reality, there are times when a "win/win" joint problem solving approach is appropriate, and other circumstances where a strict adversarial strategy is correct. In fact, switching from one technique to the other during a negotiation may be perfectly justifiable. The crux of the matter is that a good negotiator needs to use a "flexible response" strategy. That simply means that you should use every technique and strategy at your disposal to achieve your goals.

The purpose of this book is to provide a complete one-source reference containing all of the working tools you need to succeed as a negotiator no matter what position you hold, or what level of negotiation expertise you aspire to. It can serve as a complete guide on negotiation if you're relatively inexperienced in negotiation techniques, or a ready reference and refresher for veteran negotiators.

Equally important, *The Negotiator's Handbook* not only covers all of the standard strategies and techniques routinely used by professional negotiators, but also includes other key elements that are essential for negotiation success. These include often neglected topics such as pre-negotiation planning, necessary communication skills, how to conduct negotiation meetings, and what to do after you reach agreement—as well as how to proceed if negotiations fail.

Furthermore, it's important to recognize that different types of negotiations require distinctive techniques. Therefore, you'll find specific pointers for dealing with customers, suppliers, employees, bankers, agents, and others. And since negotiation sessions can get hectic, a detailed checklist is included for your use so that nothing is forgotten in the heat of battle.

Finally, it should be noted that no attempt has been made to advocate a particular method of negotiating. How to reach your negotiation goals is what this book is about, and a "flexible response" strategy is what is required. For this reason, the tactics included in this book are all-inclusive. Some of them may not suit either your style of negotiating or your ethical standards. However, to be unaware of them—and not know how to counter them—is foolhardy at best. After all, even if you're upfront and above board, people you negotiate with may be looking to gain the upper hand by any means possible. Therefore, knowing how the other party might negotiate is equally as important as knowing your own strategy. That's because, in the final analysis, your success as a negotiator rests upon being prepared for anything, and it's to that end that this book is written.

TABLE OF CONTENTS

Chapter Fourteen   How to Keep Negotiations from Stalling 232

Chapter Fifteen   Techniques for Closing Negotiations 244

PART IV   POST-NEGOTIATION STRATEGY

Chapter Sixteen   What to Do After You Reach Agreement 257

Part I

PLANNING FOR NEGOTIATIONS

Chapter 1

PRE-NEGOTIATION PLANNING

Successful negotiations start long before you sit down to bargain. In fact, no matter how skillful people are during negotiations, they're at a distinct disadvantage when going up against opponents who have done a better job of planning their objectives in advance. That's because to achieve your negotiation goals you have to not only know what you want, but also have a handle on what the other parties' objectives are.

In addition, long before you begin to bargain, you should decide what alternatives you have available if negotiations are unsuccessful, since the better the alternatives, the stronger your negotiation position will be. Needless to say, you should also make an assessment of the potential alternatives available to the opposition, since their willingness to bargain will partly depend upon what other options are available.

Something else to consider beforehand are your negotiation limits, or more specifically, what you're willing to give up to get what you want. It's easy, for example, if you're making a fairly common business purchase to decide what to pay for an item. Yet, sometimes even these seemingly routine transactions become more complex when you go to negotiate a price. All kinds of variables can come into play which may influence what you're willing to pay. However, if you haven't thought about it in advance, you may be inflexible about the price to your own detriment, or else be forced to do some quick juggling to arrive at a new figure which may result in an ill-conceived agreement.

On top of these factors, there are several aspects of negotiation planning that often get overlooked. These include how best to prepare written proposals, handle non-negotiable items, and perhaps most important—when you shouldn't negotiate at all. So let's look at each of the many elements that you have to think about before you even begin to negotiate.

1.1 WIN/WIN: WHY BEING NICE DOESN'T MEAN BEING NAIVE

It's certainly important to conduct your affairs in an ethical way, and to negotiate in what is commonly referred to as "good faith." There's general agreement that this means various forms of dishonesty aren't to be used. However, the hang-ups start over questions such as whether or not it's proper to withhold information, tell half-truths, and use similar borderline tactics.

Obviously, there are many circumstances where withholding information is valid by any standards. Proprietary data and confidential personnel files are a couple of obvious examples. On the other hand, what about information that the other party presumably needs to evaluate an offer you've made? Here, the question isn't quite so easy to answer and to a large extent it depends upon the facts of the case.

As for half-truths and other practices, it's an equally difficult task to define the line between unethical and acceptable. The bottom line is that each individual is the keeper of their own ethical standards. Consequently, where you draw the line between what are fair or unfair tactics is in the final analysis your decision. However, the standard you set for yourself will to some extent influence how you negotiate. (See section 5.1 on adapting your negotiation style to your personality.)

It's also important to be realistic in recognizing that people look at negotiations in many different ways. This often leads less experienced negotiators to make erroneous assumptions. How many times have you heard business associates say something such as, "He's trying to shaft me." or "They're trying to take advantage of us," or similar language. Actually, those statements may very well be true.

On the other hand, they may merely be a subjective opinion based upon the frustration of being unable to reach agreement on what one side considers to be fair terms. Here again, the value of establishing a negotiation plan rears its head. That's because if you carefully outline your objectives before you start to negotiate you won't be as susceptible to tricks that are tried to throw you off-balance. Instead, you can plow ahead toward agreement based on your goals, which makes it easier to ignore both the personalities and ploys of the opposition. In fact, it's when an objective isn't clearly established prior to negotiations that people become more susceptible to being manipulated.

All in all, there's nothing inherently wrong—and much to be applauded—in setting high standards for yourself in terms of your negotiation methods. However, to blithely assume that all of those you negotiate with share your views is naive. That's not to say that you can't negotiate based on that assumption, but if you do so it's imperative that you recognize that the other party may not be quite so altruistic.

Furthermore, just because others don't subscribe to your way of thinking doesn't mean that their method—as hard-nosed as it may be—is wrong. After all, in the final analysis, people you negotiate with are concerned first and foremost with their own interests and negotiate toward that end. Therefore, although it helps the negotiation process if you convince them that it's in the interests of both parties to be reasonable, your primary focus should be on reaching your own goals. After all, the other side is responsible for taking care of itself.

CAUTION: Your ethical standards can cause you problems during negotiations if you're not careful. For instance, you may find yourself getting angry at people who use what you consider to be unfair negotiation tactics. Despite how you may feel about this, it's important to separate the negotiation issues from the personality and ploys of those you negotiate with. Instead, concentrate on reaching the goals you set in your negotiation plans.

1.2 WHY ANYONE CAN NEGOTIATE FROM A POSITION OF STRENGTH

One of the most common mistakes made by inexperienced negotiators is believing they have to accept someone's terms because they have no other choice. If anything, this kind of attitude should instead be a clear signal *not to* agree to such an offer. Anytime you think your position is so weak that you may be forced to accept a patently unfair deal, then you're in trouble before you start. In all likelihood, you'll wind-up with an agreement that doesn't work out for you.

In fact, negotiations concluded under these circumstances often lead to problems for the other party as well. That's because someone who accepts a bad deal may have trouble performing their end of the bargain, and/or will be looking for a way out during the term of the contract.

It's situations such as these that ultimately lead to broken agreements, bankruptcies, lawsuits, and other forms of misfortune for both parties.

Therefore, the flip side of knowing when to say "No" to a bad deal is learning not to force one on the other party. Otherwise, they may not perform the agreement satisfactorily. (See Section 15.1 on quitting while you're ahead.)

The common view of negotiating from a position of strength is that you have a superior advantage over the other party which should allow you to get the deal you want. However, these assessments are often based on a combination of speculation and a failure to pre-plan negotiation strategy. A few examples of situations which on the surface might appear to give one side a clear advantage are:

- A large company negotiating with a small business.
- A bank when setting loan terms with a customer.
- A boss discussing a pay raise with a subordinate.
- A parent discussing allowances with a child.

On the surface, the large company, bank, boss, and parent would seem to be the party negotiating from a position of strength. Nevertheless, the small business may have a unique product, the bank customer may be a large and influential one, and the subordinate may be a "star" performer with offers in the wings. And of course, anyone who underestimates the ability of a child to turn apparent weakness into strength when negotiating with a parent is a fool waiting to be fleeced. In short, a weak position when negotiating is often based solely on surface perceptions without going any further. That is to say, if you assume you're in a weak bargaining position, that assumption will become a self-fulfilling prophecy.

A reasonable assessment of relative negotiating strengths and weaknesses can't be made without (1) establishing your negotiation objective—which in simplistic terms is deciding what you want and what you're willing to give up to get it, (2) estimating the bargaining chips your opponent holds, and (3) evaluating your alternatives if negotiations fail. Even then, if the odds appear to be overwhelmingly against you, that doesn't mean you don't have a fair shot at getting a reasonable deal. That's because no matter how much research you do, there may be unknown factors that place the other side in a weaker position than you realize.

And last but not least, your negotiating skills can be used to turn the tide during bargaining. So all things considered, never blithely assume that you're negotiating from weakness and the other party has the edge. Evaluate the situation carefully, prepare your position, know your alternatives, and proceed to negotiate. However, above all else, know when to say "No" and go from there.

1.3 ASSESSING NEGOTIATION ALTERNATIVES TO AVOID BAD DEALS

Whenever you're planning to start negotiations for any purpose, one of the first things you want to establish are the choices available to you if negotiations ultimately turn out to be unsuccessful. Otherwise, if you go ahead without doing this, you're much more likely to accept a less than satisfactory deal, simply because you feel it's the only viable action you can take.

When considering alternatives, look at the possibilities from two different perspectives. The first is what other courses of action are available if you can't reach agreement with the other party on terms that are acceptable to you. The second strategy is to look for alternatives that are different from current goals that can be suggested to the other party if negotiations falter. Actually, some of these options may not present themselves until you're well along in the negotiation process, but it's worthwhile to think about the possibilities at an early stage. These alternative terms for reaching agreement should be considered when you establish your negotiation objective. (This is covered in Chapter Two.)

It's unfortunate—but true—that alternatives are given short shrift when negotiation positions are prepared. This stems from several factors. First of all, there's an assumption that negotiations will be successful. However, although confidence is nice, it shouldn't overwhelm careful preparation.

An offshoot of the "success syndrome" is the "Why think about it now, when I can think about it later," approach. This is a handy way to avoid dealing with the unpleasant possibilities of a negotiation falling apart. Then, there's the flip side of the coin which is to rationalize that no damage will be done by leaving any consideration of alternatives until after negotiations have proven to be fruitless.

That may in fact be true in some instances. However, most business deals are impacted in one way or another by delays in reaching agreement. In fact, it's far more likely that a less than satisfactory deal will be accepted because of a failure to consider alternatives beforehand. So if you get yourself in this kind of a bind, you're likely to feel the pressure of, "We have to give the store away if we want an agreement."

With all the arguments for neglecting to consider alternatives, the seemingly most logical is the position that, "There just isn't any other alternative available." It's this reasoning, for example, that finds purchasing files filled with vendor folders labeled "sole-source supplier." Yet, in how many of these cases have questions such as the following been asked?

- Can this item be purchased somewhere else?
- Can we do without the item?

- Can we make it ourselves?
- Is there a substitute available that with minor changes can do the job?

Although there are obvious business justifications for going with a sole-source supplier, including reliability, timely delivery, product quality, and so forth, the truth is that in many cases it's simply a failure to consider alternatives. As a matter of fact, it's pretty hard to visualize someone having a lock on a product for any length of time without a competitor coming along and offering something similar.

All in all, there's much to be gained and little to be lost by always considering other alternatives, no matter how remote they appear to be. This is validated by a general rule for successful negotiations which is: "The less you care about making a deal, the better the deal you'll be able to make." That's because if negotiating a deal isn't important to you—or if you have other alternatives—you're not likely to accept unsatisfactory terms and conditions. Therefore, if you take the time to explore other options before you negotiate, you'll be better prepared to achieve your goals.

POINTER: When negotiating, never let the other party know that your options are weak. So even when the alternatives to reaching agreement with the other party aren't the best in the world, keep that information to yourself. Otherwise, your chances of fruitful negotiations will be lessened, since your adversary is likely to exploit your tactical disadvantage.

NOTE: In addition to exploring your own options, try to assess the other side's alternatives if negotiations are unsuccessful. Obviously, the fewer choices they have, the better are your chances for negotiation success. (This is covered at length in Chapter Three.)

1.4 ESTABLISHING A FLEXIBLE RESPONSE STRATEGY

Usually, people enter into negotiations with one set idea in mind, which is to buy this, sell that, or whatever else their objective is. Unfortunately, more often than not, they neglect to prepare a flexible strategy for achieving their goal. As a result, negotiations often falter, and one party or the other walks away mumbling about how unreasonable the other side was. Yet, this sort of deadlock can be averted by looking ahead and anticipating any adjustments that might have to be made during negotiations to achieve your final goal.

While planning your alternatives is necessary to decide what to do if negotiations are unsuccessful—or whether it's worthwhile to negotiate at all—preparing a flexible response strategy goes to the heart of what you will do when you sit down to bargain. Those who don't prepare a flexible response strategy often negotiate—knowingly or unwittingly—on the following assumptions:

a. *The "I'll cross that bridge when I come to it," approach.*

The problem here is that adjusting your negotiation position in the heat of battle can lead to hasty decisions that are poorly conceived and ultimately costly.

b. *The "Take it or leave it," tactic.*

When this attitude meets resistance in the form of, "I'll leave it," either failed negotiations result or hard-chargers scramble to back-off from an "all or nothing" strategy, which can quickly result in placing them in a defensive negotiating position.

c. *A "We'll work the problem together," attitude.*

This method of negotiating assumes that both parties will work together to solve any impediments to a negotiated agreement. There are times when this sort of win/win approach can be successful. Unfortunately, using this method, and blindly expecting a reciprocal response from the other party, may leave you facing a "Heads I win, tails you lose," adversary. (See Section 6.1 on the pluses and minuses of win/win.)

Preparing a flexible response strategy requires that you consider a number of factors all of which will contribute to your negotiation success. These include:

- Deciding what you're negotiating for, and what if anything you'll accept as a compromise.
- Determining what concessions you can make if it becomes necessary to do so.
- Settling who will or will not assist you in negotiations.
- Evaluating the tactics you'll use during negotiations.
- Assessing your opponent's negotiation strengths, weaknesses, and likely strategy.
- Setting the limits of your negotiation position—the point where you quit pushing for further concessions, or the point where you say "No thanks," and proceed to other alternatives.

Naturally, every negotiation takes on a life of its own from the moment negotiations are initiated. For this reason, you may continually need to make adjustments in your strategy as negotiations progress. (Section 6.13 discusses this topic in detail.)

Therefore, carefully planning your strategy beforehand presupposes that changes—both major and minor—may be needed to reach agreement. Nevertheless, doing this planning will help you to quickly shift your strategy when bargaining begins. It will also prevent panic reactions to surprise proposals, or sudden shifts in focus by the other party.

1.5 STRUCTURING YOUR OFFER TO GIVE YOU FLEXIBILITY

When planning your negotiation position, it's important to build flexibility into your offer. More often than not, when a decision is made to negotiate, objectives are set both in terms of what is wanted, as well as what will be given to achieve those goals. Then, negotiations begin, and as they proceed it becomes evident that concessions must be made if the negotiation is to be successful.

As a result, quick and often ill-conceived trade-offs are made at the negotiation table which result in a final agreement. However, rather than juggling the terms of an offer in haste during negotiations—with the inevitable errors being made—you're much better off building this flexibility into your planning. This helps avoid spur of the moment decisions, as well as some of the subtle traps that can ensnare you during the give and take of back and forth bargaining.

For example, although it's critical to control your emotions during negotiations, it's much easier said than done. This is especially true when after long and hard bargaining an agreement is in sight. It's at this point that hard-headed logic can be overwhelmed by a desire to get the deal done. As a result, emotions come into play, and terms are agreed upon that wouldn't be accepted if they were thought about before negotiations were begun.

This tendency to fade at the end is well understood by veteran negotiators, since they frequently face less skilled adversaries who battle tooth and nail right up to the point where an agreement is within reach. At this point, the skilled negotiator goes for the kill in terms of concessions, and the unaware adversary, sensing that the whole deal will go up in smoke at the last minute, caves in to these demands.

There's nothing mysterious about this, since it's human nature to become more anxious when a long sought after goal appears within reach. And quite apart from this emotional reaction, there are usually real behind-the-scenes pressures operating to encourage you to make the deal. These include everything from business necessity to a boss who has told you to "Get it done!" So if you have carefully planned your strategy to include a wide range of options for reaching final agreement, you'll be less likely to succumb to last minute demands.

Having a pre-planned range of adjustments that can be made in your offer works to your advantage in another way. If negotiations start to get bogged down, you can readily propose changes to your position which may convince the other party to accept your offer. And since these changes were already factored into your plans, there's no need for calling time-out to assess their merit before you toss them on the table. This may prod the other side into a quick acceptance. After all, it conveys a willingness on your part to be flexible, and if they appear hesitant in responding to this demonstration of flexibility, it puts them on the defensive.

How you go about structuring an offer to give yourself flexibility will largely depend upon the particulars of the negotiation you plan to undertake. But in general, set down a range of possible offers based on all of the "what-ifs" that you can conceivably contemplate before negotiations begin.

POINTER: If the situation warrants it, you might be able to hasten agreement by proposing alternative offers right at the start of negotiations. For instance, 10,000 units at "X" price, or 5,000 units at "Y." However, be careful here, since the other party may then take the offer that's most acceptable to them and begin to bargain from there. As a result, instead of speeding up settlement, you may have just given away a bargaining chip. Therefore, don't use this approach unless you're convinced that it can do no harm to your negotiating position.

1.6 DECIDING WHAT YOU CAN CONCEDE TO REACH AGREEMENT

When you structure your initial offer, it's sensible to not only establish what concessions you can make during negotiations, but also to prioritize these potential give-aways in terms of what you expect to get in return. Simply put, you don't want to give away the store for some minor concession made by the other side. (See section 11.3 on mirage concessions.)

Of course, when you prepare your offer, you should factor in the possibility that you may do either better or worse than expected during negotiations. Therefore, it's also necessary to establish minimum and maximum positions.

The "maximum" position should be the first offer you will make, which is the best you can expect to achieve in terms of a good deal. The "minimum" position is the worst deal you can possibly accept. Although these positions may be subject to adjustment based on information that develops during negotiations, it's unlikely that any agreement will be reached outside of these limits.

The major problem most folks face when preparing their offer is failing to give themselves enough leeway to bargain. This is especially true when people assume that their offer is reasonable and therefore will be accepted as such by the other party. For the most part that's a sign of an inexperienced negotiator. Incidentally, avoid making assumptions about anything during negotiations. Taking anything for granted may leave you sputtering, "I've been taken," at a later date.

The reality is that most people will presume—and rightly so—that the initial offer they receive is just a starting point, and certainly not the best deal they can get. After all, most people enjoy a bargain, and feel cheated if they can't negotiate better terms than a first offer. In addition to this, other folks just like to haggle. So frankly, it can save you a lot of grief if your first offer builds-in concessions that you can make during negotiations.

Obviously, the first offer you make must be sensible enough to be conceivably acceptable to the other party. After all, a totally ludicrous offer might convince the other party that it's not even realistic to negotiate with you.

On the other hand, the wide range of possibilities that surround every negotiation allow plenty of latitude for you to build-in concessions that make sense on the surface. Simply put, your starting point should be an offer that will send you scurrying to pop the champagne corks if it's accepted.

When it comes to factoring concessions into your offer, the specifics will vary according to the nature of what it is that you're negotiating. Furthermore, what you concede will depend upon the negotiation itself. Nevertheless, when preparing your offer try to place priorities on your concessions. For instance, those which are essentially give-aways, (perhaps a delivery date extension) as opposed to concessions which truly make an agreement less acceptable than you would prefer. (For example, a price reduction)

SUGGESTION: During negotiations, treat every concession you make as a major one. (See section 7.8 on proposing trade-offs.) Making a minor concession won't return much in the form of a quid-pro-quo if you surrender it casually. That's because your adversary won't place any value on your concession, unless by your conduct you give it importance. Furthermore, just because a concession is relatively unimportant to you, doesn't necessarily mean that it's not of some value to the other side. As a general rule, when it comes to making concessions, give ground grudgingly.

CAUTION: Although it's relatively rare, negotiations sometimes take place where one party is in such a bind that a bad deal is better than no deal at all. (A prime example is a company in financial difficulty.) If you're negotiating with someone who appears to be in such a weakened position, avoid taking advantage of the situation by negotiating unreasonable terms that will make the likelihood of performance none to nil. Furthermore, when failure to perform is more than a remote expectation, make sure that the provisions of any agreement are written to protect your interests.

A related situation involves not pushing for unreasonable concessions after you have essentially reached agreement on terms that meet your goals. The danger here is that if you try to push the limits of an agreement too far, the other party may react by walking away. (See section 15.1 on quitting while you're ahead.)

1.7 THE NEED TO SET NEGOTIATION LIMITS

With the constant give and take that negotiations involve, it's easy to get so caught up in the horse-trading aspects that your negotiation objectives become blurred. In practice, many a negotiation is concluded with one or both parties thinking, "Well, we got a good deal. Now let's sit down and figure out what it is." And when that happens, the post-game analysis may well reveal that the "good deal" isn't quite the bargain it was thought to be.

This is always prone to happen when people enter negotiations unprepared. However, even careful preparation can't rule out the possibility of carelessness arising during protracted negotiation sessions. Therefore, before you begin to negotiate you should set a firm limit beyond which you will not go. If the price you set is "X" then that's where you should call a halt if you can't reach agreement. All too often, it's easy to fall prey to ploys which push your final figure beyond the limit.

For instance, at some point, you probably have spent time listening to a salesperson extol the quality and reliability of consumer electronics, kitchen appliances, and/or automobiles. In fact, you are given a vision of a product that will be virtually trouble-free forever. That is, up until you decide to buy. Then the pitch switches 180 degrees to the virtues of a great "extended-service" warranty which you can purchase for "Y" dollars as protection against problems that aren't supposed to happen. Leaving aside the relative merits of extended service warranties, what you have done is pay "X"—the price you consider to be reasonable—plus "Y" the cost of the extended warranty.

No matter what you're negotiating, time and time again you'll be confronted with attempts to coerce you to pay (in monetary terms or other concessions) just a little more than you intended for what you want. Needless to say, this can be a costly exercise if you're not careful. The soundest way to avoid this is to stick to your guns once you reach your predetermined limit. (See section 17.3 on knowing when to walk-away from a deal.)

1.8 AVOIDING THE TRAP OF NEGOTIATION "LABELS"

Anything that throws you off-balance when you're negotiating is a distinct advantage to the party with whom you're bargaining. Consequently, you may be subjected to everything from pleading to pouting, from bullying to back-door power plays, all designed with one purpose in mind—to get a better deal for your adversary. When you add to the list of tactics that may be employed against you, the individual characteristics of the people you're negotiating with, the net result is a complex mix of strategies and personalities, all aimed at countering your efforts to get the best deal you can.

Therefore, holding your own in any negotiation session requires not only knowledge of negotiation fundamentals and a carefully prepared position. It also calls for avoiding the tendency to typecast the people you're dealing with, and/or the tactics they're using. The simple fact is that a skilled negotiator wants you to believe exactly what he or she is trying to project. If you're being bullied, it's in the hope that you'll back-off from your demands and/or make careless concessions. When people start pleading poverty, it's often with the intent that you'll believe them and settle for less than you want.

How to effectively counter any of these ploys—and successfully use them yourself—is covered in detail elsewhere within this book. However, all of the negotiation skills in the world won't get you very far if you, (a) let your emotions rule your actions, or (b) try to second-guess what your opponent is doing.

So don't lose your temper, or make assumptions about the other person's motives when you're bargaining. Instead, concentrate on your negotiation position, without worrying about what the other party is trying to do. Once you start making assumptions, or putting labels on the other negotiator's moves, you're susceptible to switching from arguing your position to countering the other parties' tactics. In short, you're going on the defensive which is exactly what the other person wants.

It serves no purpose in pinpointing people as "hard-nosed," "a soft touch," or "impossible to deal with." Everyone negotiates differently, so you have no way of knowing whether or not your perception is correct. Only when you reach agreement—or fail to—will you be reasonably sure of whether or not you were right.

1.9 EVALUATING YOUR NEGOTIATION SKILLS

Your ultimate success as a negotiator rests upon how wisely you use your negotiation knowledge. Common perceptions of successful negotiators include traits such as self-confident, pushy, and a dozen other terms that together conjure up the image of a hard-charging, aggressive individual. Yet, this sort of vision can be costly—which is a lesson that's often learned by "macho man" negotiators after being taken to the cleaners by folks playing the part of pigeons waiting to be plucked.

The simple truth is that bravado and bluster aren't the requisite tools-of-the-trade for skilled negotiators. The building blocks of negotiation success consist of being:

1. *Logical.* It's hard to argue with facts, so use factual statements to strengthen your position. Avoid using arguments that contradict each other, or unbelievable hype—even about a minor detail—since your credibility will be destroyed.

2. *Reasonable.* Be reasonable in your approach, since being argumentative encourages the other party to respond in like fashion. The end result is that it becomes far more difficult to reach agreement.

3. *Persistent.* It's easy to get steered off-course during negotiations when your adversary raises unrelated issues. Stick to your negotiation position, since persistence is fundamental to success when your opponent tries to tear your arguments apart.

4. *Patient.* For the most part, the party in the greatest rush to reach agreement is the one who will concede the most. Therefore, don't be easily discouraged if negotiations aren't moving along at the pace you would like. It may well be that your adversary is just trying to wear you down.

If you are generally logical, reasonable, persistent, and patient, then you're basically well-prepared for assuming a negotiation role. However, no matter how good a negotiator you may be, there are times when your interests will be better served if you sit on the sidelines. One obvious example is when you have a deep-seated dislike for the person you would be dealing with, and you know it wouldn't be possible for you to conceal these feelings. There are of course, any number of other reasons as to why you should hand over the negotiation reins to someone else in any given situation. (See section 2.9 on how to pick the best negotiator for the circumstances.)

Something else to consider is your particular negotiation style. Everyone's personality is different, but fortunately most folks are able to be reasonably flexible in their outlook. However, if you know that you have certain tendencies that might hamper your negotiation activities—for example, a short fuse—work on controlling these traits when you negotiate. (See section 5.1 on adapting your negotiation style to your personality.)

1.10 HOW TO HANDLE NON-NEGOTIABLE ITEMS

When you put together your negotiation position, along with identifying possible concessions, it's equally important to decide what items are non-negotiable. Otherwise, you may give-away something during a bargaining session that you hadn't planned on. As unlikely as that might seem, it's easy enough to do, especially in complex negotiations that require reaching agreement on a significant number of issues.

However, the major problem in this area isn't so much a failure to identify non-negotiable items. Instead, it's failing to recognize that when you get involved in bargaining, there are far fewer non-negotiable items than you realize.

In fact, insisting during negotiations that a topic isn't subject to negotiation frequently results in a failure to reach agreement. For example, many a bitter strike has resulted from either management or the union insisting that a particular issue is set in concrete. Yet frequently, the strike ends with the supposedly non-negotiable item being modified in the contract settlement.

There are a couple of sound reasons for not telling your adversary that a particular point is not negotiable. First of all, this immediately gives the other side a weapon to use against you. For instance, they may use this information as a wedge to get concessions from you in other areas.

This also gives them an opportunity to claim that they too have non-negotiable items. They may then proceed to bargain your non-negotiables against theirs. To make matters worse, if the other side are skilled negotiators, the odds are that their so-called non-negotiable issues aren't that at all. They are actually items raised as a bargaining chip, and anything they really consider to be non-negotiable hasn't been mentioned. Therefore, as a general rule don't tell the party you're negotiating with that something is non-negotiable.

Apart from giving your adversary a tactical advantage, there's another reason that issues shouldn't be arbitrarily identified as off-limits at the bargaining table, and that's because they may indeed be negotiable. Actually, any negotiation—other than the simplest—consists of agreeing to a broad package of individual terms and conditions that together constitute the agreed upon deal. So the problem isn't so much that any one item is non-negotiable, but rather what the other side is willing to bargain away in exchange for you modifying your demands.

As an example, suppose you own an antique automobile and you say, "I wouldn't sell this car for any price." That may indeed be true, especially if you consider any amount of money to be an insufficient exchange for your prized possession. However, what would happen if someone came along and offered you the opportunity to trade it for another classic car that you considered to be even more valuable?

The simple truth is that most anything has a price, and consequently before you enter into negotiations you should be flexible in deciding what is and isn't negotiable. Nevertheless, in most negotiations there are certain issues which you just can't budge on. For instance, perhaps you need products by a certain delivery date to meet commitments.

However, whatever your non-negotiable items may be, always remain low key about them. If the other side presses you on these topics, don't insist that you won't negotiate them. Instead, just say something that lets the other side know that you won't be easily swayed. For example, you might say something such as, "This isn't of great significance to me, but it's a pet peeve with the Board of Directors, so let's leave it on the back-burner." What you want to do is use any logical excuse that will hopefully steer the other side away from the issue. (Section 14.5 covers how to handle non-negotiable items in detail.)

1.11 TWELVE ESSENTIALS FOR WRITTEN PROPOSALS

Many types of transactions will require you to prepare a written proposal which will be used as the basis for negotiations. In fact, the quality of your proposal may very well determine whether or not you even get to the negotiation stage. Therefore, it's worthwhile to consider several essential elements that can make your proposal a success.

1. Accuracy. Is your proposal error-free? Many proposals that are sound in all other respects, fall by the wayside in this regard. This is usually due to limited time constraints when preparing the proposal. However, someone reading the proposal isn't thinking about the fact that it was prepared in a rush. Instead, they're probably wondering if someone this careless can deliver what they promise.

2. Be complete but concise. How much is enough is a mental hurdle that often leads to loading proposals with all sorts of irrelevant information. The question, "Is anything missing?" is always thought about during proposal preparation, but the counter question of, "Is this overkill?" is often ignored. Yet, sheer volume can spell the death knell for proposals far faster than a slim presentation that's loaded with convincing arguments.

3. Make it persuasive. Someone has to be convinced about something to make any proposal a winner. So support what you propose with sound reasoning, and if possible provide solid examples. In short, prove that you can produce what you are proposing.

4. Don't get fancy. Fight the tendency to offer more than is necessary to be successful. This can lead to promises that the reviewer knows can't be fulfilled.

5. **Skip the fluff.** All too often, there's an attempt to cover-up an inadequacy by padding the proposal with fluff that has no relationship to what's being proposed. For instance, a company that has a renowned scientist in its employ will include that person's credentials in every proposal. This creates skepticism when the subject matter of the proposal has no relationship to the individual's area of expertise. This leaves reviewers wondering if this is being done to beef-up an otherwise weak proposal.

6. **Don't ignore problems.** Many proposals accentuate the positive—which is good—but blithely ignore the negative aspects that must be overcome for the project to be a success. If you take the opportunity to recognize and discuss how problems will be resolved, you won't leave reviewers with the impression that you (1) don't understand the problems or (2) don't know how to deal with them. That's why it's important to anticipate questions, and provide the answers beforehand.

7. **Solve the "right" problems.** Many proposals try to succeed by covering "all of the bases" in any ball park, when the game is just being played on one field. The proposal pitch sounds like, "Here's what you want, but if it isn't, we'll do it your way." This tactic seldom succeeds, since it shows a lack of conviction, as well as doubt about what is actually being proposed.

8. **Be creative.** Although you shouldn't wander too far afield, simply laying out a response that minimally complies with what's being sought won't get you very far. After all, most proposals will offer something similar, but the one that wins will have provided a little creativity in demonstrating how to build a better mousetrap.

9. **Watch your numbers.** As any insomniac knows, sleep has always been a welcome respite from the sheer monotony of numbers. But beyond boredom, deluging a reader with numbers can leave the subject matter mired in a numerical swamp. Long lists of numbers should be placed together in a separate section to provide both better organization and ease of analysis. And don't forget to spend some time thinking about how you will format your data. For example, if you're just indicating a general trend, a graph can be more effective than a lengthy list of numbers.

10. **Combine substance with style.** As any consumer goods manufacturer can tell you, packaging helps sell the product. Therefore, take pains to make your proposal look good. A proposal strong in substance may overcome the handicap of a sloppy appearance, but you

run the risk of a reviewer who thinks that a shabby looking proposal may indicate lousy results down the road. So it's worth your while to prepare proposals that say, "The contents are just as good as the cover."

11. Remember readability.   It's easy to overlook the potential readership of a proposal. This leads to proposals that are targeted toward one person or group, without considering the fact that the actual decision-maker is someone else. This is especially true in technical proposals which are prepared on the assumption that the proposal will be evaluated only by those who understand the technical terminology. However, proposals are often reviewed by people who don't understand technical terms and the jargon of the trade. Therefore, it's prudent to prepare proposals that avoid jargon, don't confuse readers, and that aren't vague. That's not to say that a proposal should be watered down to the level of kids in a kindergarten class. However, strive to make every proposal as readable as possible without sacrificing quality.

12. Don't waste your efforts.   Preparing proposals is expensive, both in time and money. Therefore, try to concentrate your resources on those proposals with the highest possible payoff. That way, you will be investing your energies in a "high yield" effort, rather than churning out proposals and gambling on a win.

1.12 THE BEST WAY TO PROPOSE A DIFFERENT APPROACH

It's common when responding to a proposal request to offer an alternative to what is requested. However, whatever the purpose of optional approaches, there are pitfalls to avoid when including them in a proposal. First of all, if someone asks for a proposal to perform "X," don't propose to perform "Y" and totally ignore "X." That sounds pretty basic, but occasionally when people think of a better way to do something, they ignore what they were asked to do. The thinking goes like this:

- "Let's propose doing it this way to be different than the competition."
- "This method is cheaper than the one they asked for."
- "What they want isn't practical. Ignore it and offer our approach."

Actually, these and any number of other reasons may be perfectly valid, and alternative approaches can and should be included in proposals. The trick is to propose optional approaches in addition to—not in lieu of—what was asked for. It's preferable to do this in a separate section of the proposal. This avoids the risk of being shut out because you didn't respond to what was asked for.

It also pays to be diplomatic in proposing a different approach. That's because you don't want to run the risk of alienating the originator of the project—who may after all be the one who will pass final judgment on your proposal.

1.13 DECIDING WHAT YOU WANT AND HOW BADLY YOU WANT IT

One person's "good deal" can be someone else's downfall. That's why it's so important to plan your negotiation objective carefully. Knowing specifically what you want, and what you're willing to give to get it, keeps bad decisions from being made during the negotiation process. So when you sit down to talk turkey, a little preparation can keep you from ending up as one.

This is especially true when you enter negotiations where you're viewed as the underdog. Those who enter into negotiations with a "I'll take the best deal I can get," attitude don't end up with very good deals. That's because if you haven't clearly defined what you want, then your adversary will do it for you.

Where many people falter in this regard is failing to recognize the common cliche that "knowledge is power." If you know what you want before you start, then you won't be stampeded into accepting less. It also guards against a "fear of failure" factor which often leads folks to accept a bad deal as an alternative to no deal at all. By setting your negotiation limits beforehand, you know before negotiations begin what constitutes a bad deal. And by going through this exercise, it forces you to recognize the point at which "no deal" is a better alternative to a bad one.

Furthermore, when you establish goals in advance, you're not likely to fall into the "minimum target trap" that lures novice negotiators into accepting less than they could get by being better prepared. What happens is that someone who has done little preparation other than setting an acceptable price will tend to quit negotiating when they reach that figure. They then walk away satisfied with getting a good deal, without ever realizing how much money was left on the table.

Finally, proper preparation helps avoid falling victim to your emotions during negotiations. This isn't insignificant, since experienced negotiators are skilled at playing psychological warfare with your feelings. So by being prepared, you protect yourself from falling prey to persuasion tactics aimed at coercing you into an unfavorable settlement.

1.14 WHEN NOT TO NEGOTIATE—AND BE GLAD YOU DIDN'T

There's little question that the ability to negotiate is a handy talent to have in an increasingly competitive world. Even so, it's easy to overlook the fact that sometimes the best deal is no deal at all. Neglecting to recognize this reality is one of the reasons that agreements are reached that turn into very bad bargains for one or both of the parties involved.

Therefore, it's essential to heed the signals that tell you not to begin what you can't finish successfully. At a minimum, it saves the time and resources you will expend by forging ahead and failing to reach agreement. It may also place you in an unfavorable position if you negotiate at a later date with someone you previously failed to reach agreement with. But worst of all, pushing ahead when you shouldn't may result in a deal that turns into total disaster.

There are a number of reasons why it may be preferable to forego negotiations. One such instance may come about as a result of your pre-negotiation planning. You may decide that the other party would have an overwhelming advantage and could dictate terms of the agreement.

That alone doesn't mean that you shouldn't start to bargain and see what happens. It may well be that your negotiation skills—or your opponent's lack of the same—may turn the tide. Or perhaps you are just being overly pessimistic in evaluating the strength of your negotiation position. Nevertheless, there are times when after an initial look at the lay of the land it's better to forego negotiations—at least temporarily.

There are also occasions when the timing isn't just right for negotiating. Any number of examples demonstrate this. For instance, buying goods from suppliers with heavy backlogs may not be a good idea for a couple of reasons. First of all, they may not be able to meet delivery dates. Furthermore, such a supplier is well-positioned to seek excessive prices from you. In short, there are countless instances when it pays to wait to negotiate. So don't overlook the importance of timing when planning your negotiations.

One of the most common cases where folks tend to waste their negotiation efforts is in bargaining with people who don't have the authority to reach agreement. Actually, this "It looks good to me, but I have to check with my boss," tactic is often just a ploy used to extract additional concessions from inexperienced negotiators. Needless to say, always establish the authority of the person you're negotiating with to save yourself this kind of grief. (See section 3.5 for how to do this.)

Another time when it may be best to forego negotiations is when you have a longstanding business relationship that you don't want to damage. Perhaps you have the leverage to reopen negotiations and force better terms on a supplier, yet, from a long-term standpoint such a move may be unwise. There are many other factors besides contract terms that dictate whether or not it's prudent to reopen negotiations on existing agreements. Reliability, responsiveness, quality, and a host of intangibles should all be weighed prior to any decision on negotiating new terms with an existing supplier.

Of course, the same general principle applies in dealing with customers if you're on the selling side of the table. So always take all factors into consideration when you're thinking about revising existing contracts.

WARNING: Before going ahead and proposing changes to any existing agreement, be very careful to think through the advantages and disadvantages. After all, once you propose to reopen a contract, the other party may want to make contract modifications that offset any advantages you would gain.

Chapter 2

ESTABLISHING YOUR NEGOTIATION OBJECTIVES

The most important pre-negotiation step you face is putting your negotiation objective together. Failing to do this properly can have you flailing around during negotiations, not knowing how to counter the other guy's negotiation tactics.

Another aspect of negotiation planning that's often overlooked—even by savvy negotiators—is the long-term impact of any agreement. Simply concentrating on "hard-nosed" bargaining to get the best deal today can be damaging down the road. Therefore, it's crucial to consider the "what-ifs" of any agreement in terms of the future as well as the present.

Along with the planning that's required to do battle is the equally vital task of deciding who—if anyone—will assist you in your negotiation wars. Picking a negotiation team is a task that shouldn't be taken lightly, since one poor choice can result in a blunder that blows your strategy out of the water. Last, but by no means least, is the prospect of having to handle a negotiation where more than one party is involved—as if one wasn't enough. This chapter looks at how to deal with the many aspects of each of these topics.

2.1 PUTTING YOUR NEGOTIATION OBJECTIVE TOGETHER

Planning how to reach your negotiation objective is of little value unless you take the time to put all of the parts together. Of course, if you're just making a routine purchase or sale, price and delivery are generally all you have to worry about. This is especially true if you're dealing with someone you do business with on a regular basis.

However, if your transaction is relatively complex, or you will be negotiating with someone you haven't dealt with before, it's worthwhile to script out your negotiation goals.

Doing this helps in several ways such as:

- Formalizing your objective forces you to think about what you want, why you want it, and what you are willing to give in return.

- It helps you in making concessions and compromises as negotiations proceed.

- It guards against making careless off-the-cuff agreements.

- A carefully planned strategy avoids confusion which can be exploited by your adversary.

- It speeds-up the negotiation process itself.

- It can help avoid failed negotiations, since hang-ups often result from a lack of preparation.

- Most important of all, it can get you a better deal. An adversary is more likely to be reasonable if you are able to show from the start that you know what you want.

All in all, the time you invest in preparing your negotiation objective will pay plenty of dividends when you sit down to hammer out a deal.

2.2 TEN TOPICS TO COVER WHEN YOU PLAN YOUR OBJECTIVE

Every negotiation will have its own set of specific provisions that should be included in your objective, but general considerations should include the following topics.

1. Establish a target price that you will pay for what you want. This price should be what you reasonably expect to pay for what you're getting in return. NOTE: Price is used here in a generic sense to represent what is being exchanged. Many negotiations, of course, won't deal at all in monetary terms.

2. Identify your negotiation limits. As was discussed in Chapter One, you should identify a minimum position in terms of the least favorable offer you will accept. This is essentially your "walk-away" point.

At the same time you want to fashion an initial offer which is the best deal you can possibly get.

3. Decide what concessions can be made during negotiations to reach agreement. Try to rank these concessions in terms of priorities.

4. If possible, pinpoint potential give-aways that you can trade-off for concessions by the other party. These are not true concessions, but are instead issues that you will build into your offer and treat as concessions during negotiations. (Section 11.11 discusses how to do this.)

5. Indicate any time constraints for reaching an agreement. Include any that you think the other side may have.

6. Pinpoint any potential outside influences that may impact your negotiations. (bankers, government agencies, and labor unions, are a few examples of outsiders who may have an interest in negotiations that they're not directly involved in.)

7. Identify any phony issues your adversary may raise, and plan how to overcome these impediments.

8. Think about any creative suggestions you can propose if negotiations become stalemated. (For instance, are there any secondary elements you could suggest that might sweeten your offer?)

9. Establish who will be participating in negotiations. This includes not only negotiation team members, but any advisers, such as accountants or lawyers, who may be brought in to consult on particular issues.

10. Determine your alternatives if negotiations are unsuccessful.

Obviously, every negotiation won't require detailed planning. Nevertheless, you can never go wrong by being prepared for any eventuality. After all, it's far better to expect the unexpected, than to play it by ear and have negotiations end on a sour note.

2.3 WAYS TO TURN A WEAK POSITION INTO A STRONG ONE

The meek may well inherit the earth, but they won't make money at the negotiation table. That's because whenever an opposing negotiator senses weakness, you're susceptible to tactics aimed at getting you to accept an unreasonable, "take it or leave it" offer. So the more power you can project during negotiations, the more successful you're likely to be.

Incidentally, projecting a strong negotiation position doesn't mean that bluster, bravado, and bullying tactics are the order of the day. To the contrary, people soon sense when someone is simply trying to bluff their way through by swapping verbal volume for facts and figures. Nevertheless, acting like a lamb being led to the slaughter won't serve you well. So if you can't enter into a negotiation feeling self-confident about success, then you probably shouldn't be there.

The greatest fear of failure in negotiations is when someone goes up against an adversary who appears to be in a dominant position. This is common when a small company butts heads with a big business. It also tends to be a pervasive attitude when any business—large or small—seeks financing from banks or other financiers. In addition, there are any number of individual circumstances where one party appears to be going into negotiations with a distinct disadvantage.

Often, this attitude results from self-induced perceptions which lead folks to hope for the best while expecting the worst. After all, if you're looking for a loan to keep your business afloat, it's not easy to visualize yourself as an equal at the negotiation table. However, a "hat in hand" attitude only serves to make the problem worse. Therefore, as hard as it may be to do, the starting point for converting weakness into strength is to maintain your confidence. The bottom line is that "people have confidence in confident people." So no matter what you think your relative bargaining power is, if you're not confident then you better stay home.

For example, two small business owners with cash flow problems—let's call them Carolyn Cheeky and Denny Docile—both seek a bank loan. Carolyn presents a plan of action and exhibits a "routine step on the road to success" attitude, while Denny's plea is, "If I don't get the loan I'll go under." Assuming all other considerations are roughly the same, who will get the loan? Quite likely Carolyn will, because as simple as it seems, confidence can and does carry the day.

On a more general level, every so often some high-flying whiz hits the headlines after going under in a big way and leaving others to pick-up the financial pieces. Many a story is then written speculating how someone with shaky financial underpinnings managed to accrue huge debt levels before hitting the wall. Although the details vary, usually a high-flyer who crashes gets airborne by convincing otherwise sane, intelligent people to lend him money. And that isn't done by being docile.

This is in no way intended to imply that self-confidence alone will guarantee success. A well-planned strategy and basic negotiating skills are far more relevant. However, even these tools are diminished in value if you have a defeatist attitude before you start.

Furthermore, self-confidence in negotiations isn't something that's an innate gift. It's a very real craft that you can learn and practice. Let's look at some methods you can use to increase self-confidence in your negotiation position.

First of all, it's necessary to recognize that you want to project power—not weakness. Avoiding a great deal of dialogue on power, it basically boils down to real power and perceived power. Said another way, there's the power you actually possess, and the power others think you have. One good example of the difference is the real power of a CEO (Chief Executive Officer) of a large corporation, and the perceived power of that person's personal secretary. The CEO has wide ranging powers to hire, fire, and make other operational decisions. The secretary has no such organizational mandate. Yet, the secretary wields a great deal of perceived power by virtue of working for the big boss. In fact, by having proximity to the seat of power, the secretary may exert a greater influence on decision-making than many managers with loftier titles and much higher salaries.

The significance of this is that you don't actually need a strong position when you negotiate, as long as the other party thinks you have one. Being prepared, knowing your alternatives, and remaining confident, will all help give you this perception of power.

Another way to overcome the handicap of a weak bargaining position is to properly time your negotiations. Of course, this isn't always possible, but if you have the option, try to negotiate when it's most favorable for you and/or less so for your adversary. Anytime you're under pressure to complete a deal, one more element is at work to coerce you to accept less than the best possible terms. In many types of negotiations, such as repetitive purchases, advance planning can help you to take advantage of the timing factor.

One more strategy for enhancing a weak negotiating position is to keep your adversary on the defensive. You can do this during negotiations in any number of ways including:

- Ignore what is said and keep talking about your strengths.
- Attack your adversaries' weaknesses.
- Come up with novel approaches. What can you offer that others can't? Examples include long-term contracts, service guarantees, and so forth.
- Fake it. Any bluff will work as long as it isn't challenged. Be careful here though, since you might have to use your negotiation alternatives if it is called.
- Create an illusion of power. For instance, if you're seeking a bank loan, imply that there's competition for your business. Say something such as, "Another bank wanted to do business with us, but I wasn't

impressed with their ability to respond to our needs as we expand."
TIP: Don't name another bank even if pressed. Instead say, "It
wouldn't be fair to disclose who it is in light of my negative feelings."
This keeps them guessing. They may not believe you, but on the other
hand, planting a seed of doubt in fertile soil may yield a harvest of
cash.

2.4 PLANNING HOW TO GIVE A LITTLE
TO GET A LOT

The crux of any negotiation is to get the best deal you can. To do this
successfully, you want to concede as little as possible to the other side. As a
starter, always try to keep your adversary on the defensive as was just discussed. One way to do this consists of getting the other party to make the
initial offer. (See section 10.8 for an exception to this rule.)

Then, proceed to knock holes in their position with the objective of having
them back off and make one concession after the other. This isn't always as
hard to do as you might imagine, especially if the other party wants the deal
worse than you do.

A side aspect of this approach is to listen carefully to what the other party
is saying. This gives you a chance to "lock-in" on what's important to them.
Once you know their priorities, you can reap substantial benefits in areas of
the agreement that aren't a major part of their agenda.

Unfortunately, unless you're dealing with a nervous novice, don't expect a
free ride to the bank. Therefore, you most likely will have to make concessions to reach a final agreement. The trick here is to slowly and reluctantly
surrender the built-in giveaways that were included in your first offer. (See
section 1.6.)

However, you may have to go beyond this and make some real concessions.
If so, treat every concession you make as a major one, and insist on a quid-
pro-quo from the other side. The real key to success in this area isn't so much
in being clever, as it is in being patient and persistent. Stay the course and
refuse to let your adversary throw you off stride.

2.5 LOOKING AT LONG-TERM ASPECTS OF
PROPOSED AGREEMENTS

There's a very real tendency in any negotiation to bargain hard for the
present and give little or no thought to the future. Naturally, there are one-
shot deals where there's little likelihood of future business with the same

party. In these instances, future considerations aren't paramount. Yet, despite the one-time nature of these deals, it pays to be fair minded and ethical, since a reputation for taking advantage of people travels on a pretty fast track.

On the other hand, many business transactions have a life well beyond the current contract. Therefore, during your negotiation planning, one of the first things to think about is what—if any—long-term implications might arise. For instance, will it be a long-term contract, or is there a possibility of options being added that will extend the period of performance? If so, what are the economic implications of future costs for labor, material, financing, and so on?

Something else to think about is the potential for future business. Perhaps accepting a less favorable deal now can set the stage for future business that's highly profitable.

A related topic concerns the question of "buying-in" which means accepting a low price now in hopes of making it up later with (1) increased volume, and/or (2) price increases once you have an established position. Be careful here though, since low-balling (offering a price at or below cost) can backfire, especially if there's little reason for the buyer to stay with you down the road.

Incidentally, if you're the buyer instead of seller, watch out for this practice. Accepting the lowest price isn't always the bargain it appears to be. You may end-up with a supplier who sticks you with high prices on a follow-on contract. This is especially prevalent in situations where research and development (R&D) contracts are awarded. The R&D contract is bid intentionally low with the ultimate intent of making-up losses on follow-on contracts for production quantities. Be sure to guard against this practice by including appropriate provisions in any contract.

2.6 THE PITFALLS OF NEGOTIATION TEAMS

In general, the more complex a negotiation is, the greater the number of people that are involved in the process. As one consequence of this, it usually takes longer to reach agreement. Nevertheless, there's an obvious need for negotiation teams, particularly where the issues are complex and a wide variety of expertise is needed.

On the other hand, it's equally true that whenever you negotiate it's generally best to limit the number of participants to those that are absolutely essential. That's because the more people you have participating, the greater the difficulty in following your negotiation strategy. This problem gets even more complicated, since as you add people to your negotiation team, it's likely that your adversary will do the same.

Aside from the sheer inefficiency of having a large number of attendees at negotiation meetings, there are other pitfalls. For instance, specialists on both sides may monopolize matters to the extent that little progress is made toward narrowing the issues and resolving differences.

Then, there's always the danger that a member of your team may say the wrong thing and throw your negotiation plans out of kilter. In short, the number of possible missteps in a negotiation are closely related to the number of people involved. Therefore, it's sensible to be selective both in the number of attendees, as well as the characteristics of those chosen.

2.7 EFFECTIVE METHODS FOR PICKING NEGOTIATION TEAM MEMBERS

Whenever you select people to serve on your negotiation team, keep the following criteria in mind:

1. The particular skills you seek.
2. The personality of potential team members.
3. Any organizational considerations that affect selections.
4. Your overall negotiation strategy.
5. Any agreements you have on team size.

Let's examine each of these elements in detail.

1. The particular skills you seek

The type of expertise needed for your negotiation team will be dictated by what it is that you're negotiating. However, many negotiations require skills in accounting, law, and the technical area that's the subject of negotiation. In addition, subject matter experts may be needed on limited aspects of the negotiation. As a general guideline, limit the selection process to those functions that you consider to be primary for negotiation success. Whenever possible, select specialists to be included as "on call" participants when meetings take place. That way, the expertise is available if needed, without adding people with limited responsibilities as active members of the negotiating team.

2. The personality of potential team members

This is a subject that's regularly overlooked when picking members of a negotiation team. And even if someone is commonly recognized as having a "quirky" personality, that fact is usually overlooked because of the person's expertise. This ignores the reality that negotiating is a people-oriented endeavor, and picking the wrong person can do a lot of damage.

Therefore, as a general rule, look for folks who are team players with a keen sense of when to talk and when to listen. By the same token avoid anyone with a big mouth, a big ego, or an ax to grind.

TIP: If you have someone whose expertise is needed that you don't want at negotiation sessions, get their counsel before, after, and during breaks in your meetings.

3. Any organizational considerations that affect selections

One aspect of team selection that can't be completely avoided is the question of organizational politics. This is particularly true in large organizations where individual departments have functional responsibilities that may in some way be affected by the outcome of negotiations. Naturally, departments with a direct interest in the results should be consulted, and may have one or more participants on the negotiation team.

However, other groups may also be interested in the negotiations so as to protect their real and/or imagined interests. Their actual cause may be nothing more significant than a turf battle, or resentment that their group is excluded from the negotiations. But this is sometimes a tricky subject to deal with. After all, executives in positions of power that give them the opportunity to throw roadblocks in your path are a force to be reckoned with.

On the other hand, you're planning a negotiation session—not a mass rally for dissidents. Therefore, to avoid problems in this area, bring as many people on board as is necessary during your planning sessions. However, don't add them to your negotiation team unless it's unavoidable.

4. Your overall negotiation strategy

Picking a negotiation team is in part dictated by your negotiation plans. These considerations include not only what you're negotiating, but also whom you're dealing with. For instance, you may know that your opponent is easier to deal with on a one-on-one or small group basis. That being the case, it behooves you to limit your negotiation team.

The flip side of the coin is that you may have reason to believe that a large entourage will work in your favor. For example, a good-sized group can convey a psychological sense of power to others. However, don't get too enthusiastic for this sort of maneuver, since your adversary may counterattack with his own army of experts. Furthermore, the inherent problems of a large group can more than offset any possible psychological advantage.

Of even greater consequence than your opponent's attitude toward group size, are your own feelings. If you feel more comfortable with a smaller group, then that's the way to go—as long as this doesn't hurt your negotiation stance.

Finally, there are negotiations which by their very nature require secrecy. In these situations, you will want to limit your team to an absolute minimum.

5. Any agreements you have on team size

It's not uncommon for both parties to have a prior agreement as to the number of participants. In fact, it's advantageous to know who you will be facing across the negotiation table. That way, you can factor this knowledge in when you select your team. Apart from the desires of the negotiating parties, logistics alone can influence the number of participants. The facilities where negotiation sessions will be held must be taken into consideration. And, of course, if you're negotiating at a distant site, cost can also be a factor.

SUGGESTION: When you're going through the routine of selecting your negotiation team, you obviously want to limit it's scope to the number necessary to do the job. However, negotiations are complex, and technical issues may be raised that weren't considered when you assembled your team. This may force you to halt negotiations, while you regroup and get the expert advice you need. You can minimize this problem by including experts in your internal planning sessions even though they won't participate in negotiations. By doing this, they are briefed on your strategy if you have to call on them. This approach can save a lot of time and confusion.

2.8 THE QUALITIES TO LOOK FOR IN A NEGOTIATION TEAM LEADER

If you won't be conducting negotiations yourself, but are the behind-the-scenes official responsible for their success, it's necessary to designate a negotiation team leader. This person should have all the attributes of anyone thought to have leadership qualities. In addition, this individual should be exceptionally strong in traits that are conducive to success as a negotiator. These include:

- An ability to make sound decisions under extreme pressure.
- The tact to mold divergent viewpoints into a consensus.
- An even-handed temperament.
- The flexibility to adjust to changing conditions.

- A talent for projecting trust and confidence.
- A knack for sorting fact from fiction.

In addition, the designated team leader should be someone who has the complete confidence of any superior who has veto power over the negotiation results. Otherwise, this opens the door to widespread second-guessing, which can cause serious problems.

Furthermore, the person selected should be someone who supports the purpose of the negotiations. It doesn't make much sense to entrust negotiations to people who don't want to see them succeed—unless that is the underlying agenda of the negotiations. For instance, diplomatic negotiations between countries are occasionally conducted even though there is no intention of reaching an agreement. However, for the most part, negotiations are entered into with an ultimate agreement as the goal, and it helps to have a negotiator who will have that interest in mind.

Of course, it's also nice to be able to select someone with a personality that will interact well with the party they will be negotiating with. However, it's difficult enough to find someone who fills most of the bill, so how well your choice will interact with their counterpart is best left to conjecture. The only real concern here is that you don't pick someone who has a personal antagonism against the other party.

POINTER: One of the most frustrating feelings for a negotiator is to suffer the fate of being second guessed by others. Even more outrageous is the practice of senior executives short circuiting the negotiation team and dealing directly with their counterpart. This often results in haphazard agreements which both parties have to live with. The bottom line is that people entrusted with the authority to negotiate should be allowed to do their job. Otherwise, there's little incentive to put forth their best effort if they expect to be overruled. Furthermore, once other parties recognize that it's easy to succeed by going over a negotiator's head, then the negotiator's position is permanently weakened. Therefore, once negotiation leaders are appointed, they should be given full support by their superiors.

2.9 HOW TO PICK THE BEST NEGOTIATOR FOR THE CIRCUMSTANCES

There are occasions when certain people are the best choice to negotiate a particular agreement. This is so, even though the individual selected may not have the negotiation skills of other possible choices. One reason for this is that personal rapport may sometimes succeed where all other tactics fail. This isn't uncommon, and everyone has a story or two about how someone managed to persuade somebody to buy or sell after others were unsuccessful.

The rationale isn't very difficult if you think about it. Many decisions are made on an emotional basis, and although it may appear otherwise, not everyone succumbs to the lure of money. Deals are sometimes made for no better reason than the person seeking something has succeeded in winning the confidence of the other party. This is especially prevalent in instances where someone doesn't have any real need or desire to part with something. That being the case, the only real way to change their mind is to win them over on a personal basis.

Another reason for designating a particular negotiator is because that person has a track record of successful dealings with the other party. Experienced negotiators know the nuances of their adversary, and are better equipped to conclude deals faster than someone not familiar with the situation. Be careful here though, since sometimes negotiators who deal with the same party over a period of time may get sloppy. By getting to know those they deal with a little too well, they may not push quite as hard as they might in other circumstances. Therefore, under conditions of repetitive negotiations, it's useful to switch negotiators every so often.

Above all else, the most important factor in selecting a negotiator for a task which you're responsible for are your own personal feelings. After all, if you have to live with the outcome, you better be comfortable with the surrogate you select.

2.10 TIPS ON BRIEFING YOUR NEGOTIATION TEAM

It's necessary to hold pre-negotiation meetings with your negotiation team to sort out negotiation issues, assign roles, and plan strategy. Aside from topics related to the specifics of what you're negotiating, the general matters covered should include:

- Appointing a spokesperson (usually the team leader) who will have sole responsibility for making and responding to offers.
- Assigning the responsibilities of each team member.
- Establishing a timetable for completing pre-negotiation reports. NOTE: A lengthy preliminary process precedes many negotiations. A mass of financial, technical, and administrative information may have to be reviewed. This is especially true where formal proposals

are involved, so internal negotiation team meetings may be held periodically over a period of weeks and months.

- An understanding that gratuitous comments aren't to be made at negotiation meetings.
- An agreement on the procedure to be used to temporarily halt a negotiation session when a caucus is needed.
- Designation of a member to take informal notes of what is said.
- Identifying who will attend all negotiation meetings, those who will attend sessions covering specific topics, and those who will be "on call" if needed.
- Plan negotiation strategy including establishing the negotiation objective, and tactics that will be used to achieve that goal.
- Assess the other side's goals and likely strategy. (Chapter 3 covers this subject in detail.)
- All members should be advised that no private discussion of the negotiations should be held with members of the other negotiating team. This is to prevent inadvertent leaks which can undermine the negotiation process.

Incidentally, team members should be cautioned not to discuss negotiation matters internally with those who have no need to know. This precaution isn't so much a matter of not trusting other employees, but rather to guard against careless comments. After all, it's discouraging to have a customer service representative tell a customer, "I heard at coffee that we're planning to buy your company," when the President of that company doesn't know that you're planing to make such an offer.

TIP: Of course, deliberately leaking information to gain an advantage is a negotiation technique that's sometimes used. (See section 7.10 on how to do this.)

2.11 ORCHESTRATING MULTI-PARTY NEGOTIATIONS

Sometimes negotiations are conducted with multiple sources. This may be done to get a higher price, especially when there are several buyers willing to compete against one another. (This is a common technique used by agents for athletes, entertainers, and others.) The flip side is its use to obtain the lowest possible price. (This is a standard practice throughout business and government.)

The major difference between competitive bidding with several sources, and negotiations with a single source, is the greater formality of the process when multiple sources are involved. However, even this characteristic varies significantly, ranging from the relatively rigid procedures used by government agencies, to the less formal techniques commonly employed by agents.

The obvious advantage of multi-source negotiations is the opportunity to get a significantly better deal than you would by negotiating with only one party. Nevertheless, as with anything else, there are disadvantages.

For example, when several sources are bidding for the same job, there's a possibility that one or more bidders might submit unrealistically low estimates to win the contract. Guarding against this practice requires a more intense scrutiny of competing proposals than might otherwise be the case. It also requires careful monitoring of performance to make sure that quality hasn't been sacrificed for price. Another disadvantage is the level of resources that have to be employed to review multiple proposals. And, of course, negotiating with several sources can be time-consuming.

A less obvious—but very real—danger is the possibility that no one will bid. When that happens, you're not in a very strong bargaining position if you subsequently initiate negotiations with one source. After all, the message is that no one was very interested in what you had to offer. Consequently, a single subsequent source is in the driver's seat when it comes to negotiating terms and conditions. The refrain you may hear if you're selling something is, "Nobody else was interested, so don't expect me to be paying top dollar." Conversely, if you unsuccessfully solicited bids as a buyer, a sole bidder doesn't have much of an incentive to keep his price down.

Offsetting the disadvantages of dealing with multiple sources are the very real benefits of competition. Any time you can get several sources competing to sell you a product, the opportunity to get a better price is enhanced. As for getting top dollar on the selling side of the ledger, highly visible examples are the deals made for professional athletes when they have several teams interested in their services.

In general, it's best to use multi-source negotiations as a buyer when you have a common or commodity type item that can be supplied by a number of sources. Engaging in multi-party negotiations as a seller is most practical when you have a unique product or service that is highly sought after.

NOTE: Multi-party negotiations shouldn't be confused with, either auctions where the high bidder wins, or formal bidding procedures where the low price offeror is awarded the contract without further negotiation. This latter technique is frequently used by government agencies to buy commodity type items. Of course, negotiation procedures aren't inflexible, so there can be a significant overlap in how things are handled. In essence, it's not so much what you call it, as to whether or not back and forth bargaining takes place that separates multi-party negotiations from other procedures.

CAUTION: Whenever you conduct multi-party negotiations, always be sure that everyone is playing by the same rules. Every potential respondent should be given the same guidelines, whether you issue a formal request for proposals, or use a less formal procedure such as discussions on the telephone. However it's done, everyone participating should receive the same information, have the same deadlines, and be given an equal opportunity to revise their offers. Giving preferential treatment to certain respondents will destroy your credibility, making it exceedingly difficult to get anyone to participate in future negotiations.

Chapter 3

ANALYZING YOUR OPPONENT'S POSITION

Planning your negotiation objective lays the basic foundation for you to begin bargaining. However, it's necessary to build upon this base by thinking about what your opponent wants to accomplish. This requirement can't be easily ignored, since it can spell the difference between success or failure during negotiations.

Furthermore, the objectives of the other party may not be what surface appearances would have you believe. There may be underlying goals, and a failure to recognize them runs the risk of a negotiation stalemate. Of course, once negotiations begin in earnest, you will learn more about what your opponent is seeking. However, taking the time to analyze your opponent's potential strategy before negotiations begin, gives you a head start at achieving your objectives.

To do this successfully, you should attempt to pinpoint your adversaries' negotiation objectives, and then balance them against your own goals. In addition, it's useful to consider the likely negotiation strategy the opposition will employ to get what they want. This requires an assessment of your opponent's strengths and weaknesses, so that you can effectively counter arguments made at the bargaining table. Doing this will lessen the likelihood that you'll encounter surprises when negotiations begin.

It's also prudent to think about the people you will be bargaining with. Do they have the authority to reach agreement, or will major decisions be made by others who won't be active participants in the negotiation? Furthermore, if negotiations will be fairly complex, or you're uneasy about the confrontation, you may want to go through a dry-run with your own people. If nothing more, such an exercise verifies whether or not you're adequately prepared. The following sections deal with topics on evaluating your adversary before negotiations begin.

3.1 ASSESSING YOUR OPPONENT'S GAME PLAN

The basic reason for picking apart what you think the opposition will do during negotiations is to be prepared for any eventuality. Although everything may appear pretty basic on the surface, your adversary may have hidden objectives that he doesn't intend to reveal. If you can anticipate this possibility, it's much easier to adjust your position during negotiations. Otherwise, you may experience difficulty in reaching agreement, since what you're offering will be based upon surface appearances—not the hidden goals which are the true objective of the other party.

Obviously, it's much easier to reach agreement if both parties lay their cards on the table. And, for the most part, this is generally the case, since there aren't a lot of complexities behind many deals. However, there are times where what someone says they want and reality don't match. In fact, even in basic buyer/seller transactions, there may be subsurface factors which can affect the negotiation process. So it pays to give every negotiation at least a cursory analysis before you start.

For example, suppose that Company A is negotiating to sell items to Company B, who is a long-time customer. A's negotiator is surprised to discover that Company B is seeking extraordinary price concessions, since all prior negotiations had been pretty routine. And despite an earnest attempt to reason with B's buyer, he won't budge in his demands. The deal then falls through, since Company A is unable to make a profit at the price that B seeks.

Company A later discovers that "B" placed a subsequent order with "X" for a similar item of lower quality at about the price that "A" couldn't meet. It's also learned that "X" gave very favorable payment terms to "B." What "A" didn't know at the time of negotiations—which it could have learned by doing a little research—was that Company "B" was experiencing a financial squeeze. Consequently, it was looking for a lower cost supplier who would also provide easier payment terms.

Company "A" could have supplied a less costly, lower quality item, if it had known the reason "B" was seeking a lower price. However, "B" wasn't willing to reveal its financial bind, so "A" simply assumed that "B" was making unreasonable demands to take advantage of a long-term business relationship. This case shows that even where there are existing business relationships, circumstances may change for the other party. You may be made aware of them, or as in "B's" case, the facts may not be revealed. Therefore, even when there have been prior dealings, it's sensible to avoid making assumptions. Otherwise, you may face unforeseen difficulties at the bargaining table.

Of course, with any negotiation there may be strategic reasons for negotiators playing it close to the vest. For instance, they may not want you to know certain facts for fear you won't go through with the deal. (Example: a prospective buyer of land may know that a highway is planned nearby that will increase the properties' value.) Another reason for not revealing information is that it may serve to strengthen your position during negotiations. (Example: A seller needing cash might propose an earlier delivery date. If the other party knows the reason, it could be used as a bargaining chip.) Actually, there are all kinds of reasons why the other party won't reveal valuable information. Therefore, it's up to you to learn as much as you can before you sit down to bargain.

Successfully analyzing your adversaries' game plan isn't confined simply to dredging up as much information as you can, although that, of course, is part of the process. In fact, just looking at the negotiation from the other parties' viewpoint can be revealing. For instance, is a business selling a subsidiary because it's a dog, or simply because they want to concentrate resources in other areas? Is someone buying a product from you because of price, or is it quality, delivery terms, or some other factor? Pinpointing their reasoning is important, since it can influence the terms you're able to negotiate. All in all, knowing your adversaries' position before you start negotiating will enhance your prospects for success when negotiations begin.

3.2 SORTING YOUR GOALS FROM YOUR OPPONENT'S

In planning how to negotiate so as to achieve your goals, it's worthwhile to compare your objectives with what the other party hopes to accomplish. Doing this will help you to find common ground for agreement between your goals and your opponents. In basic transactions this doesn't pose much of a problem, since many negotiations involve nothing more complex than agreeing on the price to be paid for an item.

However, even here there are sometimes other considerations that can influence the price someone is willing to accept in the interests of reaching agreement. After all, when a deadlock is reached on what constitutes an acceptable price, it's often some form of concession in another area that leads to ultimate agreement. What that turns out to be is entirely dependent upon the subject matter of the negotiation, as well as the needs of the parties involved.

In fact, it may be something that's more emotional than material in nature. (Example: Ephraim Ego initially refuses the offered price for land upon which a building is to be erected, but accepts it when "A" offers to name the building after him.) Naturally, you won't be able to determine all of your opponent's objectives before negotiations begin. Some may come to light during the negotiation process itself, while both you and your adversary may have goals that are never revealed during the entire negotiation process. (See section 5.3 on searching for clues during negotiations.)

Nevertheless, it's important to at least speculate about all of the possible objectives the other side may have. This helps you tailor your offer to meet their goals. And it can come in handy if negotiations get sticky, because being able to make an offer that satisfies some unspoken demand can quickly break a negotiation deadlock.

As a matter of fact, with a little bit of creative thought, you may come up with some ideas that can help sell the deal that your opponent might not have even thought of. In any event, list all of your primary and secondary goals, including what you must receive to reach agreement, as well as terms you would like to get. Then, list all of the obvious objectives of your adversary, along with other factors that might come into play.

After doing this, look for those elements that are common to both your interests. (Example: Perhaps you both need to reach agreement by a certain date.) The more common interests you can come up with, the greater will be the possibilities for reaching early agreement. Of course, the farther apart you are in terms of the issues to be negotiated, the more likely it is that you will have some hard bargaining to do in order to get what you want.

CAUTION: When you arrive at a laundry list of what you anticipate are the real or perceived needs of your adversary, don't start-off negotiations by making an offer that satisfies every one of those demands. The reasons for this will be covered in the chapters about conducting negotiations. However, always keep in mind that until you sit down at the table and get a firm sense of how the other party intends to negotiate, it isn't wise to show your hand.

3.3 SIX CRITERIA FOR SIZING UP THE OPPOSITION

One aspect of negotiation preparation that's often overlooked is an overall assessment of the party you will be bargaining with. Yet, giving this some thought not only helps identify the strengths and weaknesses of the other side's negotiation position, but it also aids in planning your own strategy. The types of questions you want to consider include:

1. How important is this negotiation to your adversary?
2. What do they stand to lose if an agreement isn't reached?
3. What is the overall financial impact of this deal?
4. What is the current and near-term outlook for the other parties' business?
5. What kind of reputation does the other party have within their field of business?
6. What, if any, prior experience have you had with the other party? If none, what experience have others had that you know about?

Satisfying yourself on these and other points shouldn't be taken lightly, since good agreements depend not only on the transaction itself, but also on the individuals and organizations that take part. Furthermore, reaching agreement is meaningless until performance of what's being agreed to is completed. Therefore, what you're essentially seeking is to establish the credibility of the other party. Will they negotiate in good faith, and do they have the capability to perform their part of the bargain?

This type of assessment can be overlooked when there are indications that a good deal is in the offing. But the fact is, the better a deal looks, the more crucial it is to look behind the scenes to determine why the other party is agreeable to it. Always remember that if a deal looks too good to be true, it probably is.

One area where it's easy to get careless in this regard is with an on-going business relationship. When repetitive transactions take place it's sometimes assumed that things will always go smoothly. However, circumstances change, and today's best customer may be tomorrow's bankruptcy. Therefore, don't take anything for granted, and you won't have to worry about getting burned by a bad deal.

3.4 THE NEED TO SEARCH FOR HIDDEN OBJECTIVES

There are times when the other party has reasons for negotiating that aren't apparent on the surface. Of course, sometimes these hidden motives won't hamper your ability to negotiate the deal you want. They may be objectives that are relevant only to the other party.

Nevertheless, on occasion the unstated goals of your adversary can affect you; either during negotiations, or down the road at some later date. One example is someone offering a low price to make a sale. Obviously, a low price may just mean you're getting a good deal. On the other hand, it could lead to all sorts of difficulties. Perhaps delivery dates won't be met, or maybe the quality will be shoddy. Even worse, perhaps the other business will fail before you get anything delivered.

Unfortunately, unless you're the proud owner of an infallible crystal ball, it's not easy to discover what's on someone's mind. So to some extent, you have to engage in a little bit of educated speculation. That means looking for clues that indicate the other party has some intent that hasn't been revealed. To do this with any degree of success, you have to look for signs that indicate that something isn't quite right.

For instance, someone in a hurry to complete negotiations when there's no apparent rush, or who is simply a little too willing to go along with everything you ask for. Whatever the signal might be, don't neglect to heed it, and either do a little checking, or at least mull over the possible reasons for such unusual action.

Obviously, trying to second-guess someone's motives isn't a practice that's either generally necessary, or likely to be successful. So you don't have to be paranoid about every negotiation that takes place. Nevertheless, when your instincts tell you that something isn't quite right, don't ignore them.

And even though you can't pinpoint what lies beneath the surface of a sly opponent's smile, if you think something is fishy, then at least protect your interests by placing appropriate provisions in any agreement. In fact, if you suggest including safeguards in a written agreement and the other side refuses, then you have confirmed your suspicions without even knowing your adversary's motive. To put it bluntly, if you don't feel good about a deal, then don't make it.

3.5 ESTABLISHING YOUR ADVERSARY'S NEGOTIATION AUTHORITY

Many a handshake signifying a done deal is quickly replaced by a frown when someone hears, "I'll get approval for this and we'll be all set." Sometimes that turns out to be true, and what was agreed upon is approved as is. On other occasions, the other negotiator comes back to say that higher authority wouldn't accept the agreement. As a result, what looked like a done deal ends up as only a preliminary round of bargaining.

In order to minimize this problem, always establish the authority of the person you're negotiating with. Otherwise, you'll work toward an agreement only to be told at the end that someone elses' approval is needed. Of course, there are many occasions when higher approval is in fact required. However, anytime you negotiate with someone conditioned upon higher approval, always reserve the same rights for yourself—even if you have authority to conclude negotiations on your own.

The purpose of reserving approval rights for yourself is to counter the use of higher approval as a ploy to extract additional concessions from you. This happens frequently, and generally takes the form of the other negotiator saying something such as, "The boss wouldn't accept your offer, but if you'll just raise it a bit, I'm sure we can get it done." How to deal with this ploy during negotiations is discussed in section 9.1.

The important point is to know beforehand, if the person negotiating will have final authority. If he doesn't—and in many types of negotiations this is a foregone conclusion—factor this into your planning.

3.6 IDENTIFYING THE BEHIND-THE-SCENES DECISION-MAKERS

If the person you negotiate with isn't the final decision-making authority, then you have a dual selling job to do in getting the agreement you want. Not only do you have to convince the person you're bargaining with, but you also have to win over the behind-the-scenes decision-makers.

This is a prospect you may face even when you have already established that the person you're negotiating with *does have* the authority to reach agreement. In fact, don't be surprised during negotiations to have an opposing negotiator tell you that he can't accept your terms without higher approval—even though he stated at the start that he had full authority. Such a confrontation might go something like this:

Other negotiator:	"I can't accept your offer as it stands. I'll have to take it up with my boss."
You:	"Wait a minute, Joe. You said before we started, that you had the authority to reach agreement."
Other negotiator:	"I do. We can agree right now on $2,000,000."
You:	"For crying out loud, all you're telling me is that you have authority if I accept your terms."
Other negotiator:	"No, that's not what I said, but you're not even being reasonable. This deal isn't worth a cent more than $2,000,000, and you're refusing to budge from $2,500,000. As a matter of fact, if you really want to settle this, I'll give you $2,200,000 right now. Let's do it."

> *You:* "Look, I started off at $3,000,000 which was a bargain. I've dropped my price to $2,500,000 in a good faith effort to reach agreement. All you're trying to do is squeeze me. If you didn't have the authority to reach agreement, you should have said so at the beginning."
>
> *Other negotiator:* "Hold it right there. You're telling me I don't have authority, when you won't settle for $2,200,000. You're the one that doesn't have authority."
>
> *You:* "Don't give me that crap. You're just trying to hold me up."
>
> *Other negotiator:* "Look. Do you want me to take $2,500,000 to my boss, or not?"

This is a fairly typical scenario that develops during negotiations. In this instance, a carrot has been dangled in front of you implying that the boss may accept your figure of $2,500,000. That may in fact happen, if your negotiating stance has convinced the other negotiator that you aren't going to budge from your offer. However, the flip side of the coin—and the most likely course—is that the negotiator will come back with a counter offer at something less than $2,500,000.

At that point, your alternatives include, acceptance or rejection of the counter-offer, continuing to negotiate, or getting the other side's boss directly involved. However, the important point is that even when the other side has the apparent authority to negotiate, there may be higher level people either directly or indirectly involved in final decisions. So always try to pinpoint who they will be before you start to negotiate, and if possible plan your negotiation strategy to counteract their influence.

A companion tactic that you'll frequently see is an attempt by the other side to go over your head and deal with a superior. There are a number of reasons for doing this which include:

- The other side perceives you as indecisive, or as an inexperienced negotiator.
- They find you to be too good a negotiator, and are trying to neutralize your skills.
- They think their heavy hitter is a better negotiator than your higher level people.
- The other negotiator is inexperienced, and/or is trying to bail-out from having to make a decision.

- They're just trying to intimidate you into making concessions.
- They hope your superiors will put pressure on you to reach agreement.
- It's a ploy to convince you that your position is unreasonable.
- The other party thinks there is a genuine impasse, and decides that it can only be resolved at a higher level.

Handling these attempts to take the negotiator out of the loop isn't difficult to deal with, if there is cooperation within your organization. First of all, any higher authority should promptly bounce the ball right back to the negotiator's level. Of course, it should be done courteously, but the message should be clear that the other side isn't going to get what they want by circumventing the negotiator.

The only time this tactic succeeds is when higher authority succumbs to ego-stroking. In other words, they decide that they can accomplish what the negotiator couldn't. This often leads to lousy deals, and a boss bragging about how he stepped in and negotiated what others couldn't. What gets overlooked is that anyone can negotiate a bad deal. It's getting a good deal that's difficult.

The main reason to minimize the impact of other decision-makers is because their participation often is nothing more than an attempt to win concessions that couldn't be gained at the bargaining table. Consequently, even if you can't pinpoint who any behind-the-scenes decision-makers are before you start to negotiate, always be prepared to ward-off their intrusions.

NOTE: If the other side brings in a higher-level person to deal with you, don't be intimidated. Discourage any suggestions that your boss should also be involved. This allows you to keep the negotiation on the same track as if you were still dealing with only the initial negotiator. Once they are able to get a higher-level person involved on your side, they are diluting your effectiveness, and removing you as the decision-maker. That, of course, is a decision to be made by your side—not by the suggestion or insistence of the opposition.

3.7 WAYS TO RESEARCH YOUR ADVERSARY

You can never know too much about anyone you're going to negotiate with. Depending upon the circumstances, there are several categories of information that are useful. These are:

- Company specific information on the organization you are dealing with.

- Industry-wide information on business trends in the company's area of business.
- Localized data on business conditions in the geographic area where the company is located.
- Financial information on the company, organization, or individual.
- Knowledge about your adversaries' prior dealings with others.
- Opinions on the personal traits of the people you will negotiate with.

Actually, what you want to know depends primarily on the sort of negotiation you're undertaking. The important point is that the more you know, the better prepared you will be to deal with any problem that arises during negotiations. Useful information can range from something as simple as knowing that the other negotiator is short-tempered, to crucial financial data showing that your adversary is one step away from bankruptcy. Obviously, researching the opposition is time-consuming, so your efforts should be in line with the importance of the negotiation.

Taking the time/importance trade-off into consideration, there are any number of ways to get the information you seek. Some of it will be readily available from public sources. You can also use contacts that know both you and your adversary. Oddly enough, two obvious sources of information are sometimes neglected, the first being within your own organization. This failure to obtain information internally most often occurs within large governmental or corporate organizations.

In fact, within a far-flung enterprise, it's not uncommon for more than one group to be negotiating with the same party at the same time—with both groups ignorant of the other's actions. Not only does this failure to communicate prevent the exchange of valuable information, but it may also cause unwitting competition for the same resources. Needless to say, the first place to check for information is within your own entity.

A second source of overlooked material is none other than your adversary. There's often a reluctance—particularly with inexperienced negotiators—to ask for information from the other party, either prior to or during negotiations. Actually, this isn't as odd as it seems, since there's a natural hesitancy on the part of most folks to pry into the affairs of others. However, when you're about to begin negotiations, it's time to put any qualms you may have aside. Disclosure is part and parcel of the negotiation process. So don't be reluctant to ask for any information you need to evaluate the deal you're working on.

Of course, an adversary may be reluctant to give you any data which would enhance your position. That's to be expected. However, if a request for essential data is refused, proceed with caution. It may well be that certain facts are being concealed that if known could change your mind about going through with any agreement. All in all, use every method at your disposal to obtain any information which will help you during negotiations. And once negotiations begin, continue to seek answers to questions that arise as the negotiations unfold.

3.8 EVALUATING THE OVERALL NEGOTIATING CLIMATE

A major factor influencing negotiations are the attitudes of the parties toward one another. In most negotiations, both sides enter into bargaining with more or less neutral feelings about the opposition. Of course, this position may quickly change if one side or the other starts to bargain on a highly emotional basis.

In other negotiations, a far more adversarial or downright hostile attitude exists. This type of situation is most frequently encountered in the field of labor relations, although animosity can exist in any negotiation where the parties have strained relations on either an organizational and/or personal level. Given the potential for grief that an unfavorable atmosphere can create, it's worthwhile to assess the negotiating climate before you begin to bargain.

Naturally, your goal should be to establish the most favorable negotiating climate you can. Often, you can accomplish this by simply keeping your cool, even when the other party becomes combative. It helps in this regard if you realize that in many circumstances, a hostile attitude may be nothing more than posturing by the opposing negotiator. Often, it's purely role playing for the benefit of the negotiator's constituency. (Example: A labor union negotiator attempting to impress the rank and file with a hard line stance, knowing full well that the demands are unreasonable.) Recognizing this possibility allows you to keep your cool and proceed more effectively toward ultimate agreement.

In certain cases, a little bit of prevention can improve the odds for a nonhostile environment. Therefore, it's prudent to make sure that the person negotiating for your side hasn't had unpleasant dealings in the past with his counterpart at the negotiating table. If there has been hostility, you have to decide whether someone else is less likely to arouse the type of resentment that could kill a deal. Naturally, you generally want your best negotiator to handle the transaction. But, in certain instances, lesser negotiation skills may be a better choice when there's a strong possibility that personal animosity may cloud someone's perspective.

Occasionally, outside influences may cast a cloud over the negotiating climate. For example, media attention and/or governmental scrutiny may induce one or both sides at the bargaining table to adopt public positions that are contrary to their private needs. The main danger in this area is that one side or the other will start to negotiate publicly. Once that happens, even when agreements are ultimately reached, the long-term result may be less than satisfactory, since one side may feel they were taken advantage of.

In general, taking negotiations public is a recipe for unfavorable repercussions from the other side. The end result will often be either no deal or a bad deal. And even when a short-term advantage is gained, it may turn into a long-term disaster. That's because anytime a negotiator is coerced into settlement by outside pressure, his bottom line outlook may well be, "Don't get mad, get even."

Therefore, for your part, avoid the urge to take your message public in an attempt to settle a private negotiation. And if the other side succumbs to the temptation, avoid getting drawn into a fencing contest. Instead, emphasize that you expect negotiations to continue at the bargaining table to amicably resolve differences.

3.9 USING ROLE PLAYING TO PREPARE
FOR CONFRONTATION

If you're about to participate in an extremely complicated negotiation, and/or are relatively inexperienced in bargaining tactics, you might want to act out a dry-run before you face your foe in the flesh. To do this without too much formality, get your negotiation team together and brainstorm potential questions and answers on issues that could conceivably arise during the negotiation session. Then, choose someone to play the part of your adversary and sit down and go through a trial negotiation. Have the other members of the negotiation team act as observers to critique your performance.

Don't try to set-up a specific script that will be followed during actual negotiations. First of all, no matter how carefully you plan, it's impossible to predict the actual path that negotiations will take. Furthermore, bargaining back and forth involves give and take which requires you to shift focus and maintain a degree of flexibility. Conversely, adopting a rigid game plan lessens the chance for compromise when the opportunity presents itself.

However, with or without any formal role playing, it's useful to at least go over the strategy you anticipate the other party will follow. Then, formulate your plan of attack to parry your opponent's tactics. Your objective is to be well prepared without being over-rehearsed. If you have taken the time to establish your negotiation objectives and analyze your opponent's position, then there's little preparation left to be done. And if you haven't done your homework, all the play acting in the world won't improve your position.

Part II

NEGOTIATION FUNDAMENTALS

Chapter 4

CRUCIAL COMMUNICATION SKILLS FOR NEGOTIATORS

The ability to communicate effectively is fundamental to negotiation success. Not only must you have the skills to convince people that your position is reasonable, but you usually have to do this against adversaries who are convincing in their own right.

But persuasion alone is only part of the equation. In addition, you have to be able to control your emotions under pressure, absorb and decipher the opposition's arguments, and know when to talk and when to listen. Above all, you have to use communication skills to gain your objective, while simultaneously resisting the sales pitch of your adversary as he seeks to achieve his own goals.

All of this doesn't mean that negotiating is the exclusive right of those renowned for either their eloquence, or the innate ability to sell snowshoes in the tropics. Even so, understanding how to communicate in a negotiating mode can vastly improve your bargaining skills.

4.1 COMMUNICATING CLEARLY TO AVOID COSTLY MISTAKES

Above all else, it's essential to be accurate when you engage in negotiations. Therefore, always know what you want to say before you say it. Confusing

53

people during negotiations complicates matters; not to mention the fact that carelessness can cause major errors and serious financial loss.

Furthermore, careless mistakes are most likely to happen when it's least expected. The irony is that extensive measures are often taken to safeguard negotiation secrets, when more often than not they're unintentionally revealed by a too glib negotiator. Therefore, always keep in mind that everything you say during a negotiation session is being scrutinized to reveal details of your position.

Incidentally, what you don't say can be as misleading as what you do. This is particularly true when the other negotiator misrepresents your position during conversation and you fail to correct him. Of course, the misrepresentation could be either accidental or intentional. However, for practical purposes it doesn't make any difference. After all, even if challenged the guilty parties' response will be something to the effect of, "Are you sure? I thought I heard you say the discount for payment in ten days was 15%."

Failing to correct a misrepresentation may mean a raging disagreement at a later point in the negotiation process. This is especially true when it involves an essential element of the negotiated agreement.

And of course, if this misunderstanding isn't discovered until after negotiations are complete, the problem is further magnified. Needless to say, never let a misrepresentation of your position go unchallenged. (Section 9.8 discusses how to make sure your position is clearly understood.)

By the way, care in communication is just as critical during the casual conversations that take place before and after negotiation meetings. When you're making small talk, avoid discussing business, unless you're intentionally doing it as part of your game plan.

NOTE: It's important to distinguish between being precise about what you say, and deliberately being vague as a negotiation tactic. Throwing up smoke screens is a common negotiation practice. (See section 12.1 on evasion.) The heart of the matter is to always know both what you're saying, and why you're saying it. There are certainly times when it pays to be vague, but only when it results from deliberate intent—not from carelessness.

4.2 WHAT YOU CAN LEARN BY JUST LISTENING

With the possible exception of sex, there's no subject that more people claim proficiency in than listening. There are few people with IQ's above room temperature who wouldn't say they were good listeners. Unfortunately, the claims would appear to exceed performance, or there would be fewer blunders and misunderstandings in daily life.

And although failing to be a good listener brings few consequences for most people, that can't be said about negotiators. For them, listening isn't a social nicety, it's a necessity, since there's no room for giving lip service to listening when you begin to bargain.

In negotiations, apart from just getting the facts straight, listening has some real advantages going for it. For instance, letting the other side talk while you listen will reveal inconsistencies in their negotiation position. It can also uncover valuable clues on how truthful the other party is. So let's look at a few simple steps that can enhance your listening skills at the bargaining table:

- Always be attentive. It's not easy to remain alert at all times, especially during lengthy negotiation sessions. However, if you don't, important issues may be missed.

- Send a message that you're listening by eye contact, as well as an occasional nod, smile, and so forth.

- Ask questions in a non-threatening manner. Try to be neutral in your tone of voice, instead of conveying skepticism about what the other person said.

- Watch the other negotiator for non-verbal signs such as nervousness, that may signal he's not secure in what he says.

- Don't interrupt. A common error is to quickly jump on an inconsistent statement. But remember, your goal isn't to say, "Ha! Ha! I got you." Rather, it's to learn as much as you can to support the argument that your negotiation position is the more substantive one.

- Be patient. Resist the temptation to help out if the other negotiator is having difficulty in making a point. First of all, your assistance may be resented. Furthermore, you never know what valuable tidbit might be blurted out inadvertently.

- Be empathetic. Showing you have respect for opposing viewpoints will help earn reciprocal respect for yours. This will make it easier to hurdle the hard points on the road to agreement.

- Ask for clarification of anything you don't understand. When the other negotiator finishes speaking, summarize what was said. Also, ask questions about any points that the negotiator didn't cover. Remember, what isn't said can be as important as what is.

- During presentations by the other negotiation team, look for areas of agreement in your respective negotiation positions. This narrows the number of issues you have to resolve.

NOTE: Although listening carefully is a good general rule, there are exceptions. For example, during negotiations there may be times when you want to let the other negotiator know that what he's saying is nonsense. Here, being inattentive by going through your papers, or looking out of the window, can get this message across. (Section 4.5 has more on this.)

4.3 RECOGNIZING AND USING THE POWER OF SILENCE

What happens when an opposing negotiator stops talking so you can respond? You say something. You ask questions, counter their arguments, and in general support your negotiation position as the correct one. That's natural enough, since there's a general tendency to assume that silence is a vacuum that must be filled—even at the expense of saying something foolish. This, unfortunately, results in many of the ill-advised remarks heard at negotiation meetings.

Few people realize that silence—in and of itself—can be a valuable tool. As a matter of fact, if it's done properly, silence can say more than a lengthy discourse defending your negotiation terms. It can be used to signal displeasure, emphasize a point, or force the other party to continue talking. And when people talk when they don't want to, wonderful things happen, ranging from cops getting confessions to negotiators getting concessions.

Of course, silence as a negotiating tool must be used sparingly to have any effect. So you have to develop a knack for knowing at what point it will be most effective. The following examples illustrate a few of the many conditions where silence is effective:

1. To keep the other party talking.

> *Seller:* "A unit price of $185.00 is the best I can do."
>
> *Buyer:* "That's too high . . ." (The buyer then goes on to give reasons why the price is too high.) This puts the buyer on the defensive in having to explain why the price is excessive. Using silence can change this.
>
> *Seller:* "A unit price of $185.00 is the best I can do."
>
> *Buyer:* Says nothing. Chances are the seller will break this deafening silence by continuing to elaborate on the reasonableness of his price. But since he had finished supporting his case for a $185.00 price, he's in a position similar to soldiers reaching the top of

a hill as they run out of ammunition. They find the enemy sitting there with loaded guns ready to fire. The only choices are to surrender or die. Of course, the seller won't give-up, since he doesn't face the same dire consequences. However, having run out of verbal ammunition, he's forced to flounder about to further support his position. And this can lead to peace at a reasonable price.

2. To register displeasure.

Silence can also be a convincing weapon in signifying dissatisfaction. For instance, when the other negotiator closes an argument by saying something such as, "Well, what do you think? " silently nodding your head from side to side says it all. If you then let several seconds of eerie silence pass, your adversary may feel compelled to fill the void.

3. To put emphasis on what you're about to say.

When you're about to make an important point, silence in the form of a pause, can be effective in emphasizing what you're going to say. For example, suppose you're going to reject an offer. You might do it like this: "I don't know how to put this, (short pause) but your price is unreasonably high." Simply pausing in the middle of a sentence rivets the other negotiator's attention on what you're going to say. The pause can also indicate that you're wishing you didn't have to say what you did. This sends a signal that you're sympathetic, which encourages the other negotiator to work with you on reaching agreement.

REMINDER: These are just a few examples of the number of ways you can use silence effectively as a negotiating tool. However, be careful about picking your spots. You have to take the context of each negotiation you undertake into consideration. There are times that silence will be effective, and other times when its use is meaningless. You have to decide for yourself when an appropriate point presents itself.

4.4 INTERPRETING VERBAL AND NON-VERBAL CLUES

Every negotiator would love to be a mind-reader, so as to know what the opposition is thinking. After all, negotiating would be a snap if you knew whether or not your opponent was leveling with you, or just spewing forth propaganda to support his pitch. Regrettably, since there is no foolproof way to sort fact from fiction, you have to look for clues wherever you can find them. One good method is to look for verbal and non-verbal messages which indicate credibility, or the lack of it. These signals include:

- Attitude
- Appearance
- Facial expressions
- Gestures
- Tone of voice

Let's look at these one-by-one:

1. Attitude—Is the other negotiator aggressive, or friendly and forthright? Although either attitude might change as negotiations progress, initial aggressiveness may indicate that negotiations will be on an adversarial basis. On the other hand, someone who is relaxed and friendly may be a candidate for a joint problem-solving approach to negotiations. In any event, don't make a hasty assumption one way or the other, until you have a chance to feel the opposition out when negotiations get underway.

   Furthermore, although first impressions are important, it's risky to jump to conclusions. It might turn out that a meek and mild-mannered guy starts snarling at your throat the first time you disagree with him.

2. Appearance—Appearances can be deceiving. After all, eccentrics with enough money to fund a small town's budget have been known to be less than impressive in their appearance. The bottom line is that if someone's appearance is out of the ordinary, it should be read in conjunction with other signals to determine if something isn't quite right.

3. Facial Expressions—A smile, frown, or grimace can all silently telegraph your opponent's reaction to what you're saying. Be careful though, since a savvy negotiator might deliberately try to send you the wrong signal. (Example: Sammy Shrewd frowns when you mention you're willing to pay $110,000.00, hoping this will convince you the price is too low. In actuality, he knows that is a reasonable price.)

4. Gestures—Some people make very distinctive gestures when they're talking. Actually, a few might make you wonder whether they could talk if their hands were tied behind their back. Be that as it may, the

question is what if anything does this tell you? Actually, it's not wise to read too much into body language when you have money on the line. Just because your opponent sits rigid in his chair doesn't mean that he's inflexible and hard to deal with. It could be that he has a sore back from playing too much tennis yesterday.

5. Tone of Voice—How someone says something can indicate how they feel about it. Sometimes it's obvious such as, "That's crazy, you stupid fool. What are you trying to do, steal my business?" In other instances, it's difficult to tell whether someone is sending a subtle message, or you're just reading them wrong.

SUGGESTION: Any individual verbal or non-verbal clue is generally of minor value in discerning anything that might be of value to you during negotiations. This is especially true when you're up against experienced negotiators. Not only are they savvy enough not to send overt signals of their intentions, but they may also send false clues. The most common example is feigning anger to buttress their demands.

Since it's difficult—if not impossible—to decipher reality from superior acting ability, it's smart not to place too much credence on individual nuances. Of course, on occasion you may find folks who telegraph their intentions by their actions. Therefore, your best approach is to be alert to the possibilities, without wasting a lot of effort in being an amateur psychologist.

4.5 EXERCISING CONTROL OVER THE SIGNALS YOU SEND

Just as you should remain alert for subtle signals that reveal your adversaries' negotiation objectives, you must simultaneously be careful not to inadvertently reveal your own position. Instead, you want to send signals that reinforce your negotiation strategy.

One effective tactic is to use non-verbal communications to send a negotiation message. Perhaps you want to let your adversary know that you're not taking his statements too seriously. Such devices as doodling on a piece of paper, looking out the window, or whispering to a member of your negotiation team, can work pretty well. Why bother to do this? Wouldn't it just be simpler to tell him that you're not impressed with his arguments?

Actually, there are valid reasons why a little bit of discretion is called for. Your goal—and hopefully your adversaries—is to reach a final agreement that you both can live with. Each of you have independent ideas of what the final terms should be. In fact, you may be light years apart in your respective positions. Nevertheless, during negotiations you will close the gap in your differences until an agreement is finalized. And the more skillful you both are at closing this gap without creating a hostile environment, the better are the chances that you'll get there.

Sure, sometimes the debate gets heated during negotiations, but as a general rule, the less heat that's generated, the better the odds of reaching agreement sooner rather than later or even never. Consequently, when you can send subtle signals indicating dissatisfaction, you can lessen the number of issues that erupt into open conflict.

Reaching an agreement is also facilitated by maintaining as much good-will as possible. And sending a non-verbal sign that you're bored is a lot gentler than abruptly stating the same thing. In fact, even though the other party knows from your indications of inattention that his message isn't getting across, he really doesn't know why. He may even attribute it to his own presentation abilities. Alternatively, he might conclude that his demands are unreasonable, and have led to your indifference.

This brings us to the tactical reason for sending messages in subtle ways. The ebb and flow of negotiations are such that to a casual observer they appear to be going nowhere. But each of the opposing parties is constantly evaluating and revising their own position—at least internally without informing the other side.

At the same time, they are continually analyzing their opponent's stance, to determine where there may be possibilities for resolving differences. To capitalize on this, it's to your advantage to send clues that influence your adversaries' assessment of your position. After all, if they convince themselves that you're unyielding on certain points, it's that much easier to substantiate your position when the time comes.

For example, suppose you almost imperceptibly wince when the other negotiator mentions the price he wants. It's possible that in subsequent discussions with his negotiation team, someone may point this out, by saying something such as, "Did you see Charlie Cheap cringe whenever $25,000,000 was mentioned. I don't think he's going to go for that high a figure." If that happens, you have succeeded in lowering the expectations of your adversary. As a result, when the time to talk turkey on price arrives, the other side is already conditioned to accepting less than they wanted.

Aside from non-verbal clues, something as simple as changing the tone of your voice can send messages ranging from anger, to impatience, to disbelief, or most any other emotion imaginable. All of this isn't to imply that you should rush off and enroll in acting school. Verbal and non-verbal clues are but one small part of the many and varied tactics that are brought to the negotiation table.

If you're good at using them, by all means do, and if you're not, don't worry about it. A weakness in one area of negotiations is often compensated for by strength in others. The important point is to control the signals you send, so you don't inadvertently tip your hand to the opposition.

4.6 WHY LOSING YOUR COOL CAN COST YOU MONEY

Keeping control of your emotions during negotiations is necessary to prevent mistakes from being made in a moment of anger. In addition, a hostile environment makes it more difficult to move matters along toward agreement. In fact, the more heated discussions become, the more likely that negotiations will terminate never to be resumed.

It's admittedly not always easy to keep your temper in check, particularly if you're trying to reach agreement with a less than friendly foe. To make matters even worse, some negotiators intentionally try to rattle their adversaries into making mistakes.

An opponent may become hostile for a number of reasons. In some instances, it's done to obscure the fact that their negotiation position is unsupported by the facts. To overcome this handicap, an adversary may attempt to bully his opponent into submission with bluster and bravado. However, if you are subjected to this ploy, simply ignore it. Angrily reacting is just playing into the hands of your opponent. Instead, calmly reiterate your position, and wait for your opponent to cool down.

An opponent may also become hot-headed in the hope that this will cause you to make careless errors. And if you meet fire with fire that may well be what happens. Finally, less experienced negotiators sometimes become testy through sheer frustration, and the intense pressures of extended negotiations.

Although baiting an opponent is a tactic used by some negotiators, it's best to avoid using this technique yourself. Deliberately feigning anger to rattle an opponent offers far more risks than rewards. For one thing, when you rattle someone's cage, you're extending an open invitation for them to rattle back. All this will do is lead to deteriorating conditions which offer little hope for the type of compromise that's the cement for sealing any agreement. (Section 11.7 covers certain circumstances where getting grouchy may be necessary.)

Even if you are successful in getting under an opponent's skin, so that careless mistakes are made in your favor, the long-term results are going to be negative. Once someone realizes they've been shortchanged, it won't be forgotten. So the likelihood of future business dealings are down the drain. The bottom line is that there's little value in having anger and hostility surface during negotiations, either as a deliberate ploy, or the inability to control oneself.

4.7 WORKING TO ELIMINATE
SELF-DEFEATING BEHAVIOR

One of the greatest impediments to achieving success at the negotiating table is the inability to recognize and control self-defeating behavior. How you conduct yourself has a direct bearing upon your ability to convince the other party to accept the terms and conditions you propose. There's nothing mysterious about that. After all, we're all more receptive to requests from those we like and/or respect. But the human relations aspect of life tends to be rejected as irrelevant when it's time to do a business deal.

Much of this neglect stems from an attitude of, "I'm looking out for my interests. Let them worry about theirs." On the surface, that's not an unreasonable attitude. In essence, the focal point of any negotiation is to further your own self-interest and/or the interests of the party or organization on whose behalf you're negotiating.

However, what's missing is the recognition that to achieve your goals, you need to get the other party to agree with your demands. And when the positions of the parties are far apart when negotiations begin, someone has to do some heavy-duty convincing to gain their goals. Alternatively, where convincing ends, compromising has to begin if a mutual agreement is to be reached. Therefore, how you deal with your adversary will have a direct bearing on your ability to achieve satisfactory results.

One tendency to avoid is being too rigid about your goals. Give and take is required at the bargaining table, and every issue isn't either black or white. So when you're negotiating, it pays to go for the gray and seek the middle ground for agreement.

This means keeping an open mind about your opponent's objectives. Some negotiators experience vapor lock of the brain toward any viewpoint other than their own. As a result, they ignore attempts at reasonable compromise. This leads to totally unsupported arguments on the issues. However, once an adversary perceives a negotiator as being unreasonable, the possibilities for persuasion are eliminated.

It also pays to be careful about how you couch objections to your opponent's arguments. Saying the wrong thing can inspire the other party to think, "I'll show him!" The end result is an adversary who digs his heels in, which makes it far more difficult to reach agreement.

On a more personal level, whether you like someone or not shouldn't be a consideration in how you handle yourself during negotiations. Furthermore, avoid the trap of entering into an ego contest where both negotiators, instead of looking for avenues of agreement, battle to determine who is the best negotiator. The best tactic when negotiating is to keep your emotions in neutral while you drive toward achieving your goals.

4.8 WAYS TO OVERCOME COMMUNICATION ROADBLOCKS

You can facilitate making progress during negotiation meetings by working to eliminate various communication roadblocks that crop-up from time to time. The most common problem in this area is when negotiators tend to talk right past each other. This comes about when someone is so certain their position is the correct one, that they unintentionally tune-out what the other party is saying. The danger here is two fold. First of all, ignoring the other negotiator—intentionally or not—prevents you from gathering information which might lead you to (1) modify your position or, (2) gain information useful in rebutting your adversaries' assertions.

Counter this tendency by always remaining alert to what is being said. Often, especially during extended negotiation sessions, a fatigue factor sets in that lessens your powers of concentration. So watch for signs you're getting tired, and if necessary, take a coffee break, go to lunch, or adjourn the meeting for the day.

There are several simple devices you can use when you sense that your point isn't getting across. These include:

- Use humor—Humor relaxes people, and tends to make the negotiating relationship more personal. It helps build rapport, which makes it easier to resolve difficult issues. Make the humor relevant if at all possible. It doesn't hurt to make yourself the brunt of the humor, since this has the effect of making you appear less dominating.

- Shift focus—If you notice people aren't paying attention to what you're saying, change the discussion. Lengthy presentations of financial details often lull folks to sleep. So keep these to the minimum.

- Don't get too technical—Whether you or a member of your team is talking, avoid technical details that won't be understood by others.

- Paraphrase confusing points—If you sense difficulty in someone understanding what is being explained, try saying it differently.

CAUTION: Occasionally, a negotiator will attempt to simply wear an opponent down by dragging a negotiation session on and on. This is done in the hope that the opponent will give in just to get it over with. If you suggest adjournment, your opponent will attempt to dissuade you by saying something such as, "Look, do you want to negotiate or not. If you do, there's no reason to quit now." Don't let yourself be intimidated by this ploy. Simply reply by saying, "I'm as anxious as you to get this done. In fact, I want to adjourn for the day so I can evaluate what's been covered to date." Needless to say, if you're the one pressuring to continue negotiations, make sure you're well rested.

Protracted negotiation sessions also take place when there are real or imagined deadlines to meet. If you anticipate such an event, prepare yourself. Get plenty of rest beforehand, and if it's feasible have someone prepared to fill in when negotiations are in session. That way, you can take occasional breaks and extend your staying power.

4.9 BUILDING TRUST TO BREAK DOWN RESISTANCE

Building trust is a process that generally develops over a period of time as people get to know one another. However, most negotiations aren't lengthy enough for that process to work. Therefore, it's necessary to use practices that can short cut the trust-building process. In general, providing detailed factual support for your position, leveling with your opponent, and recognizing his objectives will build rapport toward reaching agreement.

One practice that helps is to raise anticipated objections to your negotiation position yourself. By doing this, you're in effect saying, "I know my objectives aren't perfect, and I'm willing to recognize that." What this does is give your adversary assurances that you're not trying to hide anything. This is a solid way to build trust quickly. What's even better, is that this type of approach has a bonus factor. Which is, by raising the issue yourself, you can also take the opportunity to overcome the objections to it. If this is done skillfully, you can put a thorny issue to rest before the other side can mount an attack on it.

Another solid trust-building tactic is to agree with something your opponent suggests early on in the negotiations. What better way to assure the other party that you're not looking to take them to the cleaners? Incidentally, many novice negotiators fear this is a sign of weakness, and signals that they're caving in to the opposition. But it isn't, and in fact you can use it to gain an advantage of your own. You do this by packaging something you want along with granting what your opponent is seeking.

For example, "I can go along with speeding-up my deliveries, assuming we put my payment terms in the contract. That's necessary, since we tie-up money in raw materials and in-process inventory with an accelerated delivery schedule. And as you know, that costs money." What you have done with a scenario such as this is to get something you want by tying it in with something the other party wants. Of greater importance, you have justified your request by linking it with your opponent's demand.

Incidentally, if you're negotiating with someone with whom you have had prior dealings, the history of performance on previous business is the consummate trust builder. If your performance has been above par, make sure you bring that fact up, even though the other party is well aware of it. And, of course, if you anticipate future dealings with the same people, how the current agreement is performed will dictate how much trust there is the next time around—or whether there will even be a next time.

4.10 LEARNING HOW TO ASK KEY QUESTIONS

It stands to reason that negotiators aren't going to just lay their cards on the table and let you pick those you want. Instead, they want to tell you as little as possible, and give only answers that support their position. So for the most part, you will have to work hard to obtain enough information to separate fact from fiction. Therefore, it's necessary to not only know how to ask the right questions, but also know the right way to ask them.

There are a number of techniques you can use to pin down your opponent. Of these, the most basic is to listen carefully to everything that's said. By doing this you can pick-up details and inconsistencies to ask about at the appropriate time. As a general rule, don't interrupt members of the other negotiating team with questions when they're making a presentation. The longer they talk, the greater the likelihood that something of value will be said. Always remember, no one gives away secrets by being silent. So even if you start to get bored, be patient. This is one of the rare instances when being bored can be beneficial.

The type of questions you want to ask will, of course, be dictated by the specifics of the negotiation that's taking place. But in general, you want to probe your opponent's negotiation position to understand his objectives, as well as verify the validity of his offer. In other words, you want to know what he wants, why he wants it, and what it's going to take to get an agreement.

You may find the following techniques to be helpful in asking questions:

1. If you're seeking information, don't ask questions which can be answered with a "Yes" or "No," unless that's what you want.

2. Ask questions that require facts to be supplied—not opinions.

3. Use a neutral tone of voice and be calm. A loud and/or demanding demeanor won't elicit positive responses.

4. If you're looking for "hard to get" information, try asking a series of "soft" questions first. This conditions the respondent to automatically reply. Then, ask the tough question.

5. If you are having trouble getting useful information, ask a question that requires a lengthy and/or technical reply. Long-winded responses often unintentionally contain valuable tidbits of information.

REMINDER: When people don't want to give you information, but don't have a valid reason to refuse, they often say something such as, "I'll have to look into that and get back to you." They may, in fact, have no intention at all of replying to your request. Their hope is that you'll forget about it as negotiations proceed. Never neglect to get a commitment as to when requested information will be furnished, and make sure you follow-up until you get it. In fact, if what you're looking for is crucial, slow down the negotiating process until it's received. Say something like, "Well, I don't see much use in going ahead until we can resolve this matter."

4.11 EFFECTIVE WAYS TO PIN DOWN VAGUE ANSWERS

Vague answers aren't much better than no answer at all. About all they really tell you is that for one reason or another, the party you're dealing with isn't being very forthright. This usually stems from one of two reasons. Either you're not asking the right questions, or more likely, you're asking questions that are too good—at least from the standpoint of your adversary.

Whatever the cause, vague answers in a negotiation session are as common as a cold, and equally as annoying to deal with. But while you may have to let the sniffles run their course, you can't let vague answers just slip by. If you want to make headway, you have to keep at it until you get the responses you're looking for. Some ways of doing this are:

1. Repeat the answer and then ask for clarification. For example, "Joe, you said material costs would be in the neighborhood of $50,000.00. What neighborhood are you talking about? Beverly Hills or the back alleys of Calcutta? I'd like to have an item by item breakdown of material costs."

2. Ignore an inadequate response initially, and then raise the same question again at an unexpected moment. You may find that you get a completely different answer, since the element of surprise works against a canned reply. If the other party objects, saying they already answered the question, simply say you didn't understand the answer. What do you do if you get the same answer all over again? Try, "That didn't make sense to me the first time, and it still doesn't." Then, rephrase the question to zero in on what you're looking for.

3. Ask follow-up questions to pin the other party down.

4. Be persistent. Keep asking until you get an answer. Don't be intimidated if the other negotiator gets angry. That's a standard tactic when someone doesn't want to answer a question.

4.12 SIX TACTICS TO MAKE YOUR ARGUMENTS MORE EFFECTIVE

Winning the verbal tug of war that takes place at the negotiating table takes more than good debating skills. After all, no matter how many points you make in support of your position, it's an exercise in futility if the other side isn't buying what you're selling. Therefore, always try to make your case with the point of view of the other side in mind. Look for clues that indicate receptiveness to certain elements of what you're proposing. Then, play to these strengths as much as possible. The following guidelines may prove helpful in making your arguments more convincing:

1. Support your arguments with documentation whenever possible. When it's on paper it appears more plausible. This is especially true if you have third party testimonials you can use.

2. Bring in experts to support your position. The more authoritative they are the better. Of course, on occasion you may find the other side bringing in their own experts to support their position and/or counter yours. (Section 14.7 discusses strategies for coping with your opponent's experts.)

3. Avoid using excessive hype or unfounded claims. The other side is more likely to pay attention to arguments that are factual.

4. Even though you shouldn't put emphasis on the weaker aspects of your proposal, it's wise not to ignore them. If it's possible to do so without looking foolish, bring them up yourself. Then, counter the weaknesses with offsetting strengths.

   For example, "Our price, as you know, is marginally higher than our competitors. That's due to the additional costs we incur to insure that our quality is superior. Let me go over the quality checks we have which are . . ." What you're doing here is raising the issue and defending it before the other side has a chance to bring it up. Doing this deals with an issue on your terms—not the opposition's. There's also a trust-building factor involved whenever you raise an issue that's to your potential detriment. It adds a degree of credibility to your argument that wouldn't be there if the issue was left for the other side to raise.

   In fact, if your adversary later attempts to use the issue you raised to attack your position, you can rebut it by saying, "I wouldn't have raised the point myself, if it wasn't perfectly justified."

5. Make sure your words and actions are in agreement. Avoid sending conflicting verbal and non-verbal messages. For instance, don't say, "Fred, we can spend all of the time you want discussing that point," as

you're glancing up at the clock, or stuffing papers in your briefcase. Along the same line, don't stumble around in presenting your thoughts. For example, if you want to rebut something that was said, but can't carry it off effectively, shift the focus to something else.

6. Use timing to your advantage. As an example, try to close the deal at an opportune moment when the mood is upbeat, not when your adversary is pounding his shoe on the table.

4.13 PINPOINTING THE REASON WHY YOU'RE BEING IGNORED

If your opponent isn't listening to what you're saying, then all that great justification you have is useless. Therefore, it's of more than passing interest to figure out why you're being ignored. The most basic reason may be nothing more than fatigue, so when you notice inattentiveness setting in after a prolonged period of negotiations, call for a break in the proceedings.

There are several other reasons why the other side may be ignoring you:

- To deliberately indicate that they aren't impressed with what you're saying.
- To rattle you into making a mistake.
- To get you to stop talking, so they can have their say.
- Your presentation may, in fact, be too lengthy which has encouraged them to tune you out.
- The environmental conditions of the conference room may be poor. (too hot or cold, noisy, and so forth)

Whatever the reason, once you notice your message isn't getting across, it's necessary to do something that will refocus attention on what you're saying. Let's look at ways this can be done.

4.14 FOUR WAYS TO GET ATTENTION

Whenever you feel that you're losing control of the agenda during a negotiation session, the following actions can serve to get the other parties' attention:

1. *Talk turkey.* In most negotiations, one or more of the issues has more significance than others. Often, of course, it's money, but it could be anything

else depending upon the nature of what's being negotiated. Whatever it is, abruptly bringing up the crucial issue will quickly get your opponent's attention.

NOTE: You don't have to do this in the context of making an offer or concession of some sort. One good tactic is to frame the issue as a question to the other party. For instance, "Jack, what are the bottom line dollars you need to do this deal today?"

2. *Test the waters.* The other side will pay heed to any statement you make that smacks of agreement with their position. For example, "Well Jack, it looks like we may agree on the specifications. If we do, then let's talk about price, since the two are obviously related." In this case, they are given an option of not agreeing to the specs, or accepting them and discussing price. This type of tactic forces the other side to respond to your assertion.

However, always be careful to use this approach in such a way that the alternative responses work in your favor. In the example given, the negotiator wants to pin down the specifications and go on to negotiating a contract price. Therefore, even if the other side wants to continue negotiating the specifications, this is working toward reaching the negotiator's objective.

Of course, your opponent may take a completely different tack in his response such as, "Hogwash, we can't settle on the specs until we resolve the question of waivers for deviations from the specs." Even with this sort of response, you have still achieved your primary objective, which was to get the other sides' attention and work toward agreement.

3. *Drastic measures.* If you want to guarantee that you get prompt attention paid to you, then start to rant and rave. If that seems a bit out of character for you, then you can try more subtle approaches. Something as simple as standing up, taking off your jacket, and rolling up your sleeves, while saying, "Let's get down to business," will do the trick. Actually, you can easily have all eyes hone in on you, by asking—directly or indirectly—why you're being ignored.

Another attention-getter is to use a bit of humor, which can also serve to relieve the tension of a long negotiation session. But be careful here, since some folks just can't carry off an attempt at being funny. Therefore, if humor isn't your strong suit, forget about it. Otherwise, you will just be encouraging the inattention that you're trying to overcome.

4. *The best guarantee of having the other side pay heed to what you're saying is to return the favor by paying attention to them.* Therefore, listen attentively to their arguments if you want them to listen to yours. In addition, make sure that you're communicating effectively, and not encouraging folks to tune you out. That means being clear, concise, and compelling in presenting your position.

4.15 THE KEYS TO POSITIVE PERSUASION

The reasonableness of your negotiation position is, of course, the prime determinant in persuading the other party to reach an agreement with you. Nevertheless, this is rarely self-evident, and it's up to you to persuade the other party that you're offering them a good deal. This is even more crucial when the deal isn't quite as good as you would like them to believe. The following techniques can be of help in convincing those you negotiate with that your position is fair and reasonable:

1. Be positive to persuade—being negative is counter productive. Act, look, think, and talk like you believe in your negotiation objectives. If you don't, you can't reasonably expect the other party to agree with you.

2. Know your facts and present them in a knowledgeable manner. To be successful in negotiations, you don't have to persuade people to like you, but you do have to earn their respect.

3. Make sure you're understood. Talk on a level the other party can understand. Often, "expert" members of negotiation teams go off on tangents, and/or couch their remarks in the language of their professional specialty. However, no one should be talking at a negotiation meeting, if they're not contributing to furthering your cause. So make sure that techno-talk is defined in terms that can be understood. It's also useful to repeat hard-to-understand concepts and terms.

4. Talk to the decision-maker. No matter who has asked a question, direct your answer to the decision-maker. That's the person who has to be persuaded.

5. Never engage in personal attacks on your adversary, either directly or indirectly. This includes not only the person you're negotiating with, but also their superiors, subordinates, and the organization they work for.

6. If possible, support your arguments with reference to third parties, since this adds credibility. For example, "The MNZ Corporation increased production 20% by using our machines." Naturally, if you have documentation providing third party testimonials, it's even more convincing.

7. Show the other side how you can solve a problem they have. If the subject matter of your negotiation is such that you can do this, you can't ask for anything more convincing.

8. Appearance counts. Whether it's a well-prepared written proposal, or a neatly dressed negotiator, people are influenced by appearance.

Chapter 5

FUNDAMENTALS FOR SUCCESSFUL NEGOTIATIONS

There are many obstacles to hurdle on the way to a negotiated agreement. Perhaps one of the most vexing that many folks face is defending price objections. Whenever you're selling anything, the other side always thinks the price is too high. And on the rare occasion when they don't, suspicions then center on whether or not there's something fishy because of a low price.

For many negotiations, price is the paramount issue. However, when price isn't a major factor—or even an element in your negotiations—it's still crucial to negotiate an agreement that has a high probability of satisfactory performance. Therefore, considerable care must be taken in negotiating each and every provision of proposed agreements.

Besides these fundamental elements, you also have to know when to say "No" during negotiations, how to respond to tactics used by your adversary, as well as figure out ways to hurdle seemingly insurmountable problems. This chapter covers these perplexing topics, along with one of a more personal nature, which is how to assume a negotiation style that best fits your personality.

5.1 ADAPTING YOUR NEGOTIATION STYLE TO YOUR PERSONALITY

Many people with limited negotiation experience think they have to assume an unaccustomed role to be a good negotiator. The mythical image they try to imitate is that of a hard-charging, hammerhead who won't take no for an answer.

Operating on this assumption, they enter into negotiations not unlike the proverbial bull in a china shop. The end result is routinely similar to what happens when a bully walks the beach. The timid slink away, while the savvy and/or strong back the bully down. Corresponding results happen in negotiations. Hard-chargers find that novice negotiators don't want to deal with them, while veteran negotiators finesse the shirt off their backs.

However, contrary to popular perception, intimidation isn't the necessary ingredient for negotiation success. That distinction belongs to preparation, since if you don't know where you're going, how are you going to know when you have arrived? Of course, you might think, "Why not be thoroughly prepared and still be a hard-charger?" The answer is really fundamental. To conclude negotiations, there must be a joint agreement between the two sides. Therefore, unless someone is getting a real bargain, why would they want to deal with an Oscar Obnoxious type of personality?

In truth, trying to bulldoze people into submission generally leads to bad deals or no deal at all. The perception of good negotiators as being hard-chargers is nothing more than a myth cultivated by image-conscious, ego driven, wheeler-dealers. Consequently, you don't have to be either blunt or domineering to succeed as a negotiator. Therefore, it's unnecessary to pump yourself up into being something you're not at the negotiation table.

Negotiation style is nothing more than the way you handle negotiations. Some folks like to delve into the nitty-gritty detail of things, while others like to go straight for the "big picture." Many people are by nature patient, while others are less so. The major consideration isn't so much what type of personality you have. Instead, what's crucial is the need to recognize where your strengths and weaknesses lie. This helps you to think about how best to negotiate based on your personal makeup, rather than forcing yourself to play an unfamiliar role. For instance, if you don't have a lot of patience, then plan your negotiation strategy with that in mind.

As another example, you may not find yourself to be particularly good at being persuasive. Yet, you may excel at evaluating information. With that in mind, your approach to negotiations might be to concentrate on countering your opponent's arguments, rather than pitching the merits of your own position. All in all, the major consideration is to negotiate in a manner you feel comfortable with—not by preconceived notions of how a negotiator should act.

5.2 ASSESSING THE OPPOSITION'S NEGOTIATING STYLE

It's risky business to try and pigeonhole people, but it gets even trickier when you try to characterize opposing negotiators based on their demeanor. First of all, it's hard to tell whether they're playing it straight, or are just using a negotiation face designed to conceal their true feelings. In reality, it doesn't make that much difference whether their actions are natural or assumed, since you have to react to whatever personality they present.

As a matter of fact, no matter what sort of negotiating antics you may be subjected to, it's necessary to stay the course and plod along on the predetermined path you have set for yourself. Nevertheless, it's useful to assess how the other negotiator bargains. Of course, the possibilities are endless, and attempting to typecast people on every characteristic down to the color of their socks is foolish.

Even so, it is useful to try and pinpoint at least the broad aspects of someone's negotiating style. Most negotiators fall into three broad groups in terms of their approach to reaching agreement. These are:

1. The "Let's get it done" type.

These negotiators are primarily interested in wrapping up a deal as quickly as possible. They will quickly make offers and nudge you toward a speedy agreement. They may readily recommend "splitting the difference," (Section 6.6 covers the pitfalls of this technique.) invoke deadlines, and in general try to minimize any objections to a prompt settlement.

Despite the apparent lack of attention to detail of a "let's get it done" negotiator, they shouldn't be hastily characterized as careless. They may very well know what they're doing—which may be to get a contract signed before you discover the potholes in their position. Needless to say, don't be rushed to agreement by these types.

2. The "Grind out the last detail" negotiator.

This type of character may have you talking to yourself before negotiations are completed. Detail-oriented negotiators tend to nitpick every aspect of your proposal. They will slowly play out their hand with the ultimate objective of wearing you down. The best remedy for coping with this kind of negotiator is a combination of patience and a little nitpicking of your own.

3. Middle-of-the-roaders.

Most negotiators tend to fall in between the extremes of the previous two types. They move steadily toward agreement in a purposeful way without being either pushy or dragging their feet.

CAUTION: Don't place too much emphasis on analyzing the style of the other negotiator. Sometimes, there's a tendency to try and place people in neat little boxes. This is a risky enough endeavor under any circumstances, but it's even more foolhardy at the negotiation table. A skilled negotiator may rapidly shift roles from one style to another. Meanwhile, while you're trying to psychoanalyze his methods, he's busy suctioning serious dollars from your wallet.

5.3 THE NEED FOR "DOUBLE-PRONGED" KNOWLEDGE

Sections 3.1 through 3.4 covered various aspects of identifying the objectives and game plan of your opponent before negotiations begin. That is, of course, worthwhile information in preparing your bargaining position. But of even greater concern is the need to obtain information when you sit down to negotiate. This data has a dual advantage. On the one hand, it gives you the ability to assess the validity of your adversaries' position. Of equal value—but often overlooked—is the need to view this information in terms of its impact upon the individual elements of your own negotiation position.

By examining the details of what your opponent proposes, and weighing these factors against your own negotiation position, you can readily identify areas of agreement and disagreement. This helps you to sort out issues you can agree on, which you can trade-off against items your opponent objects to. It also helps you in making adjustments to your position that can overcome obstacles to agreement. Let's look at how this can be done:

Background

"A," a large manufacturer, is purchasing electronic components from "B," a mid-size supplier who specializes in this type of item. "A's" pre-negotiation research has identified two other potential vendors of similar items, although the alternative items would require some modification to meet "A's" specifications. There are also open questions as to the quality of the alternative products. Therefore, "B" is the preferred source for "A's" buy.

The problem

Contract negotiations are essentially hung-up over price. "A" asks for and receives a detailed cost breakdown from "B." "A" performs a cost analysis of the data, and finds the data to essentially support "B's" price offer. However, the unit cost is still too high from "A's" perspective.

Alternative solutions

"A's" negotiation team meets and discusses the alternatives. One is to suggest a larger quantity buy, which would reduce "B's" per unit price. This is feasible, since "A" will have a continuing need for this item over the foreseeable future. Another recommendation is to change "A's" specifications, so they are less stringent. The technical members of "A's" team agree that this can be done. It's estimated that this would cut "B's" costs about 10% per unit which would bring the price within a level that "A" could accept.

The decision

"A" decides to suggest revising the specifications to lower "B's" price. "A" also decides to offer the inclusion of an unpriced option (the price will be negotiated if and when the option is exercised) in the contract with "B." "A" doesn't want to commit to a firm price for an option quantity, since it has had no prior experience with "B" as a supplier. However, "A" feels that by including the unpriced option, it will give "B" an incentive to try and lower production costs in the knowledge that "A" will want to exercise the option if "B" can offer a reasonable price.

The outcome

"A" and "B" agree to a contract at an acceptable price based on revision of the specifications. The successful negotiation resulted from "A" getting "B's" price data, and analyzing its adequacy. Learning it was fundamentally sound gave "A" the incentive to come up with an alternative solution.

NOTE: Many negotiations flounder because one or both parties don't make full use of the information they get from the other side. Frequently, there's a tendency to use data just to pick apart the other negotiator's arguments. Of course, that is a valid purpose. However, it's just as valuable to look at information from a problem-solving perspective. In other words, what does the information tell you about how the respective negotiation positions can be altered to reach an agreement that's satisfactory to both sides? Doing this, as in the case above, can lead to creative solutions to seemingly insurmountable problems.

5.4 TECHNIQUES FOR JUSTIFYING AND GETTING A HIGH PRICE

No matter how reasonable you think your price is, when negotiations begin, it's a foregone conclusion that the other side will challenge your price as being too high. There are two principal reasons for this:

1. Everyone wants to get a good deal, and accepting what's initially offered runs counter to this sort of mindset. Simply put, people like bargains, and if they are deprived of the opportunity to reduce the price, then they aren't convinced that they're getting one.

2. There's a natural assumption that your price is inflated. As the thinking goes, everyone wants to maximize their profits, so your initial price must be too high.

Because of this natural tendency to suspect that an initial price is a loaded figure, it's useful to have alternative positions prepared before you start to negotiate. This was discussed in sections 1.5 and 1.6 of Chapter One. If you do this, then you give yourself some built-in flexibility to reduce your price. Of course, if you don't have to make any significant reductions, then all the better.

Nevertheless, it's not always possible to reasonably inflate an initial offering price. For example, if you're selling a common item with a well-established market price, any price substantially above the norm won't be taken seriously—unless, of course, you can substantiate the reason for the difference. Consequently, if you're facing this sort of difficulty, you have to use other means to convince the buyer that your price is indeed fair. This is a dilemma commonly encountered by sellers with prices that are traditionally higher than the competition.

But take heart if you find yourself in this position, since salespeople consistently command and receive premium prices in competition with lower priced competitors. So whether you want to better your bargain, even though you have price flexibility, or are compelled to justify a high price which can't be lowered, you have to use techniques that justify the price. The next few sections explore how this can be done.

5.5 HOW TO OVERCOME ANYONE'S PRICE OBJECTIONS

No one is in a worse position entering into negotiations than someone who thinks their price is too high. Yet, all too often, people sit and haggle over price at a bargaining table when they have little real conviction that their price is reasonable. Needless to say, this is a guarantee of failure.

Sure, everyone knows tales of someone who supposedly can sell anything to anyone at any price. And there's little question that if one looks long and hard enough, a fool can be found to throw money away. However, super sellers are few and far between, and although fools may be somewhat easier to find, they're by no means hiding under every rock. This means, that to be successful in justifying a high price, you need to be knowledgeable— not lucky.

The starting point for anyone trying to negotiate a high price starts long before they begin to bargain. The first thing you have to know is your pricing strategy. In essence, what is your price based upon? Are there solid reasons why your product costs more than the competition? Such factors as quality, reliability, and customer service are obvious examples of areas where your product may be priced higher for substantive reasons.

On the other hand, the basis for a high price may be something more subtle, such as snob appeal or status. After all, sports cars that can reach speeds of 140 miles per hour aren't bought with that primary purpose in mind. Unless, of course, the buyer is seeking to establish a world record for speeding tickets.

The same philosophy applies to a wide range of luxury goods which aren't purchased based on any correlation between price and value. The old saw, "If you have to ask the price, then you can't afford it," rings true for many items sold on an emotional appeal. But more to the point of everyday reality, "a price is only too high if the buyer thinks it is." Which means, you can get most any price for anything, as long as you can prove its worth to the buyer.

At any rate, as a start in getting the price you want, you first must know what it's based on. After all, you're not very well-armed to defend a price if you don't know the basis for it. Therefore, if you are selling something— tangible or intangible—sit down and figure out why it's worth what you want for it. These sales points might include any of the following elements:

- Sell benefits—Be able to show the buyer the benefits to be obtained by buying your product.
- Sell value—Show how even though your price appears higher, it actually is cheaper based on its performance.
- Sell competitive edge—Convince the buyer that what you're selling will enhance their business. For instance, "Joe, you'll help your own sales by buying from us. As you know, everyone in the industry knows our reputation for quality, so our quality helps sell your quality."
- Sell personal pride—"The location of this building will enhance the professional image and status of your firm."

- Sell uniqueness—The "It's one of a kind," argument has been used to justify high prices for an awful lot of pretty common items.
- Sell service—"We'll be there when you need us."

In fact, the number of ways you can substantiate a price during negotiations is as fertile as your imagination. But besides being able to overcome objections to your price, it's equally essential to recognize that price itself may not be what the buyer is objecting to. Often, price becomes a handy excuse for someone who doesn't want to make a deal for reasons other than price. The truth is that a "Your price is too high," statement by a buyer is the business equivalent of the seasoned criminal's "I didn't do it," when accused of a crime.

However, while the criminal is innocent until proven guilty, your price is too high until you prove otherwise. As a result, when you receive an initial price objection, find out why the other party thinks the price is too high. Keep probing until you can pinpoint the basis for their objections. For instance, is it (1) based on competitive prices, or (2) the category in general. (Ex: "Commercial real estate in this city is too high.")

Get whatever information you can from the other party, and then proceed to resolve it. Then, and only then, you may discover that there's something else they object to. But until you overcome the price objection hurdle, you'll never get to the real reason.

TIP: If you have competition in what you're selling, the most valuable thing to know besides your own product is your competitor's. In fact, if it's feasible to do so, buy it, try it, and in general "kick the tires" to find out what makes it tick. After all, it's pretty difficult to differentiate your product from the competition's if you don't know what they have to offer.

5.6 HOW TO CUT A BIG PRICE INTO SMALL PARTS

One way to overcome the obstacle of a high price is to cut it down to size. What you have to do here is show the buyer that the price, is in fact, quite reasonable when it's analyzed in terms of its components. For example, if you're selling a product, you're also selling quality. Show the buyer the specifics that go into making your product one of better quality than competing products. Support your arguments with figures that prove the reliability of the item. A little bit of detailed data can be far more convincing than all of the rhetoric in the world. Figures add credibility to the argument that your price is indeed reasonable.

This type of approach can be useful in many types of negotiations. For instance, if you're selling a building, identify the many advantages that comprise the price other than the building itself. Location, traffic patterns, the building design, low property taxes, the demographics of the area, and a host of other factors all work toward showing the prospective buyer that your price is reasonable.

One of the biggest hang-ups folks face in justifying price is acting defensively about it. They end up countering price objections with, "Yea, but . . . ," and then try to prove why their price isn't high. It's generally far better to be forthright about your price. Admit that it's higher right at the start, and then go on to show why it's really lower than anything the competition is offering. What you want to do is give the buyer valid reasons that justify your price.

If you think about it, people don't make objections to price alone, other than as a negotiating ploy, or to disguise some other reason for not making a commitment. Instead, they object to a price based on a product's perceived value as opposed to a similar product and/or service. Therefore, your job is to cure their lack of knowledge by showing them how and why the sum of the parts add up to a very reasonably priced whole.

5.7 TURNING HIGH PRICES INTO BARGAIN BASEMENT BUYS

A savvy method for removing price as an issue at the bargaining table is to adopt the attitude that your price is, if anything, too low. Admittedly, this isn't easy to carry off, but it can be done in many circumstances. Remember, people salivate over bargains. An awful lot of cocktail party conversation centers around comparisons of who got a good deal on something. Therefore, if you can convince your counterparts that they're getting a bargain, you can remove price as an obstacle. To do this successfully, pitch angles that shout "bargain." One of the oldest ways in the book of doing this is to tout beating a price increase by buying now. It may seem hackneyed, but people are conditioned to rising prices. As a result, they are susceptible to buying at today's prices if they can be convinced that tomorrow's will be higher.

To be convincing in this regard, try to present evidence that supports your statements. Show that the cost of raw materials is increasing, or that a key supplier and/or the competition has recently raised prices. If nothing else, use general economic inflationary trends—assuming they support your argument. Frankly, it frequently isn't all that difficult to find support for a position that prices will be going up. The key is to present your argument with enough background data to convince the buyer that it's true, and not just a ploy to support your price.

Another angle for justifying a price as a bargain is by using comparisons with competitive items that appear to be priced lower than yours. Buyers seldom look beyond a basic price when making comparisons. After all, they're looking for the best buy they can get. However, a lower competitive price is often the result of comparing apples and oranges. The competitor's lower price may result from not offering the same value.

Therefore, always make sure, whenever a buyer touts a lower price elsewhere, to establish precisely what the buyer is talking about. Are the items actually comparable in all respects? If you take the time to dig into it, you'll often find that there are significant differences. It might be something as basic as a difference in quantities, delivery schedules, or payment terms. The fact is that with a little bit of effort, it's not all that hard to show that no matter what competitive prices are, your price is indeed the best buy.

5.8 SELLING "NEGATIVE NET COST" INSTEAD OF PRICE

One alternative that can eliminate price hassles entirely is to concentrate on the "negative net cost" to the buyer. What you're doing here is pitching angles that show how much the buyer will increase revenues and/or decrease costs by buying your product and/or service. The key here is to show the buyer in specific terms how your product at your price will save money.

Whenever possible, make direct comparisons with other alternatives that may be available to the buyer. As an example, let's assume that you're selling a non-repairable item at a unit price of $100, while a competitive item is available for $80. The key difference is that your item has a service life of one year versus six months for the competitive product. The potential purchaser uses fifty of these a year, and they have to be replaced when they fail. Your product has a yearly cost of $5,000 (50 units × $100), while the competitive unit costs $8,000 on a yearly basis (100 units × $80).

Since your unit lasts twice as long as the competitor's, the cost to the buyer is $3,000 less on a yearly basis. Therefore, the buyer is saving $60 per unit on a yearly basis by buying your product. Obviously, this is a far less complex example than the realities of the real world that you may encounter. Yet, there are many opportunities that lend themselves to this sort of justification. They may not be as easy to compute, but if you can come up with the figures, you have with one stroke turned a high price into a bargain basement buy.

NOTE: One final point relative to price is to always make sure you get substantive concessions whenever you reduce your price during negotiations. If you drop your price without any reciprocal concession by the other side, you are in effect admitting that your price was inflated. This tends to make folks wonder just how inflated the price is, and consequently encourages them to seek further price reductions. Although everyone likes to see a price get reduced as evidence that they're getting a bargain, doing it too easily creates unnecessary suspicions. The harder you make a negotiator work for a price concession, the more convinced that person will be that it was their effort—not inflated prices—that accounted for the reduction.

5.9 HOW TO WRAP PROBLEM PIECES INTO A PALATABLE PACKAGE

One problem, common to many negotiations, is when each party has several items on the agenda that they're unwilling to yield on. A fruitful way to resolve this dilemma is to try and come up with a "total package" agreement that doesn't require either side to concede on the disputed items. Let's look at an example:

Background

The "X" Corporation, a test equipment manufacturer, has a contract with "D" to repair equipment returned to "X" by customers. Under the terms of the contract, the price for each repair is negotiated separately. "X" and "D" have been unable to agree on prices for many orders. This has resulted in a large backlog of unpaid orders and is starting to create a cash flow problem for "D." Because of this difficulty, "D" hires an experienced negotiator to handle this business on a full-time basis.

The approach

Ed, "D's" negotiator sits down with Phil from "X" Corporation. He discovers that Phil won't accept the prices for several repairs because they appear to be unsupported and are higher than similar repairs done in the past. At the same time, Ed and Phil can agree on prices for a number of other orders. After Ed crunches some numbers, he sees that "D" is getting a higher price than expected on some of the orders that Phil is willing to buy off on. Based on this, he suggests to Phil, that rather than negotiate individual prices, they agree on a total price for all outstanding orders. He makes an offer to Phil on that basis and it's subsequently accepted.

The reasoning

By agreeing on a total price, "D" only received slightly less than if they got the price they wanted for each individual order. The difference was more than offset by getting paid for the old orders which were in dispute. This increased liquidity by substantially reducing outstanding accounts.

It's not unusual to find situations where by looking at an agreement on a total basis, you can overcome disputes on individual terms which are threatening to derail the chances of reaching agreement. What the specifics are will vary, and often they won't be as obvious as the example given. But by looking at creative ways to bypass problem pieces, you can often agree to disagree on the parts, while reaching agreement on the whole.

5.10 WHEN TO SAY "NO" WITH MINIMUM IMPACT

During the course of negotiations, you will receive all kinds of suggestions, offers, counter-offers, and various other proposals. Some you may agree with, others may be subject to further discussions, and many may require nothing more than a "No." However, there are sound reasons for saying "No" so that it avoids conveying a negative impact.

If you continually veto every suggestion put forth by the opposing negotiator, it won't be long before the other side starts to think that: (1) you're being unreasonable, (2) you don't want to reach an agreement, or, (3) you're just being negative to get a better deal. On the latter point, they may be right, but you don't want them thinking that, since they may start playing the same game. And once both sides cease to do little more than say "No" to each other, it's time to pack-up and go home.

Nevertheless, when properly used, a "No" can work to your strategic advantage. For example, a lot of little "No's" during the course of a negotiation will condition the other side to expect such a response. This adds a great deal of impact when you do respond positively to something they suggest. Having found you to be a tough sell, a qualified "Yes" can be used to reap concessions that might not otherwise have materialized. In other words, the psychological sigh of relief at finally hearing something positive may seduce the other side into accepting terms they wouldn't agree to with a more pliable opponent.

However, to make negative replies less threatening, try to couch them in positive terms. After all, there are lots of ways to say "No." One handy method is to couch your "No's" in the form of a "Yes." For instance, "Yes, but . . . ," or, "That would be alright if . . . ," or "I like that idea, however . . . ." You may really be saying "No" by imposing a condition for agreement that's totally unacceptable to the other party. On the other hand, depending upon the circumstances, your condition for acceptance may be a realistic quid-pro-quo that the other party can accept.

Even if you want to reply negatively without attaching any condition to it try something such as, "I don't completely understand your rationale." This rejects the contention more subtly than a blunt, "No way, Jose."

Of course, on occasion, you may just have to say "No" without resorting to any form of subterfuge. Even here, be careful that you do so without conveying any form of hostility. In the end, agreement has to be reached, and that end isn't furthered by deliberately arousing the ire of the opposition.

5.11 HOW TO WIN LATER BY LOSING NOW

Unfortunately, both parties rarely get everything they would like out of a negotiation. Yet, if all goes well, both parties will be relatively satisfied with their end of the bargain. Nevertheless, there are times during negotiations when it's advantageous to give in to something the other side wants, rather than scuttle the entire deal.

Occasionally, during a negotiation session, one party or the other is pushed to the wall in terms of making some form of concession which they would prefer to avoid. This often results in a crunch time dilemma, which is to make the concession, or forget about reaching agreement. It's most frequently this type of encounter that leads to a loss of emotional control, with resultant anger on both sides. However, this only serves to worsen an already tense situation, with neither side willing to budge.

Obviously, no one likes to be the one to give in. However, more often than not, pride is more of a factor than the substantive effects of the concession would be. Therefore, a canny negotiator can keep a negotiation moving without surrendering anything of value by being the one to concede the point. However, rather than just waving a white flag, tie the concession into some contingency. For instance, "I'll concede that point, on the assumption that we can reach agreement on . . . ." Did you gain or lose by giving in?

In effect, you won for the simple reason that although the other party may be quite happy about you conceding a point, you haven't really conceded anything. All you have done is make your acceptance contingent upon later agreement on another issue. Furthermore, you have the upper hand when it comes time to talk that point, since if things get sticky, you can say, "Hey, I was willing to give ground on the other point. Now it's your turn." Admittedly, the other party may hold their ground, but even if they do, the psychological edge swings over to you, since the other side is now depicted as being unreasonable. If this does happen, then at worst, you're at least as well off as you would have been if you hadn't made the initial concession.

However, it's far more likely that the other party will grant this concession for two reasons. First of all, it gets them what they wanted on the initial point.

Second, negotiations are now further along toward agreement, and the longer bargaining goes on, the greater is the vested interest of both parties in reaching agreement.

Incidentally, use this sort of tactic judiciously, because there is a downside. If you casually go about conceding points based on later contingencies, the other side will soon have at least tentative agreement on their substantive goals, while yours are still up for grabs. This can lead to the other side digging their feet in as you seek comparable concessions.

A simpler way to overcome roadblocks as negotiations progress is to temporarily put the sticky issue on the back burner. Simply say, "Let's get back to that later." This will allow negotiations to move along, and hopefully when the time comes to go back to the controversial topic, enough will have been accomplished so the obstacle will no longer be as formidable.

5.12 WAYS TO BE PREPARED FOR THE UNEXPECTED

There's nothing quite as upsetting during a bargaining session as having the other party adopt a totally unexpected negotiation stance. The following practices will protect you from being overwhelmed by such maneuvers.

- Temper your expectations. Don't assume everything will go according to plan. Adopting this sort of attitude will keep you from getting flustered over an unexpected swerve in the course of negotiations.
- Be prepared. Try to anticipate unexpected positions that the opposition may take.
- Have technical expertise on call. On occasion, an unforeseen stumbling block arises that threatens agreement. When feasible, have your financial, legal, and/or technical experts standing by to advise on ways to deal with these problems. When you can't readily tap this expertise, you're more susceptible to accepting what's proposed.

Apart from guarding against the unexpected during negotiations, it's sensible to include provisions to inspire performance and/or safeguard against failure after agreement is reached. Needless to say, the final results of any negotiation aren't in until performance has been completed. Unfortunately, this can be overlooked in the euphoria surrounding the negotiation of what gives every indication of being a very profitable agreement. Nonetheless, both the general economy, and individual businesses have their ups and downs. So what appears to be a bargain today, may be a big bust at a later date if the other side fails to perform their end of the bargain.

Consequently, care should be taken to include safeguards against a failure to perform. These can range from payment guarantees, to quality control provisions, to contract incentives based on performance. However, although the specifics will vary with every negotiation, the principal concern is to make sure you're satisfied that your interests are protected.

5.13 NEGOTIATING TERMS THAT GUARANTEE SUCCESS—OR MINIMIZE FAILURE

Negotiation table promises have to be converted into firm commitments, or else you have nothing more than empty promises. Therefore, written agreements should carefully confirm the rights and obligations of both parties. Most negotiations—other than routine transactions—require reaching agreement on many issues. However, it's often a seemingly insignificant item that gets overlooked that causes trouble later. This is most likely to happen when one party assumes agreement was reached on an issue, when in fact, no such meeting of the minds took place.

Sometimes, this results when negotiation rhetoric is taken to signify agreement, when actually it's merely an offer tied into acceptance of other terms. For instance, an "I'll do this, if you'll do that," sort of suggestion. However, nothing is agreed to and the discussion then moves on to other matters. Later, when negotiations are concluded, one of the parties wrongly assumes that the item previously mentioned is part of the package. Let's look at an example of how such a misconception can muddy the waters.

"A" and "B" are discussing an order for 10,000 widgets. During the discussion, "A" says, "Incidentally, I'm willing to give a 10% discount for payment within 30 days." The parties then move on to other issues, and after extended negotiations, "B" agrees to buy 4,000 widgets. Nothing is said about a discount at this time. "B" subsequently writes up a purchase order for 4,000 widgets, and includes a provision for a 10% discount for prompt payment. "A" refuses to accept the purchase order when he receives the document, since the company gives no discount on orders under 5,000 units. The end result is that angry charges are hurled back and forth and the order is never executed. Who is at fault? Actually, both negotiators were careless in failing to confirm all of the terms of the purchase order upon the completion of negotiations. "B" assumed that discounts applied to all quantities, while "A" thought "B" realized the discount applied to their discussion about the purchase of 10,000 units.

To prevent this sort of misunderstanding, always go over each and every provision at the conclusion of a negotiation session. Never idly assume that something said earlier applies to the transaction as finally negotiated. This sounds simple enough, but problems crop up when the parties fail to pin down the specifics before congratulating themselves on getting the deal done.

Chapter 6

STANDARD
NEGOTIATION STRATEGIES

Negotiators use a number of different approaches to achieve their goals. Knowing how to both use and cope with these strategies is essential for success at the bargaining table. Of course, proper preparation is the starting point, and achieving your negotiation objectives is the ultimate destination. However, the tools for getting there consist of the strategies employed at the bargaining table. And while the wrong strategy can hamper your progress, using the right tactics can speed things along to a successful outcome.

Consequently, whether or not you personally employ a particular strategy, it's necessary to recognize each and every one that may be used against you. Then, and only then, will you be able to avoid any obstacles that may be strewn in your path. This chapter discusses several basic strategies that are used to achieve negotiation goals.

6.1 WIN/WIN STRATEGY: ITS PLUSES
AND MINUSES

General negotiation strategy is usually classified as being a win/win joint problem-solving approach, or a strict adversarial proceeding. Win/win strategy asserts that the two parties are best served by working together to identify and solve the problems that hinder reaching agreement. On the other hand, the adversarial approach mandates that each party look out for its own self-interest, leaving the other party to represent its own cause.

However, as with a lot of other things in life, it's not quite so easy to put negotiating strategy into neat little boxes. It certainly sounds a lot nicer to be able to negotiate in an atmosphere where both parties lay their cards on the table and work amicably toward agreement. Nevertheless, there are some real roadblocks to this sort of scenario. The first impediment is the necessity for both parties to be open and honest about what they want. Needless to say, if one party lays their cards on the table, and the other side doesn't show their hand, the straight-shooter is left without ammunition for the forthcoming battle.

Furthermore, in many negotiations, there are no sticky problems to be solved. The only real differences of opinion are in reaching a meeting of the minds on what constitutes a reasonable deal. That, absent some unusual circumstance, is just a part of the negotiation process. Often, especially where price is involved, it's merely a matter of reaching agreement on a dollar figure that's acceptable to both parties.

In addition, there's no magic price that's the right one. One person may feel he paid top dollar by buying a business for $10,000,000. Yet, someone else may readily decide that paying $15,000,000 would be a bargain. And aside from personal judgments, there may be valid reasons for the difference. For example, perhaps the higher priced buyer is eliminating a competitor, which justifies the extra premium. Whatever the reason, the fact remains that rarely is there any objective criterion for establishing the right price and/or right terms that best serve the needs of both parties.

In reality, everyone wants the best deal they can get, which leads to another impediment to a joint problem-solving negotiation strategy—which is self-interest. Most people enter into negotiations with their own self-interest in mind. There's nothing wrong with that, since the end result will be an exchange of mutual benefit, not a charitable endeavor. As a result, maximizing your self-interest isn't necessarily furthered by worrying about solving the other guy's problems. Anyway, in most cases, his only problem is how to get you to give him the best deal he can get.

Of course, there are negotiating conditions where it's clearly beneficial for both parties to work in harmony at resolving some underlying problem which is posing an obstacle to agreement. Under these circumstances, if both parties are willing to work together with mutual trust, then a win/win, problem-solving strategy is the best approach to take. However, most run-of-the-mill business negotiations won't fall into that category.

Compounding the confusion, is the implied assumption that an adversarial negotiating strategy is one where both parties are at each other's throats. This perception has been reinforced in the past by well-publicized negotiations that have been exceedingly hostile. Some labor disputes certainly have fit in this category. Nevertheless, most negotiations are conducted in a business-like manner without animosity or anger entering into the picture. So, implications that not using a joint-problem solving approach to negotiations, presumably leads to hostile negotiations is naive at best.

Furthermore, even though you approach negotiations from a point of view that emphasizes your own self-interest, that doesn't mean you won't look for ways to overcome obstacles that hinder reaching agreement. If during negotiations, the other party indicates that a particular hurdle must be overcome to reach agreement, then it's certainly in your interest to seek ways to resolve the problem.

The bottom line as to the proper approach to take toward negotiations is to first and foremost protect your own interests. If, within that context, it's feasible to work closely with the other party to reach agreement, then by all means do so. On the other hand, if it is quite evident that the other party to the negotiation is solely interested in getting the best possible deal, then it behooves you to proceed accordingly.

6.2 STONEWALLING: HOW TO AVOID ITS FRUSTRATIONS

One of the most frustrating experiences you can encounter at the negotiating table is having the misfortune of going up against an adversary who takes a position and simply stonewalls every attempt to reach agreement. No matter what your offer, and no matter how many concessions you make, stonewallers will respond with nothing but a "No."

There are several reasons why people will use stonewalling tactics. These include:

- They have no intention of reaching agreement unless they can get an irresistible bargain.
- They intend to make a deal, but hope that by stonewalling you will make repetitive offers—each one better than the last.
- They are stonewalling to force you into losing your poise and making mistakes.
- They are trying to send a message that they are hard to deal with in the hope that you will lower your expectations.
- They don't know what constitutes a reasonable agreement, but figure it will be somewhere around the last offer you make before threatening to scuttle the deal completely.

- They are stalling because of some known deadline which will force you to increase your offer.

Although it's disappointing when you're confronted by stonewalling tactics, it's a hazard you must challenge head on. Otherwise, the stonewaller will play out this ploy to exact every conceivable concession you can make, meanwhile surrendering nothing in return. The end result will be either a bad deal for you, or no deal at all. Therefore, once you detect an unwillingness to negotiate, you have to decide how best to counter this tactic. However, under any circumstances, don't lost control of your emotions—unless you are, of course, faking it to force the other side to end their stonewalling tactics.

However, before you employ any strategy to counter a stonewaller, try to assess the reason for their behavior, since it may be something other than just a tactic to get you to make concessions. For example, perhaps negotiations may have been proceeding fairly smoothly, when you suddenly hit the wall in getting any movement on one particular issue. It may well be that there are reasons why the other side doesn't want to point out their reluctance to discuss and/or yield on a particular topic. If you give it a little thought, you may be able to make a reasonably intelligent guess as to what the unknown stumbling block is. If so, you may be able to negotiate around it.

CAUTION: Stonewalling may be used as a tactic right from the start, or be brought into play at some point during the negotiations. It's a lot easier to recognize stonewalling if it's done initially. The danger is that if someone starts to stonewall during negotiations that have been proceeding smoothly, you may be less likely to recognize the tactic. That could lull you into making unwarranted concessions. Therefore, if you make a reasonable offer which the other side dismisses out-of-hand, while continuing to stick stubbornly to a totally unreasonable position, don't make further concessions. This is merely playing into their hands, and you will never get them off of their stonewalling kick.

6.3 WHITTLING AWAY AT STONEWALLING TACTICS

The key to stonewalling success can be summed-up in one word, and that's doubt. A stonewaller wants to plant doubt in your mind that he will accept anything other than the best deal you can give him. If successful, this leads you to accept the worst possible deal you can get, since your alternative would be no deal at all. From a practical standpoint, if you have done your homework before starting to negotiate, you know whether or not your offer is reasonable. Of course, there may be something you overlooked, and/or justification for the other side not agreeing with you. However, if that's the case, your adversary will be quick to point this out. So, if they fail to do this, and stubbornly refuse to discuss the matter, then it's obvious they are just stonewalling.

If you want to succeed at overcoming stonewalling tactics, first of all, resist any self-imposed doubts that you are the one being unreasonable. Having done that, there are several approaches to take in dealing with a stonewalling adversary. One countermeasure that can be taken once you realize the other side is stonewalling is the setting of a deadline for completing negotiations. If you do this, simply state it's because the other side isn't negotiating in good faith. This has the advantage of letting them know you aren't going to put up with their nonsense.

The downside of this approach is that your adversary may well assume that you're just bluffing, and will continue to stonewall right up until the deadline expires. In other words, they will call your bluff. If that happens, then you have to be prepared to break off negotiations, perhaps by saying something such as, "We're getting nowhere, so as of now any possibility of a deal is dead. However, if you decide that you are willing to negotiate, give me a call."

NOTE: Whenever, you break off negotiations for any reason, always do so in a way that leaves it up to the other side to contact you. This gives you a tactical advantage if they do call you at a later date.

Another alternative is to ignore stonewalling tactics and just keep talking. Go on to other aspects of the negotiation if that's feasible. If the other side is negotiating seriously, then they're listening to what you're saying even though they give no indication of budging from their extreme position. Of course, if no headway is made by doing this, try making an outrageous offer of your own. Sometimes a party will start getting serious when they see that you're going to be just as unreasonable as they are.

If all else fails, lay it right on the line that if they aren't going to be reasonable in their approach to negotiations, then there's no point in continuing the discussions. It may be tough to consider walking away without a deal, but no deal is better than a bad one. One reason that stonewalling succeeds is that the more time and effort people invest in a negotiation, the more reluctant they become to call it quits. So, no matter what approach you take to counteract stonewalling tactics, don't let it go on indefinitely. If your adversary won't move off-the-mark within a reasonable period of time, get up and walk away.

6.4 THE GOOD SAMARITAN APPROACH

In sharp contrast to a stonewaller who can quickly get your blood boiling, is the "good samaritan" who sets about to prove that he's doing you a favor if you accept his terms and conditions. Although your initial reaction to this approach may be bemusement, before negotiations are concluded a "good samaritan" negotiator can also succeed in driving you up the wall.

The "good samaritan" negotiator operates on a premise of what's good for him is good for you, and takes advantage of every opportunity to convince you of that. A "good samaritan's" key to success is in lulling you to sleep with his apparent willingness to discuss anything and everything. This type of negotiator will never attack your position, or even disagree with it, but will ever so subtly simply ignore every fact and figure you put on the table.

The only way to deal with a "best deal in town" type of negotiator is to force them to focus on the facts. Cut them short once you realize what they're up to by saying something such as, "Look Charlie, I'm sure you have the greatest product in the world, but it isn't priceless. I'm offering you "X" dollars which is quite reasonable. Let's concentrate on the figures I've presented and not the superlatives." Admittedly, it may take a while to get your point across, but eventually you will. And by no means, fall prey to pleas such as, "I'm trying to be fair, and you're taking advantage of me," or similar drivel. A died-in-the-wool "good samaritan" will forever swear—even long after the deal is done—that you got the best deal in the world. In the end, the key to coping with this sort of bargainer is to beware of accepting favors at the negotiating table, since they'll come back to bite your butt.

6.5 TAKE IT OR LEAVE IT TYPES: FINESSING THEM INTO NEGOTIATING

Another approach you will face at the negotiation table is the "take it or leave it" offer. It pretty much boils down to, "This is what I'm offering. If you don't want the deal on that basis, then let's just forget about it." There are three basic moves you can make when confronted with this sort of dilemma.

1. Keep talking and ignore the ultimatum. If the other side doesn't bolt, you will immediately know they aren't serious.

2. Consider your alternatives. If they are better than the deal being offered say, "I'll leave it. Call me if you change your mind." This often induces the other party to become more receptive, and they may immediately say, "Wait a minute. Let's talk this over." But if they don't, walk out the door, and proceed with your alternative. If they subsequently contact you to reopen negotiations, then you're in the driver's seat.

3. Invent a competitor. If it's feasible, invent a competitor who will give you a better deal. Admittedly, this bluff may be called, leaving you with little choice but to accept an unreasonable offer or break off

negotiations. However, this approach can serve to establish how serious the other side is about their ultimatum.

Overcoming a "take it or leave it" offer often involves playing a game of brinkmanship. Of course, there are many more pleasant pastimes than playing a game of chicken when a business deal is on the line. However, a "take it or leave it" strategy can only succeed if you succumb to the temptation. And in the long run, avoiding a bad deal by walking away is preferable to staying and getting stuck. Furthermore, once you refuse to be bullied this way, it's less likely that anyone who hears about your taking a stand will try the same tactic on you in the future.

6.6 SPLITTING THE DIFFERENCE AND ITS PITFALLS

If you do a significant amount of negotiating, it's inevitable that you will cross paths with negotiators whose sole solution to bargaining hang-ups is splitting the difference. It doesn't matter whether the negotiation positions are poles apart or too similar to quibble about. A confirmed split-the-difference negotiator always wants to cut the dollar difference down the middle.

At first blush, this may seem like a pretty practical approach, and it is under certain circumstances. For example, if extended negotiations have narrowed the gap in positions to a point where the only disparity is a judgment call as to whether the final price should be "X" or "Y" then reaching agreement at a midpoint can be a practical resolution. On the other hand, splitting the difference is frequently used as a substitute for negotiating the merits of the relative positions of the negotiating parties. It's a tactic that is used by both inexperienced negotiators and seasoned bargainers. However, the end result can be quite different.

Skilled negotiators most often use this tactic to avoid discussing the details of negotiation differences when they know their position on the merits is weak. Conversely, novice negotiators use it as a substitute for failing to properly prepare their negotiation position. Simply put, they don't know what they're doing, so they make a ridiculous initial offer, go through the motions, and then suggest splitting the difference. So when you face a split-the-difference situation, the first thing to consider is whether it's being proposed by a pro or an amateur.

There are several pretty basic considerations that shouldn't be ignored whenever you're considering an offer to split the difference. These are:

1. What baseline are you operating from? As a minimum, you should never split the difference if the result would exceed the highest price

you're willing to pay as a buyer, or fall below the lowest price you can accept as a seller.

EXAMPLE: You're the buyer and your walk-away price (the most you would pay) is $1,300,000. Your last offer was $1,000,000, while the other side stood at $1,800,000. "B," the other negotiator, offers to split the $800,000 difference, which would result in a price of $1,400,000.

2. Quite obviously, the more reasonable your offer, and the more unreasonable is that of your adversary, the worse off you're going to be. Therefore, never split the difference unless both positions are within a range that you consider to be fair.

EXAMPLE: A reasonable price for certain items is somewhere between $2,200,000 and $2,400,000. You, the seller are asking for $2,400,000. The buyer is offering only $1,800,000, which is below your cost to produce. He offers to split the $600,000 difference, which is an unacceptable price of $2,100,000. However, if his offer was $2,200,000 and you split the $200,000 difference, then the price of $2,300,000 would be acceptable.

3. Who makes the initial offer during negotiations is important. If you make the first offer, which is a reasonable one, and the other side counters with a figure that's totally out of line, splitting the difference is out of the question until the gap in positions is narrowed.

EXAMPLE: Assume a fair price is about $1,500,000. You (the buyer) make an initial offer of $1,300,000, and the seller counters with a selling price of $2,500,000. Splitting the difference of $1,200,000 would have you paying a price of $1,900,000.

4. Avoid the "even dollar" syndrome. When negotiations take place, there's a tendency to talk in round numbers. Millions, and tens of thousands, are the sums bandied back and forth. As a result, folks forget about the smaller amounts in between. Because of this, you can make money by using uneven amounts.

EXAMPLE: Let's say splitting the difference during a negotiation comes to a compromise amount of $2,400,000. You (the buyer) might want to respond by saying something such as, "That's pretty close. I'll agree if we can make it $2,379,500." Of course, try to give some justification for the reduction. What the reason is isn't significant, as long as it has some ring of reality to it. The fact is that when folks have been thinking in terms of hundreds of thousands of dollars, smaller amounts ($21,500 in this example) tend to get treated as automatic give-aways. (Section 10.7 covers other aspects of even dollar negotiations.)

5. Reap other benefits from a split-the-difference approach. Negotiators who get hung up on splitting the difference concentrate so hard on selling that approach, that they can tend to ignore non-dollar issues.

Therefore, you may be able to negotiate a bundle of concessions in other areas that more than offset what you might lose by splitting the difference. So try to tie-in buying the other guy's dollar approach if he'll accept your other terms.

6.7 PIECE BY PIECE—THE NICKEL AND DIME APPROACH

At the opposite end of the spectrum from the "quick and dirty" aspects of splitting the difference is the negotiator who wants to settle each and every detail piece by piece. Like any other strategy it has its pluses and minuses. On the positive side of the ledger, negotiating agreement on each item serves to narrow the areas of disagreement.

The downside of negotiating this way is that it can hinder final agreement if one party gets backed to the wall. For instance, agreeing on price and setting it aside prevents a later trade-off of price for better payment terms, delivery dates, or other factors. Let's look at an example of how someone can get boxed-in by agreeing to items one-by-one.

Background

"A" and "B" are negotiating a contract for technical services to be furnished by "B's" company. Under the agreement "B" will furnish personnel to perform computer maintenance services at various locations throughout the United States. The major costs involved are for labor and travel.

The negotiation

"A" and "B" agree to negotiate the labor costs first and leave travel for later. After reaching agreement on the labor categories, and the number of hours to be furnished, a total cost of $1,280,000 is agreed to for labor. The parties then go on to travel and per diem expenses which "A" has assumed would be a piece of cake. However, right from the start hangups develop. "A" wants the technicians to stay over in a location over the weekend, while "B" maintains company policy prohibits that. There are also substantial disagreements on per diem rates. "B's" position on these issues is that it's standard company policy, which has been in place for some time, and therefore there isn't anything to be negotiated.

"A" does some number crunching and discovers that this will bring the total contract price to well over $2,000,000, which is $250,000 more than is budgeted. "A" then suggests that they go back and renegotiate the labor hours to be furnished. "B" explodes and says, "That's a done part of the deal. First we agree on something, and then you want to change it. You're not negotiating in good faith." "B" then stalks out of the meeting.

"A's" mistake

"B" entered the negotiations knowing that the labor costs would be difficult to negotiate, but anticipated no problem on travel, since it would conform with established policy. Therefore, he reasoned that "A" wouldn't quibble about travel. Therefore, "B" intended—and succeeded—in getting "A" to negotiate and settle on labor costs first. "A" for his part assumed that travel costs were equally negotiable, which they weren't. This is one reason why the best method for reaching agreement item by item is to *tentatively* agree on individual items. Example: "I'll agree with that assuming we can reach agreement on everything else." By doing this, you avoid getting boxed in on individual issues as "A" did.

The overall major weakness of piece-by-piece negotiations is that it overlooks the fact that the entire deal is a complete package. Therefore, this method is most effective when the items to be individually agreed upon have no real bearing on items yet to be negotiated.

6.8 MANAGING ISSUES SO THE FIGHT IS ON YOUR TURF

No matter how sound your negotiation position may be, making progress toward agreement can be hindered if you're continually on the defensive during negotiations. And although having a well-prepared negotiation strategy facilitates defending your goals against attack, it's also necessary to uncover the weaknesses of your adversaries' proposal. Otherwise, both sides won't be able to close the gap that's necessary to reach final agreement. Therefore, it's to your distinct advantage to maintain control of the negotiation process. There are a number of actions you can take in this regard including:

- Control the logistics of negotiations as much as possible by choosing the time and place for meetings. (See section 8.1 for more on this.)

- If possible get the other party to make the first offer. (Section 10.2 explores ways of doing this.)

- Ask questions that hone in on the weaknesses of the other side's position.

- When responding to questions from the other party, shift the focus toward the strengths of your proposal.

- Take advantage of pauses in the back and forth discussion to burrow further into aspects of your adversary's proposal. Say something such as, "Now that we've got a minute, let's look at . . . ."

- Use documentation to support your position, and ask for it in return from the other side. ("Frank, we've given you backup to justify everything we've said. We expect the same in return.")

- If feasible, use objective evidence such as third party testimonials to support your position.

- If things aren't going your way, suggest a break in the meeting for coffee, lunch, and so forth. The reason isn't important, but try to make it appear that it's not being done to give you a chance to regroup—which is exactly what it is.

6.9 VALID REASONS FOR NEGOTIATING AMBIGUOUS CONDITIONS

As a general rule, every term and condition you negotiate should be carefully honed so as to avoid any loopholes or misunderstandings. Nevertheless, there are practical reasons why you may want to leave some subjects open-ended in an agreement. Perhaps, both sides agree that the particular issue requires flexibility to enhance performance. Or maybe, it's a subject that one party or the other doesn't want to be pinned down on.

Whatever the reason, this is an area in which you should exercise extreme caution, since a carelessly executed agreement can wreak havoc down the road. This is especially true if the other party is insisting that some aspect of performance you want pinned down should be left open-ended. Of course, it behooves you to avoid this. However, in reality it must be recognized that this can't always be done.

For example, there may be an occasion where the other party will simply refuse to complete an agreement if you insist on certain terms they find unacceptable. Obviously, if you have other satisfactory alternatives, it's to your advantage to forget the deal. Yet, circumstances may be such that even without getting the provision you want in the agreement, it remains a deal that you can't afford to pass up.

When you're in this sort of predicament, you have to keep your risk/reward ratio in mind. That is, the greater the risk, the greater the benefits should be—a factor often ignored by investors to their subsequent dismay. Therefore, anytime you're stuck with accepting an agreement without a provision to safeguard against some potential liability you foresee, use this as a wedge for concessions in other areas. By doing this, you can offset the additional risk you're undertaking in one part of an agreement, with added benefits from other aspects of the negotiation. Although the particulars will vary widely, according to the subject matter being negotiated, let's look at an example that demonstrates how this can be done.

Background

"L" and "M" are negotiating a contract under which "M's" corporate consulting group will be conducting a study for "L," a large international corporation. "L" is insistent that "X," an authority on manufacturing operations, be specifically identified in the agreement as the senior investigator, and further, that "X" will furnish a minimum of 500 hours to the project during a six month period.

"M" is reluctant to agree to this for several reasons. First of all, "X" is doing consulting work on a number of projects, and does not have the time to devote 50% of his effort to one project during a six month period. Furthermore, "M" feels that "L" is dictating terms that infringe on "M's" freedom to conduct operations as conditions warrant, which may, or may not, require the services of "X" for the time period demanded. "M" also wants to retain the flexibility of using "X" on other assignments that may be forthcoming in the next several months.

Unfortunately, "L" is adamant about this, and "M" doesn't want to lose the assignment.

The flexible provision solution

"M" suggests that "X" can be identified as the principal investigator in the agreement, but proposes that a minimum and maximum of hours to be furnished by "X" be used. The minimum being 250 and the maximum 500. "L" rightly recognizing that the possibility is now open for receiving only 250 hours of X's services insists on also including a provision requiring that "Y" another senior consultant who was to work 250 hours on the project be designated as the alternate to furnish the difference between the 250 hours and the 500 that "X" does not work. "L" further wants "Y" to be designated as the project leader at such times as "X" is unavailable. "M" agrees and the agreement is signed.

"L" wisely recognized that the ambiguous provision providing for between 250 hours and 500 hours of "X's" services might well end up as the minimum of 250. Therefore, it opted to protect its interests by insisting that "Y" make up the difference.

6.10 SURE-FIRE WAYS TO KEEP FROM BEING SNOOKERED

Dependent upon the predisposition and skills of the other negotiator, you are likely to be bombarded with every trick imaginable in furtherance of the objective of the opposing party. Of necessity, the better prepared you are to fend off these tactics, the greater are your chances of coming out ahead of the game. Although there's no such thing as an iron-clad guarantee that your negotiations will always be successful, there are several fundamentals that can greatly limit the possibility of disaster striking. These are:

- Obtain third party assessments of your opponent.
- Verify all claims made by your opponent.
- Never get rattled by anything that's said or done.
- Don't make assumptions about anything the other side says or does. Get the facts and go from there. Take all of the time you need to make decisions.
- Avoid getting locked in an ego contest.
- Don't succumb to deadline hysteria.
- Don't be afraid to walk away without a deal.
- Learn to profit from every negotiation mistake the next time around.

6.11 SELECTING YOUR PROPER STRATEGIC APPROACH

Not to be overlooked in your negotiation preparations is the approach you will take when you finally sit down to begin bargaining. To some degree, this will be dictated by your knowledge of your opponent. Obviously, if you have done business with someone in the past, you have a good idea of how they negotiate and can plan accordingly. The real difficulty lies in planning how to proceed when you haven't had the pleasure—or misfortune—of prior dealings. Here, you have to proceed cautiously based on the limited knowledge you have available.

The paramount consideration that will influence the course of negotiations is the tone that's set from the start. Your objective should be to establish a foundation of trust and credibility early on in the negotiations. If you can accomplish this, it will set the stage for discussions to move along more smoothly toward a satisfactory resolution of any differences.

One of the greatest handicaps to establishing mutual trust is to enter the meeting with preconceived notions about the other party. Sure, you may have information that leads you to believe that the other party will try to nickel/ dime you to death, bully you into submission, and/or be unreasonable in any other number of ways. Naturally, you should take this into consideration in preparing your position, and determining how you will react when and if your worst fears come true.

Nevertheless, it's prudent to proceed cautiously, and feel the other party out at the beginning. After all, there are many reasons why the prior information you have may be incorrect. These include both the reliability of your source, as well as the possibility of bias. Frequently, people form judgments based upon their experience with someone that may not hold true where others are involved. Perhaps someone didn't get the deal they wanted, and arbitrarily paints the other party as the problem.

Other reasons may be as basic as a personality clash, or as complex as the nature of the negotiation. Whatever the reason, it's quite possible that you aren't aware of these factors, so it behooves you to enter negotiations with an open mind in the absence of any experience of your own with the other party.

When negotiations start, be as cooperative as possible, and feel the other side out as to how they intend to proceed. Your approach should be friendly, but businesslike, until you are given indications that the other party doesn't intend to be open-minded about working together toward agreement. If that's the case, then you should make adjustments in the tactics you use to counter the approach of the other party.

NOTE: Always exercise caution to avoid getting hung up on minor issues that may surface, and detour you away from working toward your negotiation objectives. This often happens when one party or the other insists on being proven right about some insignificant issue that will have little or no bearing on the end result. Negotiations are neither debates, nor contests, although occasionally some folks try to make them into both. If you are confronted by such a kettle of fish, nudge the other party gently back on course—even if that means conceding a point you know to be wrong.

6.12 POSITION OF STRENGTH TECHNIQUES

On many an occasion, people set themselves up to get the raw end of a negotiated agreement by assuming that the other party holds all of the cards. Therefore, they sit down at the bargaining table like a beggar with a tin cup, and then wonder why they walk away with a pittance. Obviously, one party or the other may have an apparent advantage going into negotiations. However, more often than not, this supposed position of strength is more apparent than real. Of even greater consequence, is the fact that the advantage can be nullified with a little bit of skill, along with a heavy dose of fortitude.

In business in general, the most common occurrence of entering negotiations as an underdog happens when a small company seeks to do business with a giant enterprise. The implication is that the big business doesn't need the little guy, and therefore can dictate the terms of any agreement. This often leads to a "take it, or leave it" philosophy by the big firm's negotiator.

Overcoming this sort of handicap requires some degree of bravado, but it can be done. If you think about it, no party enters into negotiations without hoping to gain some advantage. On the other hand, there's always something to be lost if negotiations fail. The one possible exception being the case of someone who has no particular desire to make a deal, but is willing to talk on the possibility that someone may make them an offer that's too good to refuse. Even here, there's at least the potential to lose a windfall gain.

So every side is faced with a real loss, or at least a foregone gain if negotiations don't succeed. This alone should be reason enough for confidence when you feel the odds aren't in your favor. After all, if you're entering negotiations expecting to get a lousy deal, then you shouldn't be there in the first place. It all boils down to knowing your limits, and not letting the other side push you beyond them. Or for that matter, letting your own emotions take control over reason, and rationalizing in your mind why a deal is better than it appears.

The bottom line in overcoming any position of strength technique thrown at you, whether it's size, financial strength, deadline pressures, or any other factor, is to know when to say "No." As long as you're willing to walk away—and can convey that fact to the opposition—you should be able to neutralize any real or imagined position of strength image. (Also see section 7.4 on how to capitalize on a weak bargaining position.)

6.13 WHY FLEXIBLE RESPONSE NEGOTIATING IS NECESSARY

The need for a flexible response strategy from the standpoint of preparing your negotiation position was discussed in section 1.4. However, no matter how carefully you prepare yourself beforehand, negotiations seldom follow a predicted path to the expected outcome. Once you sit down at the bargaining table, the other side may propose all sorts of adjustments, alternatives, and options that you weren't prepared for.

More often than not, the final outcome of a negotiation will differ in at least some respects from anything contemplated before bargaining began. In addition, the other negotiator may suddenly change his negotiating tactics in an attempt to throw you off guard. Consequently, you should always be prepared to counter any attempts to shift you away from realizing your pre-negotiation objectives.

On the other hand, you must maintain enough flexibility to adapt to changing conditions. That may even mean a major adjustment in your negotiation position. If that happens, so be it. The important point is to take your time in adjusting your position, since a common negotiation ploy is to push someone into a hasty decision. If you remain open-minded enough to consider previously undiscussed proposals, then the other side should be flexible enough to give you the time to do so. If they are not, then you can rest assured that they don't want you looking too closely at their proposition.

Chapter 7

COMMON NEGOTIATION TECHNIQUES

There are a number of garden variety techniques employed by negotiators to further their cause. These include everything from playing hardball to pious "pity me" tactics. But just learning to cope with gimmicks won't solve all of your negotiation problems. You also have to master the art of converting weakness to strength, breaking deadlocks, as well as the proper method for proposing trade-offs.

In addition, the use of options can be a valuable tool that can be used to give you negotiation flexibility in certain instances. These topics, along with how to handle the element of surprise, and avoiding getting trapped in an ego contest, are covered in this chapter.

7.1 HOW TO HALT THE GOOD COP/BAD COP CAPER

One common technique you may be subjected to during negotiations is the tried and true good cop/bad cop ploy. This is nothing more than a little role playing, where one person acts the part of a hard-nosed bargainer, while a second individual seeks to gain your confidence by being mild mannered and considerate. Needless to say, they are both working together to undermine your negotiation stance.

As business negotiations aren't conducted under klieg lights in an interrogation room, the negotiation equivalent of the good cop/bad cop caper doesn't have interrogators alternating between bullying and back stroking. The most frequent method for pulling off this ploy consists of using a hard-nosed negotiator who won't yield on anything. His or her boss then enters the picture as the understanding conciliator.

What generally happens is that the "good guy" will listen attentively to your plight, and then calmly explain why his side can only settle for what they're proposing. All of this is, of course, interlaced with syrupy pleas for your understanding. Naturally, if you fall for this trap, you end up pretty much giving the other side what they want. Of course, if the "good guy" negotiator encounters reluctance on your part, some minor concession may be offered to nudge you toward agreement.

At first glance, this type of tactic seems to be both silly and simplistic. However, it feeds upon basic emotional needs such as sympathy and understanding. Furthermore, you have likely been subjected to an extended period of negotiations with a most unreasonable person as your opponent. Having made no headway, and seeing the prospects of any agreement fading faster than the sun on a cold winter day, you are primed to be receptive to anyone who represents a voice of reason. Unfortunately, while the hard-nose was doing nothing more harmful than testing your temper, Mr. Good Guy's objective is to wallow in your wallet.

There are two extreme positions you can take to counteract this ploy. The first is to play the game yourself. The minute you are subjected to hard-nosed tactics, do a little browbeating of your own. You are now creating a tactical nightmare for the other side. Where they expected to be able to wheel Mr. Good Guy into action to extract concessions from a beleaguered and frustrated patsy, they now face a formidable foe.

It's likely that when they rethink their strategy, the discussion will focus on whether you're really a tough nut to crack, or are just playing the same game as them. Naturally, the only way to find out is by testing you. That should bring on an appearance by Mr. Good Guy, replete with his snake charmer's personality.

Now, more than ever, is the time to turn the tables. Instead of settling down and being reasonable, maintain your hard line posture. With luck, that will convince the other side that while they were only playing a game, you are a true-to-life example of a difficult person to deal with.

At this point, you can subtly introduce your own version of Mr. Nice Guy into the game—in the form of your boss or other conspirator. He can then go about finalizing negotiations on terms favorable to your side. All of this may appear to be a little unseemly, but when it comes to negotiations you have to take your foes as you find them. And if they want to play games, it's to your advantage to teach them how to score.

Of course, if you're not partial to doing a little role playing, you can use more direct means to deal with the good cop/bad cop tactic. After subjecting yourself to a lengthy enough harangue to indicate that your opposite is unwilling to discuss matters in any logical manner, insist on negotiating with someone else.

If the other party refuses, simply say something such as, "It's apparent you are unwilling to work toward an amicable agreement. If you change your mind, let me know." Then, get up and leave. The odds are you will be hearing from someone from the other side within a short period of time.

NOTE: One reason people accept bad deals is because they are extremely reluctant to break off negotiations. This is unwise, since once the other side knows that an adversary isn't going to walk, it's a better sign than a smoke signal that they can press hard for a favorable agreement. What inexperienced negotiators fail to realize is that negotiations ebb and flow, often with interludes in between where there is little or no communication between the parties. Therefore, it's important to keep in mind, that just because negotiations break off doesn't mean they have been scuttled for good. And although it's preferable for the other party to contact you to resume talks, the worst that can happen is that you may have to initiate the call.

7.2 CHANGING TACTICS BY ADDING OR DELETING OPTIONS

Although every negotiation doesn't lend itself to the use of options, they have widespread application in certain areas, most notably in the procurement of supplies and services for which there is a continuing need. The main purpose of options is (1) to guarantee a source for the optioned item, and/or (2) to insure price stability over an extended period of time.

To some extent, the advantages of options also loom as the basis for their disadvantages. For instance, having one source of supply can cause headaches if problems develop with the supplier's performance. And to a lesser extent, there is a built-in handicap anytime you put all of your eggs in one basket.

For example, perhaps your demands may temporarily increase above and beyond the capacity of your supplier to produce the item. If you don't have a second source readily available, it may take some doing to develop one, and/or you can find yourself in the position of paying a hefty price to the second source. After all, if they are savvy about their business, they know you are just using them to supply excess needs. Consequently, they expect to be dumped when your requirements decline, and will take that into consideration in establishing their price. Nevertheless, this potential problem can be safeguarded against, as long as the possibility is recognized beforehand.

Another prospective difficulty with options involves price. Just as you don't want to get locked into an option price that turns out to be too high if market conditions change, your supplier doesn't want to be snagged by a price that's too low. This contingency can be guarded against by either pegging the option price to a pre-agreed standard such as a commodity price index, or including an unpriced option in the contract. If it's the latter, then the contract should contain a provision for price to be negotiated at a later date, as well as what happens if a price agreement can't be reached at the designated time.

Although business practices should be the determining factor as to whether or not an option provision is used, options can have a secondary purpose as a negotiating tool. In certain instances, an option provision can be used to work around a bargaining impasse. This is particularly true when there's an inability to agree on a price for items to be delivered over an extended period of time. Quite naturally, the longer the period of time involved, the greater is the financial risk associated with costs to be incurred at a later date. If you are in a situation where this poses a problem, the solution may be to propose an unpriced option for later deliveries.

A lesser use of options as a negotiation tactic occurs when both parties have agreed to include option provisions in an agreement. If there are hangups on negotiating other provisions of an agreement, threatening to delete the option provision can serve as a bargaining wedge to move the other side off dead center.

TIP: Anytime you ask for written proposals prior to initiating negotiations, always require that any options be spelled out separately in the offeror's proposal. This simple requirement can save you a great deal of difficulty when you evaluate the proposal. If the other party has included options of one form or another in their basic proposal, it may be difficult, if not impossible, to segregate the technical and cost aspects of the option from the basic requirements. This is a headache, since you may not even want to consider the option, which means you may have to ask for a revised proposal setting the basic requirements apart from any option considerations. As a minimum, this is time consuming.

A further problem can develop at the negotiation table when options have been interwoven with basic requirements in a proposal. When you start to question costs, or other factors, you may find the offeror asserting that the factors you're questioning belong to the basic requirement, and/or the option, whichever is favorable to the offeror's argument. As a result, you are then in the position of negotiating a proposal where you can't pinpoint what belongs to your requirement, and what is properly part of the option. The easiest way of avoiding these problems is to insist that any options be in a self-contained section of proposals.

7.3 USING SURPRISE AS A NEGOTIATING TOOL

The element of surprise can be an extremely effective weapon in your arsenal of negotiating tools if it's properly employed. But it can only be used once, otherwise, it isn't believable. Therefore, it's wise to be prudent about its use, which means saving it for when you really need it.

Some of the ways you can change the course of a negotiation session by catching your opponent off-guard include:

1. Introducing a completely new element into the negotiation. ("We've decided to close Plant #14 if we don't have a labor agreement by the end of the month.")

2. Adding competition. ("We have received an unexpected offer from the "X" Corp., which is significantly lower than what you're proposing.")

3. To undermine the other side's position. ("By the way, Jack Arnold will be coming in shortly. Since he used to work for you guys, I'm sure he's familiar with what you're proposing.")

4. Bringing in an expert to contradict the other side's position. ("I'd like you folks to meet Sammy Smart. As you know, he's the foremost authority on the subject of land valuation.")

5. To signal a shift in your thinking. ("I know you folks here in Swill City have said you can't make any further concessions if we locate our regional headquarters here. However, it's only fair to tell you that the folks down in Sunshine County have offered us a much more attractive package.")

6. To escalate the level of negotiations. ("Ernie Urgent, our President, plans to call your president, if agreement can't be reached by Friday.")

7. To create a sense of urgency. ("We're leaving for the Far East in two days, so if we can't wrap this up, it will just have to go on the back burner.")

As you can see, the possibilities for the use of surprise are endless. Nevertheless, there are two caveats that should be kept in mind. One, only use the element of surprise when there's a stalemate, and the prospects are bleak for making further progress. Second, and paramount in importance, don't make an assertion that you can't back-up. Any negotiator worth their salt will always call a bluff. So, if you're just winging it when you try to catch the other side offguard, you better have other negotiation alternatives waiting in the wings.

7.4 MAKING A WEAK NEGOTIATING POSITION
AN ADVANTAGE

Knowing your own negotiation limits, and having the self-confidence to stick with them—as discussed in section 6.12—is the prime requisite for not being short-changed when your negotiation position is weak. However, if conditions are right, you can use a weak negotiating position to gain concessions you might not otherwise receive.

The biggest handicap you face when you're in a weak bargaining position is a lack of confidence which surfaces in an attitude of, "I'll take whatever deal they offer me." This is a typical attitude when a small business enters into negotiations with a large, well-financed enterprise. It's natural to assume that if the dictated terms aren't accepted, the larger company will take their business to someone more pliable.

Therefore, anytime you're in this sort of position, you have to ask yourself why the other party is negotiating with you in the first place. Is it just because they can dictate price and other terms to you, or are there other substantive reasons which work in your favor? For instance, perhaps you are geographically accessible, or furnish a higher quality product. The possibilities are endless in any given situation. However, if you are offering something of real value apart from being a weak negotiating opponent, then you have a valid basis for holding your own during negotiations.

It pays to be realistic when you make this sort of assessment. After all, you may be dreaming about taking a lousy deal now, with visions of profiting from the future business this relationship will bring. However, it may well be that the other party is thinking about a one-shot, low priced contract, with no intention of giving you any future work. Perhaps you are being used as a pawn to force down the price of the other guy's long-term supplier. In any event, it's beneficial to objectively weigh the merits of why the other side is dealing with you. At least then, if you choose to take the risks, you do so recognizing the possibilities.

The flip side of the coin is to weigh your own interests in entering into negotiations. Is it because you need the work at any price? If so, you better recognize that "any price" can be costly, which some businesses don't discover until they go bankrupt. All in all, the less desperate you are for the work, the better positioned you are to extract the most reasonable contract terms possible—despite any apparent weakness in your bargaining position.

Another factor that shouldn't be overlooked when you are in a weak bargaining position is the integrity of the party you are dealing with. Sound business relationships—and reputations—aren't built upon driving unreasonable bargains with people who are in a weak negotiating position.

For instance, a company that wants to develop a long-term supplier relationship may drive a hard bargain—but it will be a reasonable one. Therefore, don't ignore the track record of the other party, because if you do, it will be at your peril.

Once you have determined that you're doing business with a reputable firm, then you are in a position to ask for—and get—concessions at the bargaining table. Surprisingly enough, these can be concessions that someone in a stronger bargaining position might not be able to negotiate. For example, a small business might not have the capability to finance a project internally. However, by presenting valid arguments in that regard, the other side may well be amenable to negotiating financial terms that they wouldn't grant to a better financed adversary. Let's look at how this might work.

Background

The LCO Company, a small, thirty-five employee manufacturer has been approached by Megacorp Inc., a large manufacturer of industrial products, to supply 10,000 gizmos for use in one of Megacorp's products. Megacorp wants to develop LCO as a source, since the company needs a high quality, responsive supplier. LCO, for their part, is drooling at the prospect of getting this business, since it will effectively double the company's size.

Negotiations

The negotiations move along smoothly until payment terms are raised. Arthur Able, LCO's president points out to Ralph Realistic, the Megacorp negotiator, that LCO would need progress payments in order to finance such a large order. They jointly explore financing alternatives and determine that there are no other reasonable alternatives. It is then agreed that Megacorp will provide progress payments under the contract based on 75% of costs incurred to be liquidated against deliveries when they are made. This helps LCO finance material purchases and work-in-progress costs without having to wait until delivery to be paid.

The rationale

Megacorp knows that LCO does not have the financial capability to incur the labor and material costs to build the units if they receive no money until delivery begins, which is four months from the start date. Although Megacorp would probably not agree to progress payments with a company that had the financial resources, it was considered a sound business judgment to do so in this case. Furthermore, Megacorp knows that once the stream of deliveries starts, LCO's financing picture will improve, so that progress payments won't be needed on future orders.

Although it's possible to gain concessions by virtue of being in a weak negotiating position, it pays to be realistic in terms of your expectations. After all, the other party isn't engaged in a charitable endeavor. Therefore, any concessions they make will be based upon (1) how good a case you can present, and (2) the advantage to them. Consequently, you have to know when to ask, and when to accept "No" for an answer.

7.5 AVOIDING GETTING LOCKED INTO AN EGO CONTEST

There are all kinds of justifiable reasons why negotiations get derailed. But there's one frequent cause that has nothing to do with the merits of the respective positions. Instead, it boils down to two strong-willed negotiators getting themselves embroiled in an ego contest. What starts off as divergent viewpoints on the respective negotiation positions, evolves into a scenario where neither negotiator is willing to give ground on any basis.

What results is not a negotiation aimed at reaching mutual agreement, but a contest to prove who is the best negotiator. The irony when this happens is that the only point being proved is that neither negotiator is being very good at what they're supposed to be doing—which is negotiating an agreement.

For better or worse, negotiations are conducted by human beings with all of the frailties which that entails. Therefore, even though the best intentioned people sit down to bargain in good faith, it's inevitable that personalities may clash, or someone will perceive they're being belittled or ignored. When this happens, it's altogether possible for emotions to overwhelm logic, and a negotiation impasse to occur.

The best medicine to avoid getting locked in an ego contest is prevention. Condition yourself to concentrate on what is being negotiated, rather than on the negotiator. It helps if you view the other negotiator as a means to an end, which is getting the deal you want done. Therefore, if it means stroking a big ego, so be it. The emotional concession you make by doing this, can pay handsome dividends in terms of the contractual concessions you can win.

From a practical standpoint, if bargaining table discussions start to deteriorate, it might be wise to call a recess. There are a couple of advantages to doing this. First of all, the escalating hostility may be defused by a temporary halt to the proceedings. Negotiations by their nature are stressful, and it's natural that tensions may start to surface. A lengthy lunch break may be sufficient to defuse matters. At other times, it might be wise to adjourn for the day, or even call a halt to the proceedings.

If it does appear prudent to break off negotiations for a few days, it's best if this can be done by using some justifiable reason for an excuse. Then, there isn't a need to deal directly with how to subtly tell someone that they are ticking you off. A halt in the proceedings can have a secondary advantage in addition to giving you a mental health break. During the interlude, external pressures may be brought to bear on the other party to be more reasonable. With luck, it may come unsolicited from their superiors who want to know why negotiations haven't been concluded. Nothing deflates a big ego faster than a boss who says not so gently, "What the hell's going on!"

Another avenue of approach for taming a table-bashing egotist is to have your superiors, or some other intermediary, contact the other negotiator's boss, and explain what the difficulty is. Of course, this sort of method requires that the party making the contact have the respect of the person contacted. Otherwise, they likely will suggest that perhaps it's you, not the other guy, who is causing the difficulty.

In extreme cases where negotiators clash, the only solution may be to change one or both of the negotiators. However, this should be avoided if at all possible. For one thing, it can extend the negotiations, since old ground may have to be revisited. Furthermore, if only one side replaces the negotiator, it's sending a signal that their negotiator wasn't doing the job. Therefore, if negotiators are to be switched, it's better if replacements are brought in on both sides of the table.

7.6 COPING WITH HARDBALL TACTICS

Sometimes, there's a fine line between hardball negotiating tactics based on the issues, and the ego-based actions of a negotiator who is satisfying a personal need to have the upper hand. Actions such as threats—real or implied—or attempts at intimidation, are used in both cases. However, with an ego contest, one or both of the negotiations are the problem, irrespective of the issues. That, of course, was the focus of the previous section.

This contrasts with negotiators where the negotiator is being unreasonable simply to obtain the best deal possible from an opponent. In this latter situation, if you don't crumble in the face of hardball tactics, a fair agreement will ultimately be reached.

The core of a hardball approach is coercion designed to extract concessions. Consequently, the proper formula for defeating this strategy is to resist the pressures that are applied. Like a lot of other things, it's easier said than done. For example, how willing would you be to say, "Buzz-off!," if you were sitting on the other side of the table when these threats were made?

- "If you don't agree to pay $28,000,000 by three o'clock tomorrow, we're taking the building off the market."
- "If an agreement isn't reached by Friday, we're taking a strike vote."
- "If our lease payments aren't reduced, we're signing an agreement to move our store into the 'Spiff City Mall'."
- "Either you accept a price of $280 a unit, or we'll put this sole-source contract out for competitive bids."
- "Look, it's $5,000,000 a year guaranteed for five years, or our guy will be singing his songs for 'Soft Touch Studios'."
- "There's $2,000,000 budgeted for this contract. Either accept that now, or we'll cancel the procurement."

Everyone's gut reaction when presented with threats of this nature is to say, "Screw you, go ahead." Of course, that's an open invitation for the other side to follow through with their threat. And even if they really don't want to, a blunt challenge forces them to act. Otherwise, they would be in the position of admitting that the threat is merely a bluff, which then leaves you holding the upper hand. As a result, directly defying the other party to act is foolish unless you like living dangerously.

The best practice for dealing with a threat is to analyze it. Of course, you may need a little time to do this. However, it's best to avoid stating that you would like to recess for that purpose, because that puts you in the position of having to come back with an answer. Therefore, casually suggest a brief break for refreshments, or for that matter, any purpose unrelated to the threat.

What you want to do is to assess the threat, both from your standpoint and the impact upon the other side if it's carried out. From your viewpoint, ask yourself what you will lose if the negotiation falls through. To a large degree, your answer goes back to the alternatives that you established when you prepared your pre-negotiation position. (See section 1.3) If you have pretty good alternatives in the event negotiations fail, then your worry index shouldn't be too high. Nevertheless, that still doesn't mean you should directly invite the other side to proceed with implementing their saber-rattling scheme. That's because until they actually carry out their threat, you are still in position to negotiate a favorable agreement.

Perhaps the key to your risk assessment is the potential harm to the other side if they follow through with their threat. You may discover that their threat isn't quite as ominous as it appears to be. In conducting your assessment ask yourself these types of questions:

1. Is their threat feasible? For instance, threatening to take one's business elsewhere isn't very practical if there's no viable competition.

2. What are the potential costs to the other side even if they can implement their threat? These costs can be tangible, such as having to pay a higher price, or intangible, such as the chance of getting a lower quality product elsewhere.

3. Are the potential risks greater than the possible rewards? For example, a union going on strike where workers can be readily replaced, runs a higher risk than where substitute workers can't be quickly hired and trained.

4. Are there behind-the-scene factors that mitigate the threat? Perhaps a buyer can't afford the time delays involved in going to another supplier, or maybe the seller of a building is financially strapped and can't afford to look for another purchaser.

Once you have established to your satisfaction how real the threat is, you are in position to respond. Unless you are fairly secure about your alternatives and/or that the threat is just a bluff, it's best not to challenge it. In fact, even if your position is sound, a direct challenge isn't wise. It backs the other side to the wall, so they may feel compelled to break off negotiations even if they don't want to.

The best method for dealing with an ultimatum is to ignore it. Obviously, if the other side insists on a reply then you have little recourse other than to say something such as, "Be my guest." However, unless they are on secure footing, that's not likely to happen. Therefore, just keep the discussions rolling as if no ultimatum was issued. The more time that passes after a threat is made, the less chance there is of it being carried out. In fact, if the other side continues to negotiate after making a threat, the tactical advantage will shift to you. This is so, since the ultimate negotiation weapon is threatening not to negotiate. Once that danger goes by the boards, it's more than likely a signal that the other side will remain sitting until an agreement is reached.

7.7 PARRYING THE "PITY ME" GIMMICK

While hardball tactics are used to intimidate you, another less frequently used approach is to feed upon your sense of fair play. This "pity me" tactic can be most effective when used by a negotiator skilled at playing upon people's emotions. It's success relies on two elements, (1) the creativity of the perpetrator, and (2) the sense of fair play of the victim.

What we're talking about here aren't the run-of-the-mill pleas of poverty often heard in negotiations such as, "I can't do the job for that amount of money." Instead, these are clever excuses designed to elicit sympathy with the intent of receiving favorable treatment. This tactic is used both in negotiating agreements, and in attempting to get them modified after the performance of the work has begun.

"Pity me" ploys are most effective under circumstances where it's not easy for you to walk away and take your business elsewhere. That makes them extremely effective when you already have a contractual relationship, and are counting on the agreement being performed. Let's look at how this tactic is played out.

Background

"A," a small research company, has a contract with "B," a large energy resources firm, to do on-site testing. "A," unknown to "B," is about to sign another contract with "C" for similar work. However, "A" needs to use Fred, it's only employee with experience in this sort of testing on the new contract. That will make Fred unavailable to perform scheduled tests under "B's" contract. Arthur Alibi, "A's" president, schedules a meeting with Bob, "B's" contract administrator.

The encounter

As soon as the introductory formalities are concluded, Arthur gets right to the point. The pertinent parts of the discussion go like this:

> *Arthur:* "Bob, I'm here to ask you to postpone the tests scheduled for the first week in February. I propose they be moved to the first week in April. As you know, the weather has been bad at the test site, and with all of the snow on the ground, it would be better to do the testing when the weather improves."

> *Bob:* "Now wait a minute, Arthur. The contract calls for cold weather testing, which is why we have the February date in the first place. If we miss the February date, cold weather tests couldn't be run again until next year, and that's out of the question."

> *Arthur:* "Well, I've talked to Fred, our engineer, and he tells me that laboratory simulations could be run to factor in any cold weather impact."

> *Bob:* "I don't care what anyone said. We wanted testing done under actual conditions and that's what we contracted for. So the answer is "No" and the tests will have to be run as scheduled."

Arthur: "Well, unfortunately, we have another problem. Fred is having some personal problems and won't be able to conduct the tests. We have no one else familiar with the work."

Bob: "Look, Arthur, I'm sorry if someone has personal problems, but that's your responsibility, not mine. How you handle it is up to you. All I know is that we have a contract and I expect you to perform according to its terms."

Arthur: "There's nothing I can do. The guy has had emotional problems and isn't able to work right now. I expect him to be out eight weeks. If there was someone else I could send, I'd do it."

Bob: "You mean to tell me that this guy is the only one that can do the work?"

Arthur: "That's right."

Bob: "What a mess. Let's take a break. I'll go see about having some coffee sent in. I'll be right back." (Bob leaves the conference room, sends for coffee, and then calls Eric, the project manager on the phone.)

Bob: "Eric, this is Bob Browning. Has Arthur Alibi told you his tale of woe?"

Eric: "Yeah, Bob, and we need those tests done on schedule."

Bob: "Is there anyone else that you know of in that company who could run those tests?"

Eric: "Sure, Arthur could. He's the one who trained Fred."

Bob: "He didn't tell me that. He said Fred was the only one knowledgeable enough to do the job."

Eric: (chuckling over the phone) "I guess he probably doesn't like cold weather, Bob. Incidentally, I was talking to a guy over at 'C' Corp. at an industry conference last week. He was asking me about "A." Seems they are thinking of awarding them a contract."

Bob: "Ok, thanks Eric. I've got this muddle solved."

The solution

Bob: (Returns to the conference room) "Arthur, I've talked to Eric, and he tells me you could do these tests."

> *Arthur:* "I don't have the time to do it. I have a company to run."
>
> *Bob:* "You're telling me you don't intend to honor the contract? I'll tell you what. Either you run those tests as scheduled, or I'll terminate the contract for default. Incidentally, Eric tells me you are negotiating a contract with 'C' Corp. If word gets out that you don't honor your contracts, you won't be doing business with anyone. What's your answer?"
>
> *Arthur:* "Well, I guess I'll run the tests myself, if you feel that way about it."

NOTE: Notice that Arthur never mentioned the true reason why he couldn't run the tests, which was because he wanted to use Fred on the other contract. Instead, he concocted a tale of woe designed to elicit Bob's sympathy. This is the typical way that a "pity me" plea is designed to work. To avoid getting bamboozled by "pity me" gimmicks there are three measures you can take. These are:

- Learn as much as you can about the integrity and responsibility of the party you're dealing with before you sign on the dotted line.
- Don't let your emotions overwhelm logic when you're subjected to "pity me" pleas.
- Put the responsibility where it belongs. The other party is responsible for their performance, so don't let them transfer it to you.

Of course, there may be a justifiable basis for problems arising, both before and during the performance of an agreement. And it may be in your economic interest to agree to any necessary adjustments. There may even be occasions where you will go along with a "good faith" excuse. Just make sure it's justified, and not merely an attempt to take advantage of your good will.

7.8 THE PROPER METHOD FOR PROPOSING TRADE-OFFS

When negotiations begin, there are always one or more issues upon which both sides differ. Otherwise, there wouldn't be anything to negotiate. The number and complexity of these issues will, of course, vary from negotiation to negotiation. The ultimate objective of the negotiating parties is—or at least should be—to narrow these issues until an agreement is reached. This process involves the making of concessions until the gap in the respective positions is closed. And when all is said and done, it's your skill at trading-off concessions that will largely determine what kind of a deal you wind up with.

Giving and getting concessions can be bewildering, especially if you haven't prepared yourself beforehand. Section 1.6 discussed planning what you can concede during negotiations, and sections 11.2 and 11.3 cover how to cope with negotiation ploys such as piece by piece and mirage concessions. The focus here is on how to trade-off your concessions for adjustments by the other negotiating team.

These are several standard pitfalls to avoid when making concessions. These are:

1. Don't give away something for nothing. If you grant a concession without getting anything in return, the other side will be more reluctant to make later concessions. After all, if you condition them to think they can get something for nothing, why should they bother to give anything up in return?

2. Don't give anything up cheaply. Remember the general rule in section 1.6 which says, "When it comes to making concessions, give ground grudgingly." Your objective should be to receive the greatest possible value on every trade-off—at least from your standpoint. By the same token, you want the other side to think that they received the best deal on every concession.

3. Don't make concessions too quickly. To paraphrase an old saying, "concede in haste, and repent at your leisure." Once you grant a concession, it's gone, and if you grant them too quickly, you will end up with nothing left to give. Covering any remaining gap in the respective positions may mean surrendering some of your potential profit to get a deal. Furthermore, hasty concessions tend to indicate that your initial position wasn't a serious one. This leads the other side to wonder how much fat is built in to your first offer.

4. Remain relaxed and play a waiting game. Let the other side offer to trade-off concessions first. By the same token, don't jump to offer a concession in return if they do make the first move. This may lead them to sweeten their offer without you having yet conceded anything in return.

5. Be alert to the concessions the other side seeks. Even though in your pre-negotiation planning, you identified possible concessions you could make, the other side may be interested in other issues. If luck is on your side, these may be matters that aren't of extreme importance to you—at least until the other side expresses an interest in them. At that point, any trade-off you make in these items should be considered

to be a major concession on your part, even though in reality, you couldn't care less.

No matter what, don't be cavalier in conceding something you don't care about, since you can use these issues as bargaining chips. Anything and everything the other side seeks in the form of a concession should be bargained away as if you were parting with the crown jewels.

6. Always try to concede one of your give-away concessions in return for something substantive from the other side. In your negotiation planning you prioritized your possible concessions into those that didn't really matter, and those that would only be traded-off if absolutely necessary to reach agreement. Your objective is to swap throw-away trade-offs for red meat concessions by your adversary.

7.9 SIMPLE STEPS TO OVERCOME DEADLOCKS

Occasionally, even after concessions are made by both sides, a gap remains in the respective negotiation positions. Obviously, this impasse has to be broken or there will be no agreement. When you confront this sort of dilemma, it's helpful to step back mentally and do a little speculating. Ask yourself these types of questions:

- What's causing the deadlock?
- What will it take to break the impasse?
- Is there anything you can do to make the deadlocked deal more attractive without making any further concessions?
- Can changes be made in the proposed agreement that will eliminate the deadlock?

Although it's often assumed that an impasse is a crisis of major proportions, that's not necessarily so. The impasse may be caused by nothing greater than your adversary deciding to stand pat in the hope that you will accept his last offer. Another frequent cause, that often goes unrecognized, is that the other negotiator is stuck on hold due to some edict placed upon him by higher authority. For instance, the parting words of a boss prior to negotiations may have been, "I don't care what you do, as long as you get a 10% profit."

No matter what the source of the deadlock, always search for some common ground for reaching agreement. Try to keep the discussions going, even if you go on to other issues. Just keeping the negotiations rolling sometimes result in the deadlock issue falling by the roadside.

It may even turn out that the deadlock can be turned into an opportunity for you. For example, a negotiator who has limits placed on him by superiors, (EX: profit) may be willing to make substantial concessions in other areas. By doing a little probing to discover this sort of difficulty, you can realize gains in other areas in exchange for conceding on the point causing the roadblock.

Nevertheless, it's unrealistic to assume that there won't be occasions where an insurmountable impasse exists that won't be broken by continuing to negotiate. Therefore, sometimes the only solution is to call a temporary halt in negotiations. If this is apparent, try to adjourn only after setting a date for getting together again—unless you have other alternatives and don't want to waste any more time beating a dead horse. The recess gives both parties time to assess their relative positions and to look for a means of reaching a meeting of the minds.

7.10 WHEN YOU SHOULD GIVE AWAY
SECRETS—ON PURPOSE

Something that should generally be guarded against is the inadvertent disclosure of the details of your negotiation position. None the less, at times it can be advantageous to let your adversary gain insight as to your intentions. For the most part, this information will be conveyed across the table during the discussion of your respective positions.

Still, there may be circumstances where you indirectly want to send a signal to the other side. The most common purpose is to inspire the other side to move negotiations along if they are being too hesitant—at least from your standpoint. There are several means of doing this. One is to casually drop veiled hints during your discussions. The danger here is that your subtle message won't be picked up.

Another method is to directly convey a confidential message to your counterpart in a private conversation. Say something such as, "This is just between us, but my boss thinks we should be negotiating with the "Y" Corp., instead of you folks." The purpose of this sort of disclosure is to encourage your adversary to lower his demands, in fear that competition is waiting in the wings. Of course, whether or not this works depends upon your credibility with the other negotiator and/or his degree of inexperience.

A third approach is to give the other side deliberate access to information, while letting them think it was an accident. This involves nothing more than the old trick of leaving papers on a conference room table while you are out of the room. Naturally, the less obvious you make it appear, the less likely it is that the other party will realize it's a setup. If you have ethical considerations about doing this, you might consider the fact that the other guy isn't being forced to look. Actually, whether or not this works to get your message across depends upon whether or not your adversary chooses to snoop.

There are several sorts of messages you can convey by using this tactic. They include:

- Letting them think they have competition. (A competitor's name and phone number in your notes.)
- Implying a competitor has a lower price. (A scribbled, "XYZ Corp.—$210,000.")
- Revealing the maximum you will pay. (Another scribbled, "max. price—5 mill.") In reality, your limit may be much higher.
- Revealing an insight on their strategy. ("Tell boss, they're stalling," scrawled on your note pad.)

The obvious question is why not directly reveal what you want to say to the other party? Surprisingly enough, if you tell them they might not believe you, whereas, if they see it sneakily, it will have more credibility. In fact, that's one reason so much disinformation is leaked by the intelligence services of countries throughout the world.

CAUTION: If the other side leaves private information where it's accessible, even if your curiosity gets the better of you and you take a peek, don't believe what you see. It's a pretty common stunt, and you have no way to discern fact from fiction. This may seem like contradictory advice after being told how you can use this ploy. However, if the other side uses your disinformation, it's to your advantage. On the other hand, if you give credence to theirs, the wrong fish swallowed the bait.

7.11 HOW NIBBLE—NIBBLE—NIBBLE— GETS RESULTS

The most successful negotiators know that their counterpart at the bargaining table isn't going to give much away without an argument. But they also know that there's more than one way to get what you want. Therefore, if they run into trouble getting substantive concessions, they nibble away at them bit by bit.

Here again, is another example of human nature at work. Actually, this is a technique that you see practiced all of the time in your daily doings. A few such instances would include:

- The guy who always borrows five bucks for lunch. (He usually gets it, but he wouldn't if he asked for fifty or one hundred dollars to eat out at a fancy restaurant.)

- The teenager who nickel/dimes people into poverty. (He knows he can't hit Dad for twenty-five dollars, but he gets it a little at a time. Five dollars from Mom, ten from Dad, another five from sister Sue, and five from his buddy for gas. Of course, the gas tank was full when he borrowed the car.)

- The co-worker who is always just a minute late for work, and leaves a few minutes early a couple of times a week. (Not enough for anyone to say anything about, but a hefty chunk of time if added-up over the course of a year.)

- The neighbor who has a compete set of lawn tools. (He borrowed them from you one at a time.)

In each of the above situations, the money, tools, and time theft are all obtained by using a piece by piece approach that doesn't arouse attention. In the same way, you can reap concessions at the bargaining table if you nibble away at the edges, rather than trying blatantly to cut the pie down the middle.

For example, if you're trying to reduce the overall price, nibble away at each element of cost one by one, instead of just asking for an overall reduction. As a variation, you can often obtain concessions in areas where the other party isn't as adamant about their position. In fact, by doing some skillful maneuvering, you can obtain far better results by chipping away at your adversary's negotiation position, than by seeking a large-scale concession.

Chapter 8

THE NUANCES OF NEGOTIATION MEETINGS

Ineffective and boring business meetings are so commonplace that they are the butt of jokes and constant grumbling in the business world. However, when the purpose of a meeting is to negotiate there's little margin for error, since the consequences of a poorly run meeting can be serious. This is due to the importance of controlling the agenda, since holding your own in a negotiation meeting is essential if you want to accomplish your objectives.

Beyond this fundamental requirement, there are a number of additional benefits to be gained from mastering the dynamics of negotiation meetings. There's the very real plus of a "home court" advantage, which can give a winning edge to negotiators, as well as basketball teams.

In addition, the logistics of where and when you hold a meeting can work for or against you. There are also further factors to consider when you have to hit the road to do your bargaining. And not to be ignored—whether your meeting is at home or away—are the proper procedures for using the telephone as a negotiation tool. All of these topics are covered in this chapter.

8.1 WHY WHERE YOU NEGOTIATE INFLUENCES THE RESULTS

There are certain basics that are essential for the success of any meeting which also hold true for negotiation sessions. These include avoiding noisy or uncomfortable settings, which will diminish the power of concentration of participants. And, of course, how well the agenda is planned and executed, as well as who is invited, are fundamentals that contribute to the success or failure of any gathering.

However, meetings are scheduled for any number of purposes, and therefore differing considerations have to be taken into account. When you plan a negotiation session, there are a number of specifics that can have particular significance. First and foremost is where the meeting will be held. There are many reasons which favor holding the meeting at your home base. Yet, there are other influences that may work in your favor if you visit the other negotiator's place of business. And in still other cases, circumstances may suggest that a neutral site is the place of preference.

The following sections will address the advantages and disadvantages of each of these alternatives. The point to be emphasized here is that where the meeting is held, as well as such elements as who attends, and how skillfully the meeting is conducted, can have a real bearing on the outcome of negotiations. This is especially true where complex matters are to be discussed, particularly if you haven't held prior negotiations with the individual and/or organization. Naturally, routine and recurring negotiations don't warrant the same degree of attention. In fact, negotiations of this nature may involve nothing more extensive than the use of the phone, mail, and fax.

For complex negotiations, the location can have both psychological and practical ramifications. For instance, the mere comfort factor of negotiating in your own office or conference room can be beneficial. On the other hand, this may be outweighed by the practical advantage of seeing what you're buying, which may mean negotiating on the other party's turf.

Whichever holds true, or even if a neutral site is the proper choice, you're the one who wants to control the decision. Therefore, as part of your planning, selling the site selection shouldn't be ignored. So let's look at the advantages and disadvantages of each of these alternatives.

8.2 THE IMPORTANCE OF A HOME COURT ADVANTAGE

In many instances, the preferred location for a negotiation session will be on your home turf, since a home court advantage can have both logistical and psychological benefits. First of all, having the meeting at your location will give you greater control over such basics as the meeting room, seating arrangements, and even where people eat lunch. How to use these factors effectively is covered in section 8.6.

Furthermore, it's a real plus just to be bargaining in familiar surroundings. Not having to endure extended meetings requiring overnight travel isn't a consideration to be taken lightly. At the end of a hassle-filled day of haggling, you can exit for home, while the other side heads for a hotel. This can only help reduce your stress levels when you are engaged in an inherently stressful task such as negotiating.

But going beyond the niceties of operating in familiar surroundings, there are some real tactical benefits to be derived. First of all, it gives you ready access to any support personnel you want to call upon to answer questions that may arise. Having these people on call enhances your ability to respond to requests for information, and/or to rebut challenges to your proposal. It also simplifies obtaining documentation and other backup that can be used to strengthen your arguments.

In certain types of negotiations, it provides you with a "show and tell" opportunity to demonstrate, not only the capabilities of the product or service, but also the overall efficiency of your entire operation. For example, being able to show someone a highly efficient production line is far more effective than just saying so. Incidentally, if you do take opposing negotiators on a plant tour, make certain that company personnel are forewarned. After all, if the purpose is to emphasize the positive aspects of your business, you want to be sure everything is running smoothly when your visitors are shown around.

Of course, before you can gain a home court advantage, you must first convince the other negotiator to agree to hold the discussions at your location. There are two methods for doing this. The first is to emphasize the benefits from a negotiation standpoint such as, "Why don't we hold the meeting here, so that you can see what you're buying." The other tack to take is emphasizing the advantages of your location. This isn't hard to do if it's February, and you're in a warm weather locale such as Tucson, and suggesting a visit to someone suffering winter fatigue in Boise or Buffalo. Nonetheless, even if the climate isn't in your favor, use cultural, social, or other benefits to swing the other side to your way of thinking.

Incidentally, it helps fuel the urge to travel if you make it easy for people to say "ok." Even little things can be convincing, such as offering to make hotel reservations, furnishing ground transportation when they arrive, and so forth. In other words, you want to use every possible means at your command to justify having negotiations at your location.

Naturally, if the other party is equally insistent on holding the meeting at their location, you need to be a little more creative in justifying why that's not possible. Perhaps you can plead a fear of flying, illness in the family, or some other personal impediment. However, you better be convincing, since if the other party is suspicious, you may lose your credibility before negotiations even begin.

8.3 MINIMIZING THE "HOME COURT" EDGE ON ENEMY TURF

If, for one reason or another, you end up having to negotiate at the other side's site, it isn't automatically a disadvantage. Although a "home court" advantage is usually preferable, taking the show on the road can have benefits. Actually, in certain cases, it might be better to negotiate at the other party's location. Any number of circumstances could account for this. For example, perhaps you're procuring equipment which you want to see demonstrated, or desire to tour the production facilities where supplies will be produced. Of course, if possible, it's preferable to arrange such on-site inspections before negotiations begin.

A more common benefit of negotiating at your opponent's location is that it gives you the opportunity to ask for a wide range of information concerning your adversary's negotiation position. It's not as easy for them to make excuses such as, "Sorry, Bob, but we didn't bring that data with us." In fact, if you anticipate asking for a lot of supporting data, it might be smart to suggest that negotiations be held at your opponent's home base. In addition, if worse comes to worse, it's more emphatic to break off negotiations when you're away from home. After all, threatening to leave doesn't have quite the same impact if you're just down the hall from your office.

Incidentally, a helpful tactic to speed negotiations along when you're on the road is to let your adversary know that you have return reservations booked. This places a preset deadline for the completion of bargaining. However, don't box yourself in here, since a shrewd opponent may let things lag until the deadline approaches. The motive, of course, is the hope of winning some last minute concessions because you don't want to reschedule a flight or otherwise change your plans.

When you must negotiate at your opponent's base of operations, it's prudent to do everything you can to overcome this handicap. One common factor that's often overlooked is travel arrangements. It doesn't pay to be tired when you're about to initiate negotiations. Therefore, always try to arrive the day before, if the location is an overnight trip from your office. The extra expense of an additional night at a hotel will be more than compensated for by the fact that you will be well rested when the bargaining begins.

There are other minor factors that can aid in making a negotiation visit less of an irritant. For example, always make sure you bring along enough toiletries and other personal necessities. It can be both aggravating and time-consuming trying to find a store when you're in a strange city. In the same vein, make sure you have a rental car or other transportation of your own available. Relying on the other side to provide transportation places you at their disposal, which isn't a good position to be in at a negotiating session.

8.4 WHEN IT'S BEST TO NEGOTIATE ON NEUTRAL GROUND

There are instances when negotiations are best held at a neutral site instead of at the location of one of the negotiating parties. This is particularly common in the fields of international and labor negotiations. However, even for more routine business transactions, the use of a neutral location may be beneficial. Although the reasons for using a neutral site for negotiating sessions will be largely controlled by the specifics of the negotiation, a few commonplace reasons include:

1. An inability to agree on a site. If one side or the other is extremely reluctant to hold negotiations at the other parties' location, it's prudent to suggest a neutral setting. Otherwise, the negotiations may start off with an extended dispute over where the meeting will be held. Needless to say, this isn't a good way to get negotiations off-the-ground.

2. As a simple matter of expediency, circumstances may dictate the use of neutral ground. It may just be more convenient for both parties to schedule a bargaining session at an off-site location.

3. To provide an atmosphere more conducive to reaching agreement. Pleasant surroundings tend to put people in a better frame of mind. Therefore, holding an important negotiation session at a location that can combine business with pleasure has practical advantages.

4. When a third party has a vested interest in the negotiations. For example, a third party involved in financing a deal may dictate that the meeting be held at the financier's place of business.

TIP: Whenever you're negotiating at a neutral site that's unfamiliar to you, give yourself as much time as possible to get comfortable with the surroundings. Feeling at ease with the setting will set the stage for concentrating on the negotiation without being distracted by the environment.

8.5 TIPS FOR SWITCHING NEGOTIATION SITES IN MIDSTREAM

On occasion it may be expedient to switch the meeting site after negotiations have begun. For example, if negotiations are at an impasse it's necessary to look for every possible way to break a deadlock. One such course of action may involve a change in the meeting location. Of course, changing the scenery won't necessarily resolve critical issues that are preventing an agreement. However, a new location might encourage a fresh outlook on the differences separating the parties. So, although changing the location of a meeting might not be a cure-all, it can serve as a substitute for breaking off negotiations completely.

A more likely reason for changing sites arises from the context of a particular negotiation. For instance, it may become apparent during a meeting that for fact-finding or other purposes the negotiations would be easier to conduct on the other parties' premises. This isn't always so obvious before negotiations begin. For example, perhaps the personnel and documentation needed to answer questions would be more readily available by shifting locations. Or maybe a previously unanticipated desire to view facilities necessitates a change.

Of all the possible incentives for changing the locale of a negotiation meeting, none is more paramount than switching from your opponent's place of business to your own. Although it's generally preferable to negotiate on your home turf, you may not always have initial success in convincing the other party to do so. Therefore, you may find yourself reluctantly agreeing to negotiate at the other side's office. However—particularly with protracted negotiations—it may be possible to switch sites to your place of business.

Of course, convincing your adversary of this requires some form of justification. This isn't hard to do if you are both based in the same city. Something as simple as "Why don't we meet in my office tomorrow?" will suffice. It gets a little trickier when switching locations will involve overnight travel. Therefore, for you to have any success, some sort of solid substantiation is necessary. Nevertheless, with a little thought you should be able to dream something up. The best approach is to convince the other negotiator that switching sites is to his benefit. This can take many forms such as:

- "We've got tons of backup that supports those figures. Let's move the meeting to Seattle on Monday, and we can dig up whatever you want to see."
- "The best way to convince yourself that we can meet your production deadlines is to take a look at our facilities."

- "I talked to our engineering people, and they suggest you come to Phoenix on Friday for a demonstration."
- "Look Sarah, I can't agree with your final offer, but I've talked to Mr. Jamison, and he's willing to listen to what you have to say. Why not make the trip and give it a shot?"
- "Jim, as I mentioned when we started negotiations, I have to be back in Tampa on Wednesday. I'd hoped we would have this wrapped-up by now. Let's move the meeting to Tampa next week. I'm sure we can agree on everything after a couple of sessions."

8.6 USING MEETING ROOM LOGISTICS TO YOUR ADVANTAGE

Often overlooked, but nevertheless a critical contributing factor to the success of a negotiation session is the facility used for the meeting. As has probably been your misfortune to experience, any meeting held in a room that's too hot, cold, or overcrowded, isn't likely to be a smashing success in the eyes of the suffering participants. The physical surroundings can affect everyone's power of concentration. Therefore, as a starter, make sure the facilities to be used are adequate to meet the needs of those attending.

Such simple elements as comfortable seating and good lighting can indirectly influence negotiation results. After all, someone who is forced to endure less than adequate conditions isn't likely to appreciate that fact. This sort of resentment can manifest itself in the attitude of the other side during bargaining sessions. At the least, they may wonder what kind of a deal they will get from someone who can't even provide decent meeting facilities. Furthermore, they might decide to reciprocate by making the negotiation a less than pleasant experience.

Beyond the necessity of adequate meeting facilities, there are certain strategic advantages you can gain by properly setting up the meeting site. For example, seating arrangements are important. You want to be seated in the commanding location, which is either at the head of the table, or at a central position where you are nearest to everyone in attendance. Your closest advisors should be seated next to you, or immediately to your rear. This will allow you to confer in a whisper, or unobtrusively pass papers back and forth.

By the way, as a meeting moves along, and the topics being discussed change, your team member's participation will vary. Therefore, try to plan ahead and juggle the seating of your team during meeting breaks. For instance, if the focus of the discussion shifts from financial to technical, make sure the technical member is in close proximity to you.

The obvious procedure for guaranteeing that everyone sits in the proper place is to have name cards set out at the table prior to the meeting. Otherwise, the other negotiating team will waltz in and plunk themselves down where they see fit. So even if everyone knows each other, don't neglect this formality. Incidentally, it's also a good idea to have your negotiation team members seated in the conference room before the opposing group arrives. That way the seating arrangements will be guaranteed beforehand.

HINT: When you're negotiating at your opponent's site, chances are that you won't have control over the seating arrangements. Obviously, if by some stroke of good fortune the seating is still up for grabs, quickly commandeer the head of the table position. Nevertheless, if that's not possible, sit at the opposite end of the table to give yourself equal status.

CAUTION: When it comes to the question of meeting facilities, someone in an attempt to be creative may decide that making the meeting conditions unbearable can provide a tactical advantage. For instance, perhaps keeping a room too hot or cold will discourage dragging out negotiations. In rare cases, this may work. However, for the most part, deliberately making a meeting facility intolerable has far more risks than rewards so it's generally wise to avoid trying this ploy.

8.7 WHO AND WHAT TO BRING WHEN YOU'RE ON THE ROAD

Whenever you're negotiating at either your opponent's location, or at a neutral site, you have to take into consideration the size and scope of the negotiation team that will accompany you. Needless to say, any large scale negotiation shouldn't be compromised by any dollar and cents determination as to who should and who shouldn't go. Saving a few travel dollars can be quickly offset by a preventable error that wouldn't have occurred if the proper expertise was on hand.

On the other hand, you don't want to bring along so many people that your entourage is the size of a small convention. Not only is it unwieldy to manage a negotiation team with a large number of participants, but it also invites the other side to respond by assembling an equally numbing number of attendees. The inevitable result is that it will take longer to reach agreement than if fewer people were in attendance.

Although your negotiation team will be limited to the number of people you bring along, your adversary will be operating under no such constraints. Consequently, an attempt may be made to intimidate you by the sheer weight of numbers. This could lead to a power play where the other side brings a small army to the negotiation table. A simple expedient to prevent this is to agree beforehand as to the number of attendees each side will have.

In general, you want to have people on hand that complement the expertise the other side is bringing to the bargaining table. Simply put, if they will have an acoustics expert present to justify their technical position, you want one along also to rebut vague technical assertions. Otherwise, you will be subjected to all sorts of inflated claims which you don't have the knowledge to reject. This sort of tactic can quickly place you on the defensive, which is a position you don't want to be in.

In addition to the people you bring with you on a road trip, there are several procedural precautions you should address when you will be negotiating away from familiar surroundings. First of all, every negotiation is subject to unexpected twists and turns. Therefore, during a bargaining session, you may suddenly find the need to consult someone who isn't along with you. Therefore, before you leave your place of business, make sure that anyone you are likely to contact can be reached when you need them.

It can really be frustrating when you're trying to overcome a sticking point in negotiations and are unable to reach the party you need on the phone. You are then placed in a position of going ahead without the advice you want, or slowing the progress of negotiations until you are able to track down the information you need. This may not seem to be particularly important and it often isn't. However, if a negotiation gets bogged down because of a time delay, other elements may be raised in the interim that further muddy the waters. Inevitably, the more smoothly you can keep a negotiation moving along, the easier it will be to conclude a deal. Therefore, taking care of minor details has a greater significance in negotiations than might otherwise appear to be the case.

On the subject of details, it's worth mentioning that all of your negotiation papers should be in your carry-on luggage on airline flights. You may also want to bring along a lightweight laptop computer and/or a portable fax. Of course, if you will be in a major city many hotels have business equipment available for travelers. The important point is to make sure you will have on hand anything that you will need before your trip starts. That way, you won't be faced with any surprises that can cause problems you don't need. After all, negotiations are difficult enough in themselves without avoidable difficulties adding to your burden.

8.8 THE IMPORTANCE OF SETTING A MEETING AGENDA

Prior to any negotiation it's important to prepare a detailed agenda of topics to be covered. In this regard, it's useful to include key questions the other side might ask, along with the appropriate responses. This sort of exercise will allow you to answer queries about your position with a greater degree of confidence. As a result, your replies will be quicker and more convincing. This adds a degree of credibility that is absent when someone has to ponder a reply and/or seek advice from others before responding.

Your agenda should be prepared in consultation with all the members of your negotiation team. This is important, since you want everyone presenting a united front when you sit down to bargain. As a part of setting the agenda, be sure to assign responsibilities as to who will answer inquiries in particular areas when negotiations commence. This avoids the possibility of assumptions being made, and team members inadvertently contradicting one another—to your dismay and the glee of your opponent. A short list of items to be included in your agenda are:

- Date, time, and location of the negotiation meeting.
- The names and job responsibilities of the other side's attendees. (This should be coordinated with the other negotiator beforehand.)
- The names and negotiation meeting responsibility of each of your own team members. Be specific about who is responsible for what.
- Your negotiation objective.
- Questions the other side may raise and how they will be handled.
- Questions you want answered about the other side's proposal.
- Concessions that can be made if necessary to reach agreement.

The length of your agenda will, of course, vary with the complexity of the negotiation, as well as the negotiation experience of your team members. The importance of setting an agenda isn't so much in having a script to follow, as it is in verifying that everything has been done in terms of your pre-negotiation planning. Frequently, the importance of an agenda is overlooked, since negotiation meetings aren't as susceptible to a set format as are business meetings in general.

8.9 THE BEST WAY TO START A NEGOTIATION MEETING

A negotiation can go a lot easier if you're in the proper frame of mind to begin with. As a minimum, it pays to be well rested and alert. Needless to say, that means getting a good night's rest so you start off fresh. As basic as this requirement is, it can sometimes be neglected. This frequently happens when every final minute is used in preparation for the negotiation. What gets overlooked is that concentrating on making sure that you're thoroughly prepared, may leave you too tired the next day to know what you're talking about. Therefore, be sure to let go in terms of your pre-negotiation preparation, so that you have the physical and mental stamina to properly present your position.

Negotiating on the road can also contribute to having you enter a conference room in less than your best condition. This can result from either not planning your travel so you are well rested, or from a longer than expected night on the town with your negotiation team. Suffice it to say that any celebrating should be saved for after negotiations are finished. That way, you will have a better chance of having something to celebrate.

As for beginning the negotiations themselves, try to ease into it with some social banter. This helps relieve the tension on both sides of the table. Furthermore, when discussions do begin in earnest, don't start off by being critical of your opponent's proposal. All this will serve to do is raise the level of tension. Even though the initial offer by your adversary may be totally unacceptable, how you go about rejecting it has significance. It's best to convey the notion that it isn't all that bad. For example, say, "We generally like your offer. However, we'd like to see . . . ," rather than a totally negative, "Your offer is so low, it's insulting."

In the first place, it's just an opening offer, so unless the other party is a pretty naive negotiator, it's not likely to be something that's immediately acceptable anyway. After all, that's why you're negotiating in the first place. If there wasn't anything of consequence to discuss, the entire deal could have been handled on the phone. Therefore, bluntly rejecting it doesn't serve any purpose other than making the other side mad.

Furthermore, how you initially proceed will set the tone for the entire negotiation. Consequently, a little tact at the beginning will aid in keeping the hostility level low throughout the bargaining period. Of course, things may eventually heat up, but the longer a negotiating session goes without anger coming to the fore, the better off you'll be in the long run.

8.10 NINE STEPS FOR A SUCCESSFUL NEGOTIATION SESSION

Keeping the following fundamentals in mind will assist you in making the most of a negotiation meeting.

1. Invite only the people who need to be there. Keep your experts on the sidelines until needed. Always try to agree with your negotiating counterpart on the number of attendees.
2. Try to schedule the meeting for the convenience of the other party. The more you do to oblige them before negotiations begin, the more

likely they are to oblige you once they start. So a little bit of courtesy beforehand can pay big dividends.

3. Keep the meeting on track. When the discussion starts to wander from the issue at hand, interrupt with a question to get it back in focus.

4. Don't lose control of your emotions even if provoked.

5. Designate a note taker for your team so that anything said isn't lost in the shuffle.

6. Listen attentively when the other side presents their arguments. Don't keep jumping in to counter everything that's said that you don't agree with. If you keep cutting them short, you may not get to hear something that would be to your advantage. In addition, this encourages them to do likewise when you're talking. However, if you have listened to them politely, when they interrupt you, you're able to say, "We listened to your presentation, and we would appreciate the same courtesy in return."

7. Establish the details in terms of who is going to do what in terms of supplying any agreed to proposal backup or other documentation.

8. Summarize what has been accomplished at the conclusion of each negotiation session. Also get agreement on what will be on the agenda when the meeting resumes.

9. When negotiations conclude, agree on who will write up the written document. Volunteer yourself, since if you write it up, you control what it says. This, by the way, isn't a trivial matter. (See section 16.3 for more on this.)

8.11 HOW TO DOMINATE MEETINGS WITHOUT ANYONE REALIZING IT

You want to maintain as much control as possible during negotiation meetings, since this allows you to steer a steady course toward reaching your objectives. However, overtly attempting to dominate the discussions will result in resistance from the folks on the other side of the table. Therefore, your ultimate goal is to control the meeting without seeming to do so. At best, this isn't easy to do. However, it can be done if you go about it the right way.

The first step is to assert yourself promptly at the beginning of the meeting. Starting off strong will help to establish your dominance, but you don't want to be negative, since this will immediately create a hostile atmosphere. For this reason, if at all possible, try to start your presentation with a pitch as to how you can solve a problem for the other side. In fact, the more you can offer in terms of resolving the differences in the respective negotiation positions, the more you will be listened to.

Doing this also tends to create credibility in what you're saying, as well as demonstrating that you intend to be businesslike in working toward settlement of any differences. You may even want to stand up when you start your opening pitch as an added means of placing emphasis on what you are saying. And as the meetings move along, try to be the one to suggest coffee and lunch breaks, as well as daily recess of the meetings. This not only helps to assert your dominance, but it also lets you take breaks when you need them for strategic reasons—such as when the meeting isn't going too well for your side.

Of course, there are two sides to every coin, and the other party to the negotiation will want to have their say. This is the time when your control of the meeting is most likely to slip away. Naturally, you want to listen to the other side's presentation, since it takes two parties to reach agreement. However, if you get to a point where nothing substantive is being said, reassert your authority by asking questions. Try to pick out significant items that are difficult at best to respond to. This will tend to put the other side on the defensive, and will give you an opening to reassert your authority. Actually, if you raised a tricky enough question, the other negotiator may be relieved to have you take over the discussion.

All in all, maintaining control of a negotiation meeting is best done by (1) being prepared for any eventuality, and (2) remaining alert and ready to assert yourself whenever an opening comes about.

NOTE: When unexpected questions are raised by the other side, the lead negotiator should be the one to initially respond. Let your people know this beforehand, so there's no confusion about it. It may be that you want one of your experts to be the one to respond, however, that should be your decision as the negotiation team leader. Otherwise, you will lose control over the discussion.

Incidentally, often the best answer to an unexpected question is something tentative or noncommittal, such as, "We'll look into that and get back to you." This avoids erroneous and/or misleading responses that you may have to back off from at a later point in the negotiation. Actually, sometimes a question may go no further than your promise of a future reply. This is especially helpful if you don't have a good answer to give, either now, or in the future. It may seem unrealistic that someone is going to ask a question, without following up later when they don't get a reply. However, sometimes questions are asked innocuously without realizing their impact. Consequently, if little or no significance was attached to the question, there's a strong possibility the other party won't realize and/or care that they didn't get a response.

8.12 THE PITFALLS OF PHONE NEGOTIATIONS

The telephone is, of course, a standard tool of the negotiator. Many routine, repetitive transactions involving little negotiation other than on price and delivery are handled exclusively by phone and/or fax. However, with more complex negotiations the telephone is more likely to be used as an adjunct to face-to-face negotiations. In fact, where extensive negotiations are to take place, conducting them exclusively by phone has its drawbacks.

First of all, the telephone is by its nature impersonal. Therefore, phone negotiations don't give you the opportunity to use the full force of your personality in making your presentation. A further handicap is that the phone doesn't allow you to observe the other party. As a result, you aren't able to discern the little nuances that body language and facial expressions can reveal. Frankly, exaggeration and lying are a lot easier to do in the absence of eyeball to eyeball contact. As a result, don't rely exclusively on the telephone to negotiate anything other than the most routine transaction.

On the other hand, the telephone is extremely useful as part of your overall negotiation strategy. Many negotiations involve a great deal of give and take including a number of meetings over a period of time. And while the bulk of the issues may be resolved in personal meetings, much information that contributes to inching toward agreement is transmitted over the phone.

For example, it's very helpful to use the phone if you want to make a proposal that you would prefer not to do in person. For instance, if you intend to propose something that in all probability will be rejected by the other side, it's pretty impractical to schedule a meeting just to be shot down. Yet, by making such a pitch on the phone, you can determine the level of resistance. If it's not as high as you anticipated, then perhaps a meeting can be scheduled to discuss the possibilities.

It's also handy to use the phone to bait the hook with a tempting offer. Using the phone to make a preliminary offer gives you an opportunity to hold a follow-up meeting to emphasize your point. Of course, this tactic will only succeed if your meeting can satisfy the anticipation built up by your phone call. In short, don't promise more on the telephone than you can deliver in person.

CAUTION: Of course, many of the routine details surrounding a negotiation will be conducted on the telephone. This includes transmitting documents by fax which can help immeasurably in speeding up the overall process. However, for no better reason than its ease of use, care should be taken when using a fax machine as part of the negotiation process. It's speed and convenience can lead to carelessness in terms of what is transmitted. Therefore, take precautions to carefully monitor any negotiation documents to be transmitted by fax. Here, as with any other means of transmission, what is sent should have the prior approval of the negotiation team leader or his designated representative. This practice will avoid errors which at best may be embarrassing, and at worst costly.

Chapter 9

BASIC NEGOTIATION TABLE TACTICS

At the negotiation table you will be subjected to a wide array of tactics, all aimed at getting the upper hand for your adversary. How well you fend for yourself in countering these tactics will influence the course of the negotiations—as well as the end result.

Your overall objective is to keep the negotiation in focus, and proceed in an orderly fashion toward accomplishing your negotiation goals. This may require diplomacy in the face of hostility on the one hand, and skill in presenting your position on the other. How best to accomplish these goals is what this chapter is about.

9.1 ASSESSING THE OTHER NEGOTIATOR'S CLOUT

As you may recall, sections 3.5 and 3.6 discussed the importance of establishing the negotiation authority of your counterpart, as well as identifying any behind-the-scenes decision makers. This is of more than passing interest, since if you don't know where the authority lies to approve an agreement, you may just be spinning your wheels. Of course, as was discussed earlier, the person you're negotiating with may not be the one with final authority to approve the deal. This is by no means uncommon, especially in larger organizations where higher level approvals are the norm rather than the exception. In fact, even agreements negotiated by senior level personnel are often subject to scrutiny prior to being executed.

Nonetheless, even when negotiators don't have final authority, their degree of influence with those possessing the power to accept or reject an agreement is significant. So even though you have to convince the other negotiator of the merits of your offer, that only gets you halfway home. Because then, you have to rely on the clout of your counterpart in selling the deal to his superiors. Therefore, it's worthwhile to evaluate how much clout your opposite number has within the organization he represents. Otherwise, you have no assurance as to whether the negotiation session is a final event, or merely a preliminary round that will have to be replayed with the other negotiator's superiors.

So before negotiations even begin, determine if the other negotiator has final authority, and if not, establish who does have the final say. As will be true in many cases, you will likely be told that some higher level of review is required. If so, as mentioned in section 3.5, reserve the right to secure higher approval for yourself. This is a good guarantee against the use of higher authority simply as a ploy to extract further concessions from you after you think you have a done deal. In other words, if the other side plays a higher approval game, you want to be in a position to counter this ploy.

Once you establish that a negotiated agreement will be subject to higher level approval, you then have to think about how much power the other negotiator has. If you're dealing with someone who doesn't have any clout at all, then you might be better off insisting from the start that someone participate in the negotiations who has authority to make commitments. This is a touchy subject though, since you don't want to appear to be dictating what the other side should do—especially if they're in a position to take their business elsewhere.

Therefore, make sure you're able to make such a demand stick before you broach the subject. And even then, do it diplomatically by saying something such as, "Frank, since Mr. Howard is going to have to approve this anyway, wouldn't it be better to get him involved from the start?" This, or some similar approach may work, but if it doesn't, then you have little choice but to start negotiating and see what happens. Naturally, if things get bogged down because of the powerless position of the other negotiator, then you can become more insistent.

In assessing the power of the other negotiator to sell a deal to his superiors, look at such factors as the person's experience and position within the organization. Additionally, watch for clues that indicate the individual may have substantial power beyond what would be expected from someone in that particular job. An obvious example, is anyone who for a variety of reasons happens to be well connected to the key decision makers in the organization.

In any event, the persuasive powers of the other negotiator are a critical factor in moving a negotiation along toward agreement.

Aside from determining the real or apparent authority of the opposing negotiator, the most common problem you will confront in this area is an attempt to use the approval of higher authority as a gambit to get you to make further concessions. This is the old line which goes, "My boss won't buy $80,000, but we can accept $99,000."

This is frequently used as a ploy even when the negotiator does in fact have the authority to reach final agreement. The most common mistake you can make when this happens is to continue to bargain, since it will represent a tacit acceptance of the negotiator's assertion. Once that happens, your opponent will likely try to extract further concessions using an unseen superior's veto authority over every offer you make. This may continue until you finally threaten to walk away from the deal. Then, and only then, will an agreement be reached. In the meantime, this ploy may have succeeded in substantially increasing the amount of your offer.

The best way to handle "the boss won't buy it," arguments is to insist that the absent decision-maker take an active part in the negotiations. Say something such as, "Look, if Ms. Tuttle objects to my offer, then Ms. Tuttle should be here to talk turkey. I want to hear directly what her objections are, because I'm convinced that my position is fair." If the other negotiator refuses, then simply say, "Well, my offer remains the same until the person finding it unacceptable tells me first hand why they object to it."

This sort of approach forces the other negotiator to (1) bring in the boss, (2) break off negotiations, or (3) accept the offer you made—which was allegedly rejected by higher authority. If the choice is the latter, then you will know that the other side was playing a game with you. If not, it's most likely that a higher level person will then appear and attempt to convince you that your offer isn't acceptable.

As an alternative, the negotiator might break off negotiations with you and have his boss attempt to negotiate an agreement at a higher level. No matter what is threatened, if you have made your best offer, simply refuse to budge from your position. In negotiations, agreements aren't always reached until one or both parties are convinced that the other side is at the limit. With both this ploy and others, you will often find that deals only get done when it gets to the point of looking like there may not be a deal.

When what is negotiated at the bargaining table is rejected on the basis that higher authority won't agree to the deal, the alleged veto power is often being exercised by a boss, but other variations are used. Technical experts, accountants, lawyers, boards of directors, and bankers, are all used in different situations as the reason why an agreement can't be reached. Of course, this may be true, but unless and until you receive first hand verification of this, you won't know for sure whether or not it's just a ploy. And even then you can't always be certain, at least until the objection is scrutinized and considered valid by someone with comparable expertise on your side of the fence.

The tactic of using a third party straw to object to an offer is so widespread that it's worthwhile to take a look at such a scenario to see how best to deal with it.

Background

Harold S., a buyer for a small manufacturer, is negotiating with Robert C., a contract administrator for a supplier, to purchase raw material used in the manufacturing process. The negotiations are being conducted at the supplier's facility.

The boss says, "No" ploy

After extended negotiations, which have narrowed the differences in the respective negotiation positions, Harold makes an offer of $450,000 for the material being procured. Robert C. says the figure looks ok, but he has to check with his boss. He exits the conference room and returns in about ten minutes. The conversation goes like this:

Robert C.: "I checked with Mark L. (his boss) and he tells me we can't accept anything lower than $550,000. However, I told him that you won't budge, so he said that seeing you were such a good customer, he'd eat half the loss and settle for $500,000."

Harold S.: "Impossible, we bought the same quantity last year for $420,000. $450,000 is the best I can do, and I told you that an hour ago."

Robert C.: "I know Harold, but . . ." (Robert and Harold go back and forth for another forty-five minutes but Harold refuses to budge.)

Robert C.: "Look, I'll give it another shot." (Leaves, returns, and says) "Mr. L. is pretty ticked off, but I got him to agree to $480,000. Let's wrap-it-up before he changes his mind."

Harold S.: Appearing exasperated says, "Bob, I don't see any point in going any further. I've got a plane to catch in two hours. If your boss doesn't want the deal, then he better come in and tell me himself right now. Otherwise, I'm leaving."

Robert C.: "Sit tight, I'll be right back." (He returns in five minutes accompanied by Mark L.)

Mark L.: Shakes hands with Harold, sits down and says, "What seems to be the problem Harold?"

Harold S.: "I don't have a problem. I've made my best offer of $450,000. That's $30,000 more than we paid for the same quantity the last time around. If you can't accept that, then there's no point in continuing the discussions."

Mark L.: "Our costs have gone up significantly since last year Harold. Let me just take a minute to go over some figures with you." (Mark then starts to go over a cost breakdown which is basically nothing more than a rehash of data already discussed by Harold and Robert.)

Harold S.: After listening for a few minutes to make certain he isn't going to hear anything new says, "Hold it Mark. We've already covered this ground. Do you want the $450,000 or not?" as he starts to put his papers in his briefcase.

Mark L.: "I don't see how we could survive with that number. However, I don't want you to think I'm just being stubborn. Let me take this to the division Vice President and see what he says."

Harold S.: "How long will that take? I've only got an hour left before I have to leave."

Mark L.: "I'll be back in ten minutes. Why don't you people grab a cup of coffee?" He returns fifteen minutes later, sits down and says, "Well, I've got good news Harold. The boss says if I want to take the responsibility for any loss we have on this deal, I can settle for $460,000. That's just about what you wanted, although to tell you the truth, we're going to lose money on this contract." He sticks out his hand and says, "Do we have a deal?"

Harold S.: "It's a deal for $460,000. I'll process the paperwork when I get back to the office on Monday."

NOTES: 1. Although Harold finally settled for $460,000, which was $10,000 more than he said was his best offer, he was satisfied with the results. That's because when he learned before negotiations began that higher level approval would be needed for any agreement, he kept something in reserve to give away. In reality, which only Harold knew, his walk-away figure was $475,000. Once you establish that higher authority will be involved in approving a negotiation, it's worthwhile not to make your maximum offer while you're negotiating at lower levels. This gives you a cushion to fall back on if the other side tries to squeeze you as in this case.

2. Another important point is that Harold refused to go back to square one and start negotiating all over again at a higher level; namely Mark. He listened only long enough to (1) be polite, and (2) to establish that Mark wasn't going to say anything that hadn't already been discussed with Robert. Once you make what you say is your best offer, if the other side can get you to start negotiating all over again at a higher level, then you're sending a signal that your position wasn't firm.

3. Of course, this scenario could have been played out differently. Mark could have refused to move from the $480,000 figure. This would have left Harold with the choice of leaving, with the hope that he would be called with a better offer, or upping his offer toward his $475,000 maximum. And of course, Harold could have tried to split the difference between his offer of $450,000 and Mark's $460,000. How any negotiation plays out in the end depends upon the players and their judgment as to when to call it quits. The bottom line is that both sides have to know what is reasonable in any given circumstance. It's as important to know when to quit trying to squeeze a deal dry, as it is to know when to turn down an offer as unacceptable.

9.2 USING PERSONAL PUBLIC RELATIONS TO SCORE POINTS

Everyone likes to be liked, and that's as true of a negotiator as anyone else. Therefore, a little bit of politeness and apple polishing can give you an edge at the bargaining table. Of course, it's a little naive to assume that just because you're nice to someone, they're going to give you the deal of the century. Nevertheless, showing courtesy and respect toward your opposition can pay dividends in a number of ways. These include:

- When negotiators have to sell negotiated agreements within their own organization, they may work harder at it if they like you.
- Most negotiations have an acceptable range for reaching agreement. Good personal relations will deter the other negotiator from squeezing you to the limit.

- Deals can and are killed for no better reason than the people involved don't like each other.
- A good relationship gives you a better chance to get your points across at the bargaining table.
- A positive attitude at the negotiation table can help enlist the other negotiator in a cooperative endeavor to close the gap in your respective positions.
- If people like doing business with you, they will more likely than not want to deal with you in the future.

The long and the short of it when it comes to negotiating is that there's little to be gained and much to be lost by treating the other negotiator as a mortal enemy. So even if glad-handling isn't your strong suit, at least attempt to be calm and businesslike, no matter how hot under the collar your counterpart gets. A little patience and a lot of persistence are a distinct asset for any negotiator to have.

9.3 AVOIDING PERSONAL CRITICISM WHILE TAKING A FIRM APPROACH

Combine differing opinions and personalities with the need to reach a mutually satisfactory agreement on diverse issues and the potential exists for emotional outbursts to erupt. Yet, anger and hostility will only serve to push the two sides even farther apart. Therefore, even though it's necessary to be firm when challenged at the negotiation table, this can and should be done with dignity, irrespective of any actions taken by the other side to provoke you into losing your composure.

Probably the most common problem in this area is how to rebut the other negotiator's assertions without being negative. The paramount consideration in this regard is to attack the position—not the person. Even when this is recognized, it's easy to err simply by a choice of words which unintentionally assail the sensitivities of the other party. In essence, it's not only what you say that counts, but also how you say it.

A useful device to defuse potential anger when disagreeing with your adversary's position is to blunt your disagreement by cloaking it in positive terms. Let's look at some good and not so good ways to start off rebutting what you don't agree with:

> *Bad:* "You're wrong . . ."
> *Good:* "You're right, but . . ."
> *Bad:* "I totally disagree with what you're saying."
> *Good:* "I essentially agree with you, however . . ."

Bad: "Your offer is an insult."

Good: "I think your offer is fair, and we can settle right now if . . ."

Bad: "I don't buy that argument at all."

Good: "I couldn't agree with you more, however . . ."

Bad: "That stinks. Here's how it should be done."

Good: "Let's kick that suggestion around a bit. It's doable as far as I'm concerned if we could just . . ."

Bad: "That's ridiculous."

Good: "That's a great idea, and perhaps we could strengthen it further by . . ."

Your arguments against whatever has been proposed will be the same in any of the examples above. However, by putting them forth in a positive manner, you not only avoid angering the other party, but you also are more likely to receive a favorable hearing on what you propose. This may seem to be a small matter in the general scheme of things, however, the more adept you are at preventing provocation, the greater are your chances of ultimate success.

9.4 ARGUING EFFECTIVELY WITHOUT HOSTILITY

There will be times during many negotiations when disagreements over the respective positions become confrontational. However, here the key is to argue the merits of your position while avoiding hostility and anger. This can be a tall order, especially if the opposing party is prone to mounting negative attacks. Nevertheless, trading insults won't further your cause, so maintain your cool under any circumstances.

It helps to keep your emotions in check if you recognize that disagreements are part and parcel of the negotiation process. So instead of meeting fire with fire in terms of a hostile adversary, instead look for the reason behind the hostility. A few ways to defuse anger at the negotiation table include:

1. Suggest alternatives that can resolve the problem. Often the other person's anger is based upon sheer frustration at being unable to overcome differences on a particular issue. If you can propose an alternative solution, this can serve to defuse matters.

2. Try to steer the discussion to less volatile matters. This doesn't resolve the difficulty, but it will serve to quiet things down. Later on in the

negotiations, the tricky issue can be taken up again, perhaps from a different angle that's less likely to evoke an angry response.

3.   Attempt to put a positive spin on disagreements. Assure the other party that by working together, you're sure that an amicable solution can be found.

4.   Be flexible in looking at topics from the perspective of the other negotiator. If both parties adopt a rigid, "no compromise" attitude, it makes it difficult—if not impossible—to resolve disagreements.

5.   Add a touch of humor if the opportunity presents itself. A little bit of levity at the proper moment can help to cool things down.

6.   If the other negotiator is being unreasonably hostile, you may want to directly confront the situation by saying something such as, "If we both remain calm and discuss matters in a reasonable manner I'm sure we can reach an amicable agreement." Sometimes, a statement such as this will shock an angry opponent into more reasonable conduct. However, if you are being berated to the extent that you find it to be intolerable, threaten to leave if necessary.

9.5 COUNTERING YOUR ADVERSARY'S TACTICS

All sorts of tactics may be employed against you during a negotiation. The bottom line is that these ploys are designed to throw you off balance, and divert your thoughts away from your game plan. First of all, successfully countering any tactic requires you to recognize it. In fact, that in itself, may be enough to destroy the tactic's effectiveness. Details on countering various tactics and ploys—as well as how to use them yourself—are contained in various sections of this book. Nevertheless, it's worthwhile to summarize some of the tactics that are so common as to be almost generic to the negotiation process. These are:

- intimidation   As a general rule ignore it.
- lying   Ask for supporting evidence.
- bluffs   Call them to avoid being victimized.
- delay   Force the issue if the other side is stalling.
- deadlines   Ignore them. They're only issued to force you to react.
- ultimatums   Toss them back with a, "That's your decision," retort.
- threats   Challenge them.

These general approaches for dealing with various tactics aren't, of course, an automatic response to be used in every situation. You have to evaluate the overall impact of the tactic, as well as the best way to deal with it under the circumstances of any particular negotiation.

Incidentally, an often overlooked consideration is the need to distinguish between tactics that warrant a response, and those that are better off being ignored. During the course of a bargaining session, you may be subjected to a varying assortment of puffery, bluffs, threats, and so forth. The bulk of this negotiation game playing will have little or no impact on reaching your goals, once you recognize the ploys for what they are. For this reason, in most cases, it's best just to ignore any inconsequential gimmicks used by your opponent. That, in itself, sends a message that you won't be rattled and/or conned.

9.6 SEARCHING FOR THE LINK THAT LEADS TO AGREEMENT

More often than not during negotiations, one or two key issues become roadblocks to reaching agreement. The bargaining then evolves into extended discussions on these hang-ups, with both parties sticking steadfastly to their position. The end result is generally either some form of last minute compromise, or failed negotiations with no deal being struck.

When a deadlock looms over a particular issue, there are several useful approaches to overcoming this hurdle. First and foremost, try to look at the deadlock from the point of view of the other party. Ask yourself why the particular issue is so important to that person. This helps to overcome a tendency to view things from one's own perspective. This can lead to the sort of tunnel vision which has both parties refusing to budge from their position.

In point of fact, there are very few differences that can't be resolved if both parties view the difficulty as a hurdle to be overcome, rather than adopting a stonewalling attitude and refusing to compromise. It helps in resolving differences if you carefully listen to the other party's objections. Sometimes when this is done, the basis for objection may not appear to be particularly sound. This leads to the conclusion that the other negotiator is just being stubborn about the matter.

What is often overlooked when this happens, is that the reasons given for objecting to something, may be merely masking the actual reason for disagreement. This frequently happens when a negotiator has had certain constraints placed upon him before the negotiations began. For example, limitations in terms of the maximum price the negotiator can accept may have been imposed by a boss.

Sometimes, a negotiator will readily admit that restrictions on his authority are causing the difficulty. Once this is known, then, of course, it can be dealt with. However, a negotiator may not be willing to point this out. This reluctance may be based on the negotiator's opinion that to do so would destroy his effectiveness. Alternatively, the restriction may be such that revealing it might cause the other side to refuse to negotiate any further.

Whatever the reason, once it becomes obvious that there is likely to be little movement by your opponent on a particular issue, it is useful to look for other ways of attacking the problem. For instance, are there changes you can propose that would compensate you for accepting the other side's position on the deadlocked issue? A little bit of thought might turn up a satisfactory trade-off that can resolve the deadlock. Such overtures often bear fruit, since they allow the other side to reach agreement without surrendering on the sticking point. Consequently, it's generally a good idea when deadlocks occur to search for alternatives that circumvent having to bargain a deadlocked issue until someone concedes, or negotiations break-off.

9.7 TACTICS FOR KEEPING CONTROL OF THE NEGOTIATIONS

"I'll talk about anything as long as it's from my point of view," is a bit of an exaggeration as to the degree of control you want to exercise over the bargaining you do. Naturally, it's important, as well as polite, to listen to what the other party to the negotiation has to say.

Nonetheless, the greater the influence you have over the course of the negotiation, the better the chances of achieving your objective. Therefore, it's helpful to keep the discussion focused on the issues you want to discuss. Generally, this means emphasizing the strong points of your position, be it price, quality, customer service, or whatever else that happens to be.

The reasons for this are simple enough. First of all, the strengths of your negotiation position are the easiest to defend when your adversary attempts to poke holes in your arguments. Second, the strong points of your position are what will sell the other side on the wisdom of accepting your offer.

To keep the negotiation focused on what you want to emphasize, continually steer the discussion toward those issues. You will have to make an effort to do this, since your adversary will likely be (1) advocating the strengths of his own position, and/or (2) attacking what he perceives to be the weak points in your offer. There are all sorts of methods you can use to strengthen your arguments. These include:

- Comparisons   "Our price is lower than any competitor."
- Documentation   "We've got extensive back-up you can look at, which justifies our labor costs."
- Testimonials   "Here's a letter from Stickler Corporation attesting to the work we did for them."

- Experts   "Professor Neverwrong is willing to vouch for the reliability of our technical approach."

- Experience   "We've been in this business longer than anybody else."

- Uniqueness   "Forget I'm his agent. Where else will you find a ballplayer like this?"

- Special factors   "You want accelerated deliveries, and that means higher overtime costs."

- Demonstrations   "We'll have our engineering people do a demonstration test for you this afternoon."

The number of factors you can use to strengthen your arguments and control the course of the bargaining are limited only by your ingenuity. Of course, as you pound away at praising the virtues of your offer, your adversary will attempt to counter what you're saying by putting you on the defensive. This will often take the form of asking you all sorts of questions. Of course, the factual ones you should be able to field quite nicely. However, in an attempt to shake your confidence in your position, you may be asked tricky questions designed to destroy the validity of what you are touting.

The simplest way to counter loaded questions is to not answer them—at least not directly. "Are you still having quality problems?," is the sort of question that shouldn't be answered with a "Yes" or "No." And all sorts of "what if" questions are best countered by avoiding speculation, and insisting that the speculative disaster will never occur. For example, "What happens if your material costs are higher than expected?," can be responded to by emphasizing a history of projects completed within cost.

Another pitfall to avoid is answering questions that weren't asked in the first place. Being helpful and informative is one thing, but setting yourself up for trouble by volunteering information that wasn't requested isn't a very smart move. It's tough enough to handle the questions that will be thrown your way without giving responses to those that weren't even asked.

9.8 MAKING SURE YOUR NEGOTIATION POSITIONS ARE UNDERSTOOD

You will encounter enough difficulties at the negotiation table, without adding to the burden by having avoidable misunderstandings. This frequently occurs because one side or the other, doesn't make their position clear which leads to it being misinterpreted. On occasion, this erupts in charges and counter charges as to who said what.

Not only does this slow down progress toward agreement, but it can lead to mistrust and suspicion, which certainly aren't conducive to a settlement of the differences in the respective negotiation positions. In fact, on occasion, misunderstandings aren't discovered until an agreement is about to be signed. Then, upon reading the provisions, one of the parties is apt to explode and say, "We didn't agree on that. What's it doing in the agreement?"

Consequently, you should take care to spell out carefully anything you propose, and likewise be certain that you understand precisely what the other side is offering. This is especially important with complex negotiations involving a large number of issues.

One fertile area for disagreement is when something is accepted by one party with certain qualifications attached. Discussions then proceed on to other issues until agreement is in hand. Then, and only then, does the other party recognize that there was an initial qualification attached to the acceptance of a particular provision. This type of misunderstanding usually results from statements such as, "I'll accept your material costs assuming we can agree on a 7% profit." The negotiations continue and ultimately the parties begin to talk profit. The party who qualified their acceptance of the material costs then raises that issue in arguing for a 7% profit. The other side—having forgotten about the qualification—gets irate over the fact that the agreement on material costs will be reopened unless the profit is 7%.

Avoiding these dilemmas is simple enough. First of all, always have a note taker present to record everything agreed to as the discussions wend their way toward agreement. Then, if questions subsequently arise, the notes can be referred to. In addition, whenever there is agreement on a point, it pays to repeat what has been agreed upon—including any reservations or qualifications—to be certain that both sides are clear on the matter. Furthermore, if a particular provision is particularly complex, you may want to take the time to put it in writing and have you and your counterpart initial it. This can avoid confusion at the end of a difficult negotiation when it's time to put together a final document.

CAUTION: Taking the time to insure that agreed upon items are understood is a good preventive device against backtracking by the other side. As a ploy to extract further concessions, an opponent might allege near the end of the negotiations that he had never agreed to the resolution of a particular issue. This sort of tactic isn't so likely to be tried if pains are taken to document agreements as negotiations move along.

9.9 HOW TO KEEP THE NEGOTIATION IN FOCUS

The very complexity of a negotiation can make it a time-consuming endeavor. Therefore, on this basis alone, it's necessary to keep the discussions chugging along toward eventual agreement. However, for reasons both trivial and purposeful, the bargaining can get bogged down with little headway being made. Consequently, it's to your advantage to avoid getting caught in this trap.

From an unintentional standpoint, you can find yourself dealing with a negotiator who tends to wander off on tangents. This may be a result of the person's personality, or the fact that the other negotiator doesn't have his negotiation objective very clearly defined.

On the other hand, negotiators may stall deliberately. For instance, unknown to you, they may be simultaneously trying to negotiate a better deal with someone else. As a consequence, there is little interest in seeing your negotiations move forward while they have other options available.

Another likely reason for people to stall is when they assume that time is in their favor. Perhaps the other negotiator is aware—or assumes—that you have some degree of urgency in reaching agreement by a certain date. As a result, the strategy employed against you is to drag the negotiations to the deadline in the hope that this will yield a better deal.

Whatever the reason, once you sense the other side is stalling, apply pressure to keep the talks moving along toward resolution of the differences separating the two sides from agreement. A good way to do this is to set aside any peripheral issues, and concentrate on the main areas of disagreement.

Of course, if no matter how hard you try, the other side persists in dilly-dallying along, you may have to issue an ultimatum. If so, do it without any show of anger. Say something such as, "Tom, we don't appear to be making any headway. If we can't wrap this deal up today, then perhaps we should forget about it." This may succeed in prodding the other side into action. But ultimately, if nothing else has worked—and there is no great advantage in your continuing the discussions—it may be time to simply say, "See you later, alligator."

NOTE: Whenever you're negotiating against a crucial deadline that's known to your opponent, you are bargaining with a distinct handicap. Therefore, whenever possible, don't reveal deadlines. However, if it is general knowledge, or can be reasonably assumed, you can turn your drawback into an advantage as discussed in section 14.9.

9.10 USING INTERRUPTIONS TO YOUR ADVANTAGE

As a general rule, unnecessary interruptions only serve to distract the attention of negotiators from the task at hand. At the same time, planned interruptions can be of great value. For this reason, they are a tactic to be reckoned with when used by the opposition. (Section 12.3 covers how to counter inter-ruptions initiated by your adversary.)

On the other hand, you can use interruptions for the following purposes in furtherance of your cause:

- To bolster your arguments.
- To give you a chance to regroup.
- To change the focal point of the discussion.
- As a power play.

Let's look at each of these possible uses.

1. One of the most effective uses of interruptions is to support your position with the unexpected appearance of experts. This is true either when the opposition is waging an attack on a particular seg-ment of your proposal, or when you desire to strengthen what you're advocating by having an expert waltz in to corroborate your position.

   Of course, the key here is the element of surprise. What you are attempting to do is establish dominance over the particular issue being discussed. If your planning permits it, an outside expert has the maximum impact in terms of credibility. In fact, if you have really done your homework, there's nothing quite as effective as the use of an expert who has also consulted for your adversary in the past. That is, of course, assuming the consultant's work performance was satis-factory. Naturally, this isn't usually possible, but it pays to keep this application in mind for circumstances where it might be effective.

   Incidentally, to use experts properly, it's necessary to identify crit-ical areas where support may be needed during the planning stages of negotiations. This allows you to make the necessary arrangements, since you can't pull the proper expert out of thin air by snapping your fingers.

   Generally, the experts you use to support your negotiation posi-tion will be your own employees. And, for the most part, they will be either in attendance at negotiation meetings, or on the premises waiting to be summoned. The essential point to be emphasized is that expert testimony is most effective when properly timed. In the first place, if the other side is aware that you will be using a subject matter expert, they quite likely will be sure to have their own in attendance to counter-balance your expert's arguments.

   In addition, expert opinions carry maximum weight when they are timed to coincide with (1) immediately rebutting what the other side just said, or (2) offering expert support to what you're advocating at the moment. This tends to create a dominant stand for your side of the issue, which can lead to immediate resolution of the dispute in your favor.

Furthermore, if the other side doesn't anticipate such a move, they won't be in a position to effectively rebut what is asserted. Therefore, whenever possible, don't telegraph your intentions to use experts to support your negotiation position. Incidentally, the procedures for protecting yourself when you're the victim of the other side's experts are covered in section 14.7.

2.   Interruptions give you a valid opportunity to regroup and organize your thoughts during the course of negotiations. There's nothing to prevent you from asking for a brief recess at any time during bargaining sessions, but sometimes it's advantageous to make it look inadvertent. For example, you can prearrange to be interrupted if you have someone dredging-up information which you want to receive in privacy when it becomes available.

A planned interruption is also useful for briefing your boss and others on the progress of the negotiations, or for soliciting advice. Having someone come in and say you have an important phone call, avoids implying that you don't have ultimate control over the negotiations, and therefore have to consult with others.

3.   There are times when you can use an interruption to change the focal point of the discussion. For example, if you have spent the morning in an unpleasant defense of some weak point in your negotiation position, a change of direction would be welcome from both a personal and practical standpoint. However, you can't just bluntly try to change the focus, since that only adds credence to the notion that this is a weak spot that's vulnerable to attack. But if you can arrange to be interrupted on some pretext that is a valid basis for changing the subject, suspicions aren't likely to be aroused. One possibility is the arrival of someone with information of interest to the other side. This gives you the opportunity to assume control of the discussions and move away from the trouble spot.

4.   Interruptions can also be used to pull a power play on the other negotiator. This is done by the sudden arrival of a high level official at the negotiation. Who it is isn't important, other than that it be someone with stature in the eyes of the other negotiator. A boss inquiring as to how things are going, and suggesting the importance of getting the negotiation concluded quickly, will do nicely. What you want to do is convey the impression that people in positions of power within your

organization are concerned that things aren't moving along. This technique works well to prod the other negotiator into working harder toward reaching agreement—especially if the implication is cast that if negotiations aren't concluded quickly, they may be abandoned.

9.11 SURE-FIRE WAYS TO SAVE FACE WHEN YOU GOOF

The complexities and stress of negotiations can often lead to mistakes being made. Assuming the errors are caught and corrected before a final agreement is signed, major damage can be avoided. Yet, as a minimum, mistakes discovered during negotiations can cause significant embarrassment, and perhaps undermine your credibility in the eyes of the opposing negotiation team.

The major headache with errors during the negotiation process is when mistakes are discovered in provisions that have already been agreed upon. This happens most frequently in the financial area. For example, if agreement has been reached on a cost element, (such as material or labor) correction of the error may result in higher costs than otherwise anticipated. To say the least, it's a little discomforting having to tell the other negotiator that you have discovered an error that will increase agreed upon costs.

Unfortunately, you have little choice but to recognize such errors openly by saying something such as, "I goofed because . . .", taking pains to carefully detail how the error happened. After the dust settles, and the other negotiator has finished expressing his displeasure, provide enough evidence to prove that an error was indeed made. Otherwise, the other negotiator may well think you're trying to put something over on him.

To further quell the anger of your adversary, be sure to apologize for the mistake. You may also want to practice a little bit of self-deprecating humor to help humanize the predicament. Of course, if the error requires renegotiation of items already agreed to, it helps if you can offer some sort of compromise that will minimize the effort involved. For instance, agreeing on a total cost figure without renegotiating individual cost elements. Whatever the case, the easier you can make it to correct an error, the less resistance you are likely to encounter from the other side.

Incidentally, many errors during negotiations result from hasty calculations as both sides bounce figures back and forth. Needless to say, don't rush calculations so that foolish errors will result. Another preventive tactic to avoid the embarrassment of correcting math mistakes is to negotiate individual cost elements on a qualified basis, subject to final agreement at the conclusion of negotiations. This keeps the other negotiator from saying, "We've already agreed to that," whenever a mistake is discovered.

NOTE: Due to the potential for conflict, which in extreme cases could scuttle a deal, insignificant errors in calculations may be best left as is. If an error in a previously agreed upon item isn't going to cost you much, or if you can compensate for it elsewhere in the agreement, it isn't worth the hassle to try and correct it. As an alternative, you may tell the other negotiator that you have discovered a minor error, but are absorbing the loss. This sort of gesture can help create good will, which in the long run may be worth more than the hassle of recalculating and renegotiating to adjust for the error.

TIP: If during the course of negotiations, you discover an error made by the other negotiator, don't make a big issue out of it. Call it to the other side's attention, and amicably work together to resolve any problems it has created. Your good natured acceptance of any inconvenience resulting from the error will serve to strengthen the negotiating relationship between you and your counterpart.

Of course, there are errors, and then there are errors. On occasion, an unscrupulous negotiator may make deliberate mistakes in the hope that they will go undetected. However, even in these situations, it's unlikely you can prove whether it was an inadvertent mistake, or a deliberate attempt to deceive. So, all in all, it's best to avoid making any accusations. If you do have suspicions that an error in your opponent's favor may have been deliberate, simply take extra care in analyzing everything before you reach a final agreement.

9.12 STRATEGIES FOR REGROUPING WHEN IT ISN'T GOING YOUR WAY

As a negotiation moves along, you may find that things aren't going well for your side. Often, to get the process back on a more satisfactory track, it's necessary to take some action to regain the initiative. What precisely you do will depend upon the circumstances. Some tried and true techniques are as follows:

1. Take a break. Try to do it unobtrusively such as suggesting a coffee break or lunch, or using planned interruptions as discussed in section 9.10. However, if this isn't possible, take a recess anyway. There are likely to be occasions during negotiations when you want to discuss certain points with team members in private. Don't be hesitant about recessing to do this.

2. If you're really on the ropes, you may want to break-off negotiations to completely reassess your position. Sometimes, as negotiations proceed, you may discover facts from the other side that will warrant an adjustment in your negotiation objective. Rather than trying to do

this in helter-skelter fashion, it's prudent to take a break and go over your position in detail. This will avoid the possibility of a substantial error being made by trying to make hasty adjustments at the negotiation table.

3. Shift the focus of the discussion away from the sticking point. Negotiations frequently get bogged down over one or two issues. Often, by going on to something else, the troublesome point will work itself out, be forgotten, or better able to be resolved at a later point in time.

4. Sometimes when you're losing the upper hand, you can regain it by offering a concession in return for your opponent's concession on the stumbling point.

5. If you feel your position is weak in a particular area you may be able to strengthen it by bringing in an expert. This is a particularly useful strategy when you're dealing with technical matters. An outside expert, rather than an employee, will have a greater degree of credibility.

6. If a particular segment of your proposal is being attacked, use documentation to support it. When at all possible, third party evidence carries greater weight than internally generated facts and figures.

Part III

CONDUCTING NEGOTIATIONS

Chapter 10

THE NEGOTIATING PROCESS FROM OFFER TO ACCEPTANCE

Other than relatively simple negotiations, a succession of offers and counteroffers will usually take place before a final agreement is reached. Your skill in both making and rejecting these offers will have a significant bearing on the end result, since both content and timing of offers is important. In addition, reaching a satisfactory conclusion will require you to support your negotiation position against all sorts of challenges, and make necessary adjustments in your position when circumstances require it. This chapter addresses these concerns.

10.1 THE "HARD-NOSED NEGOTIATOR" MYTH

Contrary to popular opinion, the successful negotiator isn't one who is skilled at browbeating the opposition into submission. In fact, if you think about it, most of the traits necessary for success in deal-making carry the opposite connotation. The ability to practice compromise, exercise patience, and cooperate in problem solving, are indicative of someone able to reason—rather than the tools of a bully. The truth is that negotiations require the ability to sell—not to assail.

There's little question that your patience may well be tested, especially if the other negotiator is intent on intimidating you. However, the better you're able to ignore this tactic, the less likely that it will continue—unless that's the only way the other party knows how to negotiate. If you do run into an adversary who emphasizes hard-nosed methods, it probably results from one of the following causes:

1. The other negotiator has an aggressive personality, which carries over to the negotiation table. Anyone with a short fuse, is likely to lose control of their temper at the first sign of disagreement at the bargaining table. Although it isn't pleasant to deal with such people, unless they are intolerable, it's generally to your advantage to ignore their behavior. That's because negotiator's with short fuses, not only lose control of their emotions, but they also frequently lose sight of the negotiation position they are stridently trying to uphold. This results in mistakes which can well work in your favor.

2. Some relatively inexperienced negotiators wrongly assume that a hard-nosed approach is the key to achieving success when negotiating. However, folks who adopt this sort of posture will often cool-off once they realize that you won't be bullied into giving them a bargain.

3. On occasion, negotiators may adopt a hard-nosed approach, when they are led to believe that you can be intimidated. This is most prevalent when they enter negotiations with the belief—real or imagined—that they are dealing from a position of strength which will allow them to dictate terms. Standing your ground from the start will quickly disillusion anyone operating on this assumption.

4. Intimidation may also be used by an opponent in an attempt to cover weaknesses in a negotiating position. The hope is that being belligerent will deter you from asking questions, and otherwise probing their proposal in depth. If you set your own course, and refuse to be deterred by this maneuver, the defensive wall can be broken down which will leave you holding the upper hand.

Of course, whatever the reason, if the anger and hostility of other negotiators becomes intolerable, say so, and if necessary call a brief halt to the negotiations. A cooling-off period will let them know that you are there to reach agreement—not to engage in a jousting contest.

10.2 WEAVING YOUR WAY TO GETTING—NOT GIVING—THE FIRST OFFER

There are advantages in having the other negotiating party make the initial offer. First of all, it gives you an immediate idea of how far apart the respective positions are. For example, if your opponent's initial offer differs substantially from what you consider to be reasonable, you have several options.

On the one hand, you can state that the offer isn't even in the ball park, and then proceed to a factual discussion aimed at undermining the offer. Your objective here is to get the other party to make another offer, without you having even given an inkling of what your position is. This isn't likely to be successful unless you're dealing with a novice negotiator, but it's certainly worth a try. The worst that can happen is that the other negotiator will avoid being lured into a detailed discussion of his offer until you, in turn, lay your cards on the table in the form of a counter-offer.

As an alternative, you can simply give the offer a broad brush rejection, and come back with a counter-offer which is equally farfetched. The purpose of this isn't to be spiteful, but rather to hedge your bets until the negotiations proceed far enough to establish the opposition's intentions. Obviously, if their initial offer is way out of line, they either haven't done their homework, or even more likely, are using an unreasonable offer as a negotiating ploy.

Consequently, if you respond with a reasonable offer that is very close to your negotiating limit, you are putting yourself in an unnecessary bind. That's because after a little back and forth discussion, the other side may suggest splitting the difference. Naturally, you have to refuse, since you will be splitting the difference between your reasonable offer and the excessive proposal made by the other side. This would place you in a difficult position to get the negotiation gap closed because you have little left to concede in exchange for the other side making movement from their initial offer.

Actually, whether or not you are successful in getting the other side to make the initial offer, or do so yourself, always make sure that your first offer gives you leeway to make concessions as negotiations proceed. Otherwise, you will be making it much harder to reach agreement. Most people aren't happy unless they can get some concessions from the other side. They assume that a first offer isn't going to be a favorable one, and therefore aren't satisfied unless they can negotiate more favorable terms than the opening offer.

Another advantage of having the other party make the first offer, is the chance—however slight—that you may receive a better offer than what you would be willing to settle for. If so, your negotiations may well turn out to be short and sweet. Surprisingly enough, considering the advantages, who makes the first move is often based on nothing more complicated than being the one to ask the other party for their offer.

A good way to do this is to pop the question as soon as the opening pleasantries of a negotiation session are concluded. As part and parcel of your request, it's also beneficial to set the stage for how you expect the negotiations to proceed. What you want to do is state that you intend to be reasonable in an attempt to reach a speedy agreement, and assume the other side is similarly disposed. A typical request for an offer could go like this:

"John, I want you to know that we intend to be reasonable in trying to reach an agreement, so why don't you give me an offer we can accept without a lot of back and forth nonsense."

If John makes an offer close to what is acceptable, a counter-offer that leaves a narrow gap could be made by saying something such as, "That's just a little more than I can buy John, but if you can raise your figure $20,000, we've got a deal." On the other hand, if John's offer is way out of line, indignation can be expressed in the form of, "I told you we would be reasonable, and you throw that kind of figure on the table. Let's go over the details of how you arrive at that." This approach immediately focuses the discussion on the opposition's offer, without you having made a counter-offer.

Of course, the details of how an offer is solicited will vary with the circumstances. What's of concern is to maneuver yourself into position to ask the other side for their offer at the start of negotiations.

NOTE: In many situations, an initial offer may have been requested and received before negotiations begin. This is standard practice in many business transactions where price is the predominant element. If you have received an offer prior to negotiations, attempt to start-off the session with facts showing the unreasonableness of the offer. This will force the other side into a defense of their offer, rather than allowing them to attack the soft spots in the facts and figures supporting your position.

10.3 MAKING OFFERS AND HAVING THEM STICK

In limited situations, it may be appropriate to make an initial offer that is far in excess of your negotiation objective. One such circumstance being to counter an equally unreasonable offer, as mentioned in the previous section. However, for the most part your offer should be within the range of credibility, while making allowances for any concessions that are needed to reach agreement. In the first place, an initial offer that is credible, may be accepted outright by your opponent, or with just minor adjustments having to be made.

Even more important, the credibility of your initial offer sets the tone for the negotiations. For instance, if you make an offer that's so out-of-line it's not believable, your opponent will pay it little heed. Furthermore, it might encourage the other negotiator to be just as unreasonable. This will only serve to widen the gap in the respective positions, which is a forerunner of a long and difficult negotiating session.

Another pitfall of an unreasonable initial offer is that it will require a great deal of movement in the form of concessions to ultimately reach agreement. This, of course, means you have to raise your offer in relatively large chunks if you're the buyer, or conversely, lower it substantially if you're on the selling side of the table. As a result, when the other negotiator sees substantial movements in your position, it arouses suspicion as to just how much fat is built-in to your position. This can lead to an attitude of, "Hey, if this guy can change his position like that, let's see how far I can get him to go." Consequently, even when your opening offer has been whittled down to a reasonable figure, your opponent may still negotiate in the belief that you will go even further.

Along with establishing credibility by making an offer that's reasonable, you also have to be able to defend your offer if you want to make it stick. If you have done your pre-negotiation preparation, it shouldn't be hard to do this. Documentation supporting your offer, expert opinion, and comparisons with similar deals, are all part and parcel of proving the validity of your offer. In other words, if you make a reasonable offer, and are able to defend it against attack, then you should be able to reach agreement somewhere within your range of acceptable terms.

10.4 SEVERAL WAYS TO ENCOURAGE QUICK ACCEPTANCE OF YOUR OFFER

The longer negotiations drag on, the greater the odds that agreement may never be reached. So for this reason, as well as the time, money, and uncertainty involved with conducting extended negotiations, it's advantageous to encourage a quick acceptance of your offer. There are a number of techniques you can use to do this. They include:

1. Make your offer conditional in terms of time. For instance, "Mr. Adams, I'll make you a one-time offer good until 5:00 P.M. tomorrow." Putting a time limit on an offer puts pressure on the other side to give it prompt consideration. However, they may assume you're just bluffing, and wait it out to see what happens. This is especially true if you don't offer a valid reason why a time deadline must be imposed. Therefore, make this technique more effective by establishing some necessity that justifies your deadline. It's particularly helpful if this reason is something that appears to be beyond your control. For example, "Jim, I'll make you one last offer of $5,000,000, but it must be accepted by Friday, since that's when my loan agreement expires."

2. Offer incentives for prompt acceptance. Adding value to an offer in exchange for early acceptance can be used to encourage a quick

response. For instance, "If we can close this deal today, we'll absorb the shipping charges over the course of the contract." Here again, this approach is made more convincing by using a sound basis to justify your offer. Otherwise, if agreement isn't reached within the deadline, and negotiations continue, the other side will have an expectation that your incentive will be included in the agreement when it's reached. NOTE: Anytime you offer something of value, it's extremely difficult to backtrack and take it off the table—no matter what conditions you attach. Therefore, don't casually make conditional promises, since with or without the condition, you have signaled a willingness to make what you promise a part of any resultant agreement.

3. Establish an imperative deadline. This can take many variations. It can be based on third party commitments, ("My subcontractor can't meet deliveries, unless we have an agreement this week."), higher authority, ("The President has given us until Wednesday to finalize this, or the money is going for another research project."), or performance factors, ("The manufacturing capacity we need won't be available unless we can start within two weeks."). In essence, the basis for a deadline may be real, or only the result of your creativity. Whichever it is, the essential point is that it be believable.

10.5 THE PLUSES AND MINUSES OF A TOTAL PACKAGE OFFER

When the subject matter of a negotiation involves only one or two elements that merit discussion, usually the offers and counter-offers are structured as a total package. In other words, rather than negotiate the parts to arrive at a final agreement, in these cases there's little to be gained by negotiating individual elements. However, even when a negotiation consists of many factors that could conceivably be taken up one-by-one at the negotiation table, it may be advantageous to negotiate on a total package basis rather than struggling to reach agreement on each of the many individual parts.

The most common reason for negotiating on a total package basis is its practicality. The fewer elements that require a meeting of the minds, the less likely the opportunity for time-consuming disagreements. Therefore, this approach is an excellent tactic for avoiding the hassles that often occur when discussing price. Frequently, when two parties attempt to reach a price agreement by negotiating each individual cost element, hang-ups arise because of a failure to agree on the reasonableness of the parts comprising the whole. For example, consider the following cost breakdown:

a. Direct Labor	$ 50,000
b. Labor Overhead (150% of a.)	75,000
c. Direct Material	150,000
d. Material Overhead (20% of c.)	30,000
e. Total Direct Costs (a. through d.)	$305,000
f. General & Administrative Overhead (30% of e.)	91,500
g. Total Cost	$396,500
h. Profit (15% of g.)	59,475
i. Price	$455,975

Let's assume that a fair price is somewhere between $425,000 and $450,000. It's highly likely that the buyer could make an offer somewhere within that range, and without a great deal of discussion an agreement could be reached. On the other hand, suppose the parties decide to arrive at a price by negotiating each cost factor individually. The buyer upon review of the supporting data for the material costs is of the opinion that only $140,000 is justifiable. The seller argues that the other $10,000 is a contingency to cover defects. The seller further argues that if the material costs are reduced by $10,000, then direct labor costs will increase 10% ($5,000) to cover rework of defective parts. The two parties bargain back and forth with neither side willing to concede the point on principle. Let's look at the impact of reducing the material costs by $10,000, (from $150,000 to $140,000) and increasing the direct labor costs by $5,000 (from $50,000 to $55,000).

	Original	Revised
a. Direct Labor	$ 50,000	$ 55,000
b. Labor Overhead (150%)	75,000	82,500
c. Direct Material	150,000	140,000
d. Material Overhead (20%)	30,000	28,000
e. Total Cost	$305,000	$305,500
f. General & Administrative Expense (30%)	91,500	91,650
g. Total Costs	$396,500	$397,150
h. Profit (15%)	59,475	59,572.50
i. Price	$455,975	$456,722.50

As a result of reducing material costs by $10,000, and increasing direct labor by $5,000, the price has actually increased by $747.50 due to the application of overhead and profit percentages to the $5,000 increase in direct labor. Although the actual dollar figures in the example are relatively unimportant, they do serve to illustrate several important points.

1. Whenever individual cost elements are questioned, a considerable amount of disagreement can arise, which makes it more difficult to reach agreement. In fact, in extreme cases, negotiations can fall apart because of bickering over details which have only a minor impact on the overall price.

2. Unless a proposed price is unreasonable, it's generally preferable to negotiate on a total price basis. There are exceptions, with the most notable being when contracts are on a cost plus fee basis. In these cases, since the final profit to be earned is based on costs, it's important to carefully negotiate the costs involved. Of course, costs also have to be analyzed when there is no other basis for establishing a reasonable price. This happens whenever historical cost data, and/or comparative prices don't exist. However, whenever a total price can be reasonably established without delving into analyzing individual cost categories, a lot of headaches can be avoided.

3. Individual elements of cost are often interrelated, as in the example where reducing material costs meant the seller would incur additional labor costs to rework defective items, since he would no longer be buying $10,000 worth of material to allow for defects. Therefore, changing one element of cost can impact other areas. Incidentally, this is a common negotiation argument even when it's not true.

4. There is sometimes a tendency to overlook the fact that it's the final price that matters, not whether any one element is higher than the buyer deems to be reasonable. This sort of hang-up frequently occurs in any discussion of profit. More than one negotiation has disintegrated because a buyer took exception to the profit being made by the seller, even though comparable prices offered by competitor's were higher. The proper focus should be on price, not whether a low cost producer is making a higher profit than a less cost-efficient competitor.

10.6 COPING WITH A "BEST AND FINAL" OFFER YOU DON'T WANT

Often, with much fanfare, a negotiating adversary will announce that the offer he has just made, or is about to make, is his last offer. Naturally, the intent of doing this is to convince you that you are now in a "take it or leave it" position. Of course, if the offer happens to be acceptable to you, then by all means accept it. However, more often than not, the offer isn't palatable. This supposedly leaves you in the position of accepting an unsatisfactory offer, or ending up with no deal at all.

The truth is that more often than not a "best and final" offer is neither the best that can be made, nor the last offer that will be forthcoming. What it really constitutes is an implied ultimatum that if you don't accept the offer, negotiations have ended. Consequently, when you face this sort of bluff, the proper move is to call it. This can be done by rejecting it outright and saying something such as, "That's not acceptable because . . . ," meanwhile giving a recap of the reasons why you won't accept it. This method of refusing an alleged final offer bounces the ball right back into the other negotiator's court. He essentially then has to either break off negotiations, or continue the discussions. If it's the latter, then there is tacit acknowledgment that there is still room for an improved offer.

An alternative tactic is to just keep on talking as if the ultimatum hadn't been issued. If the other side continues to negotiate, then here again their threat to walk has been exposed as a bluff. What most folks worry about when they are presented with a "best and final" offer is that the other side will break off negotiations if it's not accepted.

However, on closer examination, the threat isn't as serious as it seems to be. So what if they do take a walk? There's nothing to prevent you from calling them in a day or two and either resuming negotiations, or accepting their last offer if you feel it meets your objectives. If they are getting a reasonable deal, they're not about to hang up the phone on you.

The bottom line is that this sort of a threat isn't as serious as it seems. The greatest hazard it creates is that someone will bite the bait and accept less than satisfactory terms solely because of a fear that otherwise there won't be any deal at all. And anytime the choice is between a bad deal, or no deal at all, the savvy negotiator will gladly let the other party take a hike.

CAUTION: If you are the one in a position to make a final offer, make certain that it is exactly that—at least as far as things stand at the present moment. In other words, if it isn't accepted, be prepared to get up and leave. Otherwise, if you continue to negotiate, your credibility is gone. As a result, when you get to where your last offer is in reality the best you can do, it isn't likely to be believed.

Of course, if you do bluff and it's called, that doesn't prevent you from changing your position if and when negotiations do resume. You can waltz around the fact you backed-off your position by citing some new information that came to your attention.

The general rule for "best and final" offers is to refuse them if you're on the receiving end, and walk away from the table if you make one that's not accepted. Of course, make sure that you don't arbitrarily reject a fair offer, just to see if you can squeeze a few more dollars out of the deal. In the long run, such tactics only serve to alienate people whom you may have to work with in the future.

10.7 OVERCOMING "EVEN DOLLAR" NEGOTIATION HANG-UPS

You may recall that in the discussion on splitting dollar differences in section 6.6, it was mentioned that negotiators generally use round numbers. It was pointed out that in splitting the difference, you could benefit by using odd figures. However, using uneven numbers have an even greater significance involving credibility.

An amount such as $124,542.76 appears more credible than $125,000. There's an aura of computational accuracy that implies it isn't just a random number thrown out for feelers. This is especially true in negotiations where offers and counter-offers are bandied back and forth. Negotiators naturally suspect that the figures tossed out aren't computed with any degree of precision. Therefore, if you deviate from this expectation by using odd dollars and cents, you can add an extra measure of believability to your numbers.

Using uneven numbers have other advantages, such as making it easier to move more slowly when dollar concessions are made. Because your figures appear to be computed down to the last cent, it's easier to argue that you've moved as far as you can. Let's look at a capsulized version of how this works.

Background

Albert and Benjamin are in the final stages of negotiations, with only the final price still being discussed. Albert's last offer was $450,000, while Benjamin was at $521,376.54.

Discussion

Albert: "Ben, I can go to $480,000, which is half of the difference. Let's close on that." (Of course, he didn't quite split the difference in half, but negotiators love to pick-up the extra buck.)

Benjamin: "Let me look at the figures, and see what I can do." Ben returns after a brief recess and says, "I went over everything in detail with my number-crunchers. Frankly, my first offer of $521,376.54 was rock bottom. However, in the interests of settling this thing, I'll go to $509,898.34. Let's wrap it up there."

Albert: Looking and sounding peeved says, "Now wait a minute. I raised my offer $30,000, and all you gave up was $11,000. We won't get anywhere at this rate."

Benjamin: "In the first place, Al, it's more than $11,000. (only $478.20 more) But that's not the point. I made an initial offer based on the minimum I could accept. To chop that $11,000, I had to go back and cut the labor I need to do the job. I've got the figures right here to support that. You agreed that the amount of labor I was using was reasonable, and now you come along and want me to cut it further. We're not playing a numbers game. I proposed what we need to do the job. I can't cut that just because you're looking for a bargain."

Albert: "You can't tell me Ben that you don't have at least a 10% contingency factor built-in to your proposal. Taking 10% off of your $521,000 would put you around $470,000. I'm offering $480,000."

Benjamin: "My $521,376.54 was my best estimate to do the job assuming everything went according to plan. If something goes wrong, I'll be eating the costs. It's as simple as that."

Albert: Appearing disgusted says, "I'll go to $500,000 even, but not one penny more."

Benjamin: After another twenty minutes of back and forth discussion says, "Let me take a final look." He returns a half hour later, slumps down in his chair and says, "I went over everything again, and frankly there's nowhere else I can cut. All I can do is take something off our hoped for profit and make a final offer of $506,375.20. That's it period. All you need to do to settle at that figure is move about one percent from your $500,000."

Albert: After a bit of a protest agrees with Ben's final figure of $506,375.20.

The important point here is to convey credibility when you present your numbers. This gives you a framework to sustain your arguments which doesn't exist when round numbers are tossed back and forth.

NOTE: Along with a failure to use precision in numbers, your choice of words can also have a bearing on the reception an offer receives. Never make the careless mistake of couching your offer in language that doesn't denote finality. Qualifiers such as "about $255,000," "approximately $2,000,000," or "roughly $10,000,000" are to be avoided. They send a signal that your offer isn't final, whereas every offer you make—even if it's the tenth offer—should be presented as if it were your last.

10.8 USING THE SHOCK VALUE OF A "QUICK HIT" OFFER

Negotiations often get bogged down in hassling over minor details, which have little impact in terms of a final agreement. One way to move things off of dead center is to make a sudden offer at a totally unexpected moment. There are a couple of benefits to doing this.

In the first place, it immediately moves the course of the discussion away from the subject at hand. This is particularly useful if the other negotiator happens to be targeting one or more particularly weak points in your negotiation position. If nothing else, your sudden offer forces the other side to pause and consider it. Of even greater consequence, if the bargaining has been particularly difficult, your unexpected offer may have appeal as a way to break a deadlock.

Although, as previously mentioned, it's usually better to have the other side make the first offer, there are also circumstances where it may be preferable to make a "preemptive strike" initial offer geared toward securing quick agreement. The reasons for doing this will be closely related to the details of any individual negotiation. A few such instances are:

- If you face a deadline unknown to the opposition, putting an offer on the table can move things along.
- To feel out the opposition by making a high initial offer. Their reaction can be useful in gauging the future course of the negotiations.
- Certain facts not known to your adversary increase the value of what you're negotiating for. Therefore, you may want to make an attractive first offer to get the deal under wraps.
- If your negotiating position is strong enough to dictate terms. Under these conditions, the longer you negotiate, the more you signal a willingness to make concessions.
- If the value of the subject matter under negotiation is difficult to ascertain, making a first offer will let you set the base price for negotiations.

- If the circumstances are such that making the first offer will be seen as a sign of good will. This is particularly true where the other side is a more or less reluctant partner to the negotiations.

10.9 HOW TO PARRY COUNTER-OFFERS EFFECTIVELY

Rejecting counter-offers can be dealt with in a variety of ways. To some extent it depends upon how realistic the counter-offer is in relation to the offer you made. If it brings the respective positions relatively close to agreement, you may simply want to stand firm on your offer, and see if you can get the other negotiator to move a little bit more. As an alternative, you may suggest splitting the difference, (see section 6.6) to conclude the deal.

The more difficult problem arises when the counter-offer comes nowhere close to your offer. Let's look at various alternatives that can be used to respond when this happens.

1. The most obvious rebuttal of a counter-offer is a straightforward rejection. However, unless the terms are outrageous enough to be laughable, a blunt, "No" isn't satisfactory. A flat rejection may well lead the other negotiator to believe that you're just stonewalling. This, of course, will only serve to harden the stance of the other side.

   Therefore, whenever you reject an offer, give valid reasons for your rejection. This not only adds credibility to your rejection, but it also puts the other side back on the defensive in terms of refuting your reasoning. Incidentally, comparisons work especially well in justifying the rejection of a counter-offer. Hence, if it's at all possible, compare the proposed counter-offer—or any of its components—with similar projects, prices, or whatever else constitutes a comparison in the particular case.

   EXAMPLE: "Mr. Arnold, your offer is way out-of-line. Comparable leases in buildings within the business district are 30% lower than what you're proposing. I've got a list here which shows what others are paying for similar footage with terms comparable to what I offered you."

2. When you receive a counter-offer on a project that is complicated and comprises many elements, take the time to analyze it in detail. It may well be that certain aspects of the counter-offer are satisfactory, while others are unreasonable. By looking at the components, you can then decide whether or not to reject the offer as a whole, or opt to attack it piece-by-piece. The latter method gives you the advantage of accepting the good points, and rejecting those that you don't agree with.

EXAMPLE: "Carl, I've gone over your offer in detail with my cost accounting people. We can live with your material costs, as well as the overhead rates proposed. However, both your direct labor costs, and the hours proposed to do the job, aren't even in the ballpark. In order to get this thing resolved, let's concentrate on the labor. For one thing, you've proposed 3800 hours of senior technician time . . ."

NOTE: When you reject an offer in this manner, try to launch right into the problem area. Doing this shunts the discussion onto the issue you want to attack.

3. On occasion, you may find it preferable to reject a counter-offer by simply downplaying its significance. Be lighthearted about it, without being insulting. This approach indicates that you don't take the proposal seriously, and are treating it as a counter-offer that's being thrown on the table for posturing purposes.

EXAMPLE: "Adam, if I didn't know you better, I'd think you were blowing smoke in my ear. You can't be serious about a counter-offer that puts us two million bucks apart. Give me something more realistic, so we can get down to some serious negotiating."

4. If the circumstances fit, you may just want to plead poverty. Adopting a position that you can't afford the deal based on what the other party is recommending does two things. First of all, it plants the idea that you may not be able to financially handle what's proposed. The bottom line is that the other side either has to consider giving you a better deal, or risk seeing you walk away from the table. Alternatively, your opponent may just think your objection is based upon the price being too high. This puts the other side back on the defensive in terms of justifying the value of what's being offered.

EXAMPLE: "The bottom line on your counter-offer is that I'd go broke if I agreed to it. If I pay $2,300 a piece for your sub-assemblies, I'll end up losing $200 a unit on every machine I sell. It's that simple, so for us to do business, you'll have to do better than that."

5. Another way to deal with a counter-offer is to come right back with your own counter-offer. However, be careful not to try and close the difference in the positions too quickly, or you'll find yourself giving up most of the cash. So just adjust your offer slightly from your original position. This sends a signal that you're not likely to move much from your original position, while at the same time it indicates your willingness to negotiate.

EXAMPLE: Your company offers a price of $5,495,000 to perform computer support services for the ZZZ Corp. They make a counter-offer of $4,900,000. You immediately respond with, "We can go down to $5,480,000, but that's about as close as we can cut it."

NOTE: The less you move from your initial position in one jump, the greater the possibility of convincing someone else that you don't have much room to maneuver. Conversely, when people make a substantial move from their initial offer, it signals that they have plenty of leeway to play with.

6. If you want to bring matters to a head rather quickly, you can reject a counter-offer with a veiled threat to walk away from the table without making a deal. Perhaps this will force the other side to get serious in a hurry. However, it's prudent to have other alternatives in case they decide to stand pat and call your bluff.

   EXAMPLE: "Victor, if you can't do better than that, there doesn't seem to be any point in continuing the discussions." NOTE: Remember, that if the other side keeps you negotiating further, without making a better counter-offer, they know you are only bluffing. So after a short while, if they don't give you a better proposal, you might want to emphasize your point by packing your papers and saying something such as, "Like I said, Vic, there's no point in going further, unless you are willing to move. So what do you want to do?" In other words, to make this work successfully, you have to be willing to head for the door. Otherwise, you will have lost your credibility, and will likely be in for a long and difficult negotiation.

10.10 WHEN TO WITHDRAW YOUR OFFER

Unlike the little boy who picks up his bat and ball and goes home when he doesn't get his way, withdrawing an offer once it's made isn't as easy—unless you too intend to go home, even without reaching agreement. If there's a lesson in this, it's not to make an offer on the assumption that it can just as easily be withdrawn. The truth is that once an offer is on the table, the other side views that offer as your current position, even after it's withdrawn. The circumstances are rare where you can make an offer, withdraw it, and then subsequently negotiate an agreement better than the withdrawn offer. Common sense says that if you offer $100,000, withdraw it, and then offer $90,000, you won't be taken seriously.

Nevertheless, there are valid grounds for withdrawing an offer that's currently on the table. These include:

1. When circumstances change. We live in an ever-changing world, and during the negotiation process events may occur which make your existing offer a bad one. The reasons may range from a sudden financial setback to a change in your competitive business climate. From a negotiation standpoint, it's useful to distinguish between offers that

are withdrawn due to a reason that makes further negotiations useless, and those where it's justified to continue negotiations under the changed circumstances. In the first instance, other than breaking-off the discussions as amicably as possible, there's little else to do.

On the other hand, if you want to continue the negotiation process with the changed circumstances being taken into account, you have to make your case for withdrawing your offer. It becomes necessary to explain the specifics of why your offer is no longer valid. Obviously, if the cause is something beyond your control, there's a greater likelihood the other side will be reasonable about it. But if it's something such as an internal business problem, your opponent is likely to hold your feet to the fire if the changed conditions will mean a new offer less attractive than the one that was withdrawn.

2. Withdrawing an offer is sometimes used as a negotiation tactic in the hopes of forcing the other side toward agreement. However, for the most part this is a silly maneuver, since it's seldom taken seriously when an offer is withdrawn and the discussions continue on. Therefore, if you are in a position where you attempt this tactic, be prepared to walk away from the table in the hope that the other side will contact you. If your ploy works, they should either agree to your terms, or at least make a better offer than they had previously proposed.

A better strategy than a sudden offer withdrawal is to make an offer conditional when it's first proposed. Say something such as, "I'll go to $90,000 if we can settle today." This is particularly effective if you can provide a factual basis as to why the offer will be withdrawn if it's not accepted. For instance, "I can offer you $524,000 if we settle this week. Otherwise, I'll have to withdraw my offer and recompute the figures, since new labor rates take effect next Monday." Obviously, the greater the credibility attached to your reasoning, the better the chances of convincing your adversary.

3. There comes a time in many a negotiation where little progress is being made, and the prospects for agreement become increasingly bleak. At these times, when you are ready to pack it in, you may have to choose between (1) ending negotiations with no intention of resuming them, (2) leaving your offer on the table, with an invitation to contact you if they decide to accept it at a later date, or (3) withdrawing your offer, with the understanding that it's being done because no progress is being made.

Naturally, ending negotiations without leaving the door open should only be done when, all things considered, that is the logical choice. As for choosing between leaving your offer on the table, or withdrawing it, to a large degree that will depend upon what stage negotiations were in when they ended. If you have made what is in fact your final offer, then you might as well just leave it open with an offer to contact you if it's subsequently acceptable. However, even here, time constraints should be given for acceptance of the offer. For instance, say "My offer remains open if you choose to accept it within the next two weeks."

10.11 FACT FINDING: SUPPORTING YOUR POSITION WITH PAPER

The better prepared you are to defend an offer, the more likely the chance that it will be accepted. Many negotiations involve detailed evaluations of the back-up data which support an offer. As a result, it's important to be able to justify your position with documentation when it's challenged. Otherwise, the other negotiator will assume that you're flying by the seat of your pants when you lay your cards on the table.

Where folks often fail in this regard, is not so much in having data to support what they assert, but being unable to produce it in a timely fashion. When questions are raised about run-of-the-mill matters, such as material and labor costs, the frequent response is, "I'll have to dig that up for you." Of course, in many instances that's a valid response, since a large dollar value negotiation may have reams of paperwork to support it. However, in other instances it results from a lack of planning in terms of being able to anticipate the need to prove your case.

Being able to quickly produce supporting data when questions are raised serves several purposes. First of all, it indicates efficiency, and in the eyes of the other negotiator, efficiency at the negotiation table translates into credibility. The longer it takes to come up with supporting documentation, the more a thought process is likely to form which says, "These people don't know what they're doing." Furthermore, the quicker you respond to a request for information, the sooner you can put the subject to bed and go on to something else. Finally, keeping the negotiation process moving smoothly helps prevent the sort of bottlenecks and deadlocks which can cause a negotiation to languish, or even fall apart.

10.12 TEN WAYS TO DEFEND WRITTEN PROPOSAL TERMS

Whenever you're negotiating based on the submission of a written proposal, you can readily expect all sorts of challenges to your presentation. You can use negotiation table discussions, both to elaborate upon complex aspects of your proposal, as well as to furnish explanations when questions are raised. Of course, your ultimate success in defending the proposal will depend upon your ability to support your position with whatever it takes to make your point. However, you have a lot of flexibility in terms of how you do this. Basic strategies that you can employ to defend proposal terms include:

1. Using support documentation such as vendor quotes, bills of material, and detailed cost breakdowns to reinforce your arguments when costs are questioned.

2. Show the provision being questioned is routinely accepted by other parties that you do business with.

3. Prove that what you're doing is a standard practice in your type of business and/or industry.

4. Show it's to your opponent's advantage. Try to use a "this is for your protection" argument.

5. Use a "higher authority" mandate. Argue that superiors such as a boss, corporate headquarters, or some other higher level has imposed the requirement.

6. Prove it's a third party requirement imposed by government regulations, a lender, or some other entity with the power to require the disputed provision.

7. Offer outside expert testimonials to support objectionable proposal provisions.

8. Use a "my lawyer put that in there" argument. Sometimes people accept this with sanctity, never thinking to run it by their own legal counsel.

9. Try a policy argument. "I can't change that because it's company policy."

10. Non-negotiable necessity. As a last resort, you can simply assert that the offending provision isn't negotiable. If necessary, trade-off acceptance of the provision for something the other side has proposed which you don't like.

10.13 MAKING MID-COURSE CORRECTIONS IN YOUR OBJECTIVE

No matter how carefully you plan before negotiations begin, on occasion you may discover that adjustments have to be made in your negotiation position. This is likely to happen when negotiations commence, and information is revealed by your opponent that you weren't aware of. It may be something substantive which wasn't anticipated, or a different perception of the other side's goals as revealed during face-to-face bargaining. In either event, you should always be flexible about adjusting your negotiation position as the negotiation process proceeds.

Frequently, negotiations grind to a halt because one side or the other refuses to yield from a pre-negotiation position, even though it becomes obvious that an agreement can't be reached on that basis. Yet, there are often times when a little bit of creative thinking can come up with a solution to a seemingly unsolvable problem that threatens to wreck the negotiations. However, several factors should be considered whenever a substantial change in your original negotiation objective is a possibility. These include:

1. Don't jump at a sudden offer—as good as it may seem—if it's substantially different from what you were expecting.

2. Don't make major changes in your negotiation goals without analyzing the impact on both yourself and the opposition.

3. Don't change your position just because you assume you have a hopeless deadlock. Evaluate carefully whether or not accepting something other than originally planned is better than no deal at all.

4. Take whatever time is needed to evaluate any realignment in your negotiation position.

CAUTION: Occasionally, during negotiations, your adversary will suddenly make an offer to sell goods and/or services other than what you undertook to negotiate. Use extreme care when this happens, since it may not arise out of sudden inspiration on the part of the other negotiator. It may instead be just a deliberate attempt to either throw your negotiation strategy out of whack, or a simple sales pitch to sell you something you really don't want. Frequently, the unwanted items are coupled as a package with the subject matter of the negotiation. An attempt is then made to force you to buy what you don't want to get what you came to bargain for. Your best bet when faced with this dilemma is to insist that you wrap-up the planned negotiation separately, and then look at any add-ons that are offered. However, if the other side insists that coupling is the only way they will go, recess the negotiations and reassess the entire package.

10.14 SAVVY WAYS TO GIVE GROUND TO GET AGREEMENT

When negotiations open, there will, of course, be a disparity between the two negotiating positions. Both skill and patience will be needed to close this gap in a manner that gives you a satisfactory settlement of the differences in the respective positions. Obviously, you want to work toward having the other side make any significant concessions that are necessary to bring the negotiations to a conclusion. However, in most cases, you won't be able to just stand pat until they finally agree with you. Therefore, your goal should be to concede as little as possible, while maximizing the concessions you get in return.

For starters, you should always insist on getting a concession you want, in return for anything you concede. This is pretty basic, however, in order to avoid hassles, and/or foster cooperation, inexperienced negotiators have a propensity to promptly concede items that are of little or no significance to them. What gets overlooked is their trading value in getting concessions from their adversary. Therefore, something that's of little value to you shouldn't be automatically assumed to be equally worthless to your opponent. In fact, the very fact that they are looking for the concession signifies that they have more than a casual interest in it.

One good way to speculate on the importance your adversary attaches to potential concessions is to look at the negotiation from the point of view of the other side. What matters to them? Is price a paramount consideration or does it have secondary importance? What about such factors as product quality, delivery, and/or financing terms? The more thought you put into this sort of analysis, the more likely you are to identify factors that are important to the other side, and less so to yourself.

Although your pre-negotiation planning will include a determination of what concessions you can make to reach agreement, as well as speculation on what concessions your opponent will seek, it's only after negotiations begin that you can really pin down what's of utmost importance to the other side. For this reason, resist early attempts at trading-off concessions until you are able to pinpoint what is and isn't negotiable. Once you are reasonably certain of the relative value of your potential concessions in the eyes of your adversary, then, and only then, will you be positioned to consider trading concessions to get agreement. And even then, always remember to give ground grudgingly, and get something for everything you give.

Chapter 11

STANDARD
NEGOTIATION PLOYS

The terms of a final agreement are to some degree dictated by your skill in minimizing your concessions during negotiations, while simultaneously maximizing what the other side surrenders. This is by no means an easy undertaking, but it's less of a hurdle if you learn to hold your own in a negotiation table tug of war.

Nevertheless, when and how to make concessions is only part of the equation. You also have to recognize when to stand firm in your position, and even when it's wise to get angry. You may even have to take a stand that can place the negotiations in jeopardy. Although you may not feel particularly comfortable at using certain negotiation ploys to advance your cause, you at least should be able to react properly if you're on the receiving end of such tactics. This chapter discusses both how to use certain ploys, as well as how to defend against them.

11.1 BLUFFS: MAKING THEM AND
CALLING THEM

Bluffing, of course, can be either a successful technique, or a terrible failure if the bluff is called and it leaves the bluffing party holding little other than a red face. In the final analysis, a bluff is only as good as the ability to convince someone that it's not a bluff. In negotiations, it's often not the initial stage of the bluff that makes for success, but rather the ability to carry the bluff further after it's initially challenged. Let's look at a simple example:

Background

Alex, the owner of a small chain of stores, is negotiating the sale of the business to Ken, who represents a major chain interested in buying the business. After extended negotiations, the bargaining has gotten down to a disagreement over price.

Discussion

Ken: "We can't go any higher than $15,000,000."

Alex: "I've been telling you all along that the price is $20,000,000, and I won't accept one cent less. Let's just forget the whole thing." (This threat that the negotiations are over is the initial bluff, which is being made in an attempt to get Ken to raise the offer.)

Ken: "Well, sorry we couldn't get together, Alex. If you change your mind, get in touch with me." (Ken is calling the bluff to see if Alex will continue to negotiate. Actually, Ken's company will pay the $20,000,000 asking price, but only if they have to.)

Alex: "It's just as well it didn't work out. I'm not ready to retire yet anyway." (Alex wants to sell the business, but he knows Ken's company really wants his stores, so he decides to walk away and see what happens.) Two weeks later Ken calls Alex and agrees to pay the $20,000,000 asking price. Alex, by responding to the challenge when his bluff was called is successful in getting what he wanted.

Once a bluff is initially called during negotiations, it's ultimate success depends upon having the nerve to carry it out. In Alex's case, he walked away when his bluff was called and won. As is equally apparent from the example, he could also have failed in his quest for a higher price. Bluffing is fraught with danger, so playing this form of brinkmanship shouldn't be taken lightly. When a bluff is made, you have to be prepared to accept the risk of it being called.

On the other hand, if negotiations have reached the stage where the risk is minimized, bluffs can and do work. This is particularly true in situations where it's highly unlikely the other party will call your bluff. For instance, if you know the circumstances are such that the other party needs the deal far worse than you, there's less of a likelihood that they will do anything that would jeopardize the negotiations. Nevertheless, people can't be programmed like robots, so you can never be completely certain that a bluff won't be called. Therefore, if you're not prepared to live with the consequences, don't include bluffing in your bag of tricks.

The flip side of making bluffs is handling them when you're on the receiving end. There are a couple of alternatives for doing this. You can either immediately challenge them and see what happens, or simply ignore them and force the other side to react. In the latter instance, if negotiations continue and the other side takes no action relative toward their bluff, then you're over the hurdle.

Of course, what makes a bluff a success is the inability to separate fact from fiction. In other words, do they mean what they say, or are they bluffing? The following sort of statements are typical negotiation threats that may be either genuine, or just a bluff made to force your hand:

- "It's either what I've proposed or nothing."
- "Do you want the project for $3,000,000, or should I look elsewhere?"
- "You have until three o'clock today to accept my offer, or the deal is dead."
- "I'll declare bankruptcy if your union goes on strike."

In making a judgment as to whether a threat is genuine, or merely a bluff to gain a negotiating edge, you have to look at all of the facts surrounding the situation. Would the other side face difficulties if they carried out the threat? Do they have satisfactory alternatives available if the deal falls through? Beyond the facts of the case, you have to draw conclusions relative to the personal make-up of the other negotiator. If the person is recognizably irrational and hot under the collar, then the threat might be carried out, even though the factual scenario would indicate otherwise.

When all is said and done, the bottom line is that if the other party didn't have an interest in doing business with you, they wouldn't be there in the first place. So if you're faced with a bluff that represents an unreasonable demand, ignore it. If it turns out not to be a bluff, and ends up as a deal breaker, you're probably just as well off in the long run.

11.2 PIECE BY PIECE CONCESSIONS: THE GOOD AND BAD POINTS

In conducting negotiations, you have to consider whether to make concessions one by one or attempt to reach agreement by bundling concessions and making a package deal. Doing it piece-by-piece holds out the promise that you will get maximum value for the concessions you make. It also negates the fear of giving up something unnecessarily during the negotiation process.

However, a long series of offers and counter-offers where each side reluctantly concedes one minor item after the other is time-consuming. It also tends to build-up the sort of frustration and hostility that can trigger a complete breakdown in the negotiations. Conceding item by item can also leave you trapped if you get to the point where you have little left to concede, and the other side continues to press for further concessions. In addition, when offer after offer is made—each one a little better than the last—it's difficult to convince your adversary when the well has run dry. Conversely, a total package offer lets both sides avoid the necessity of dealing directly with individual sticking points in their positions.

To a large degree, how you proceed will be dictated early on in the negotiations. If the initial offer of the other side is relatively close to your negotiation objective, you should be able to conclude a deal by making a wholesale trade-off to reach agreement. If, on the other hand, your opponent's initial offer isn't close to what is reasonable in your view, then you are probably going to have to move him toward your position with a series of concessions.

For all intents and purposes, the most practical approach is to attempt to negotiate the entire package in one fell swoop, meanwhile guarding against failure by keeping something you can concede in reserve. This keeps you from having to surrender red meat to get agreement if you hit a snag.

11.3 MIRAGE CONCESSIONS: WHAT YOU SEE ISN'T WHAT YOU GET

One thing to guard against when you trade-off concessions is to be sure you're not giving up something of value without at least getting an equivalent concession from your adversary. This can happen when the other party makes a concession that on the surface appears to be substantive, but in reality is little or nothing at all. There are three basic questions you should always consider whenever the other side offers to make a concession. These are:

1. Are they giving you something of value? Appearances can be deceiving, and nowhere more so than at the negotiation table. Both sides are trying to obtain the best deal they can, which, for one thing, means conceding as little as possible in the form of concessions.

    On the other hand, it can be anticipated before negotiations begin that some form of concessions may be necessary during the actual bargaining. As a result, both parties to the negotiation are likely to start off with initial positions that over-inflate their objectives. The end result turns out to be the granting of concessions that represent movement from what was an unrealistically attainable objective in the first place. Therefore, in many negotiations, at least the initial concessions represent nothing more than eliminating the fluff from each side's negotiation objective.

Assuming your initial offer has been formulated to give you the flexibility to make inconsequential concessions that don't cut to the core of your negotiation objective, you won't be harmed by this sort of trade-off. However, you can run into trouble if (1) you neglected to factor give-aways into your pre-negotiation objective, or, (2) you trade-off give-aways carelessly, leaving yourself at the bottom line of your negotiation position, while your opponent still has plenty of room to maneuver. To guard against the latter, make sure that you fight hard for every concession you grant. Not only is this a safeguard against getting stuck with nothing to give, but it also psychologically promotes the idea that you are conceding fat rather than fluff.

Even when negotiations get to the point of granting hard-core concessions that neither side wants to make, you can still be the victim of valueless concessions. They can take all sorts of forms including everything from promises that are impossible to perform, to those that are prohibited by law or government regulations.

2. The second question to ask yourself when a concession is offered by the other side is what are they asking in return? Your success in trading concessions will to a large extent dictate how good a deal you end up with. One common trap in this area is an offer of a dollar for dollar trade-off. This creates a problem when the other side's position is nowhere near your price objective.

   For example, if $200,000 is the maximum price you will pay, and the seller offers to split the difference between his last offer of $300,000, and your offer of $150,000, you would be paying $225,000. The significant point here is that even what appears to be a trade-off of equal value can be detrimental. Therefore, when you consider what kind of concession the other side is asking for, you have to view it in terms of your overall objective, not just in the form of a quid-pro-quo exchange of concessions.

3. Any promised concession is only as good as the commitment to see that it's actually carried out. Many concessions consist of items that will be part of the performance of the subject matter being negotiated. Therefore, whenever a concession is to be part of the performance of a negotiated agreement, make sure that the specifics are pinned down in a

written agreement. Otherwise, you may find yourself not getting what you bargained for.

11.4 THE PROS AND CONS OF PERFORMANCE INCENTIVES

Performance incentives are a useful tool to turn negotiation table promises into reality. It's one thing for a negotiator to spout all sorts of superlatives about past performance on similar projects, and quite another to expect that this puffery will be translated into performing your contract satisfactorily. However, if the subject matter of the negotiation is appropriate, you may be able to use performance incentives to motivate the other party toward delivering what they promise.

Incentives are commonly used to encourage technical performance that meets or exceeds the agreed upon specifications. In their most basic form, the technical requirements that must be met are identified, and if the contractor does better than the requirement, additional profit is paid for the above average performance.

In some cases—particularly research where firm specifications can't be agreed upon—target goals are established. Here, since there is uncertainty as to whether or not the target specification can be met, not only can there be provisions for additional profit for meeting or exceeding the specifications, but there also can be provisions for little or no profit if the target goals aren't reached. Of course, how incentives are structured depends upon the nature of what is being bought and what performance characteristics are desired by the buyer.

In addition to incentives on technical characteristics, it's also possible to have incentives on the cost of doing a project and/or delivery dates. In fact, any type of incentive is possible with the only real limitation being the creativity needed to design an incentive arrangement that will motivate the level of performance that is desired. To better demonstrate how incentives can be used, let's look at a few very basic examples.

Technical incentive

The "X" Corp. (the buyer) is negotiating with "Y" Corp. (the seller) to design and build a component that will be part of a new product. The specifications call for the component to weigh six pounds. Since weight is a crucial parameter in the end product, "X" offers to pay an incentive of one dollar per unit on all production units if the component can be designed and produced to weigh less than four pounds each.

Delivery incentive

"A" Corp. (the buyer) contracts with "B" Corp. on March 1st for the production and delivery of 4,000 widgets on or before December 1st. However, since it's to "A's" benefit to receive delivery before that date, "A" agrees to pay "B" an additional one percent of the contract price for delivery on or before September 1st.

Cost incentive

"L" Corp. engages "B" Corp. for research and development work on a cost plus incentive fee basis. To encourage cost effectiveness, the contract contains a provision where "B" can earn an additional fee of twenty cents for every dollar by which final costs are less than a target cost of $1,000,000. Assuming the final costs are $800,000, "B" can earn additional fee or profit of $40,000, (20% of the $200,000 difference between the target cost of $1,000,000, and the final cost of $800,000).

NOTE: Of course, incentives on any combination of cost, performance, and delivery can be included in the same agreement. Furthermore, the complexities of such arrangements can go far beyond the simple examples shown here. It should also be noted that incentives can be a two-way street. That is, provisions can be included where a contractor will receive less money if performance is below the level established in the contract.

CAUTION: There are several cautionary measures that have to be taken into consideration whenever you're considering the use of incentives. These include:

1. The number and type of incentives. If the incentive structure in an agreement isn't carefully planned, it can do more harm than good. For example, if you have a number of performance incentives, you have to decide where you want to place the emphasis in terms of priorities. Otherwise, the contractor may strive to meet certain incentive goals at the expense of others.

    For instance, if you have an agreement containing incentives on height, width, and length, and height is the most important of the three, your incentives should be weighted to place the greatest emphasis on reaching the targets established for height. Otherwise, if the three incentives are weighted equally, your contractor may profit by ignoring the most difficult of the three, and instead concentrate on achieving the goals set for the other two. Whenever possible, you should guard against such practices by putting a provision in the contract to provide that no incentive payments will be made on an individual incentive unless certain specified goals are met for all of the criteria that have incentives.

2. The criteria for determining whether or not an incentive has been met should be carefully thought out. If the incentive goals you write into the contract are either weighted wrong, or are too lenient, it may result in paying incentive dollars without getting the performance characteristics you're seeking. On the other hand, if the incentive goals are so stringent as to be virtually unattainable, there will be little or no motivation for your contractor to work toward achieving the goals.

3. The language of the incentive clause in the contract is crucial. It should be complete enough to clearly specify how performance will be measured to determine any incentive payments, yet simple enough to be clearly understood. This will help avoid conflict over the interpretation of the provision when it's time to tally up what incentives have been earned, and the amount of incentive payments that are due.

HINT: Apart from using incentive provisions to inspire maximum performance, you may have occasion to use them as a negotiation tactic. This can be done by raising the specter of having incentives in the agreement, as a means of getting concessions in other areas in exchange for dropping your performance incentive demands. However, if you decide to try this ploy, be sure that incentives can actually be used effectively in case your bluff is called. Otherwise, you will have to find a way to back-off your incentive provision suggestion without looking foolish.

11.5 EXERTING BRINKMANSHIP WITHOUT GOING OVER THE EDGE

There will likely come a time during a negotiation when the other side is stonewalling, or simply stalling due to a lack of decisiveness. Or perhaps you have a deadline to meet, and the negotiations aren't proceeding fast enough to suit your purposes. For these, and other reasons, you may find yourself forced to push the bargaining toward a prompt conclusion. As a consequence, this may require you to intensify negotiations to the point where you essentially have to threaten to walk off into the sunset if agreement isn't reached.

This sort of dilemma can cause you to pause, since the possibility exists that the other side will simply say, "So long," leaving you with nothing for your efforts other than a lot of frustration, and the realization that not all negotiations end in agreement. Nevertheless, it's important to recognize that there are any number of reasons why the other party may be more interested in dilly-dallying than working toward agreement. These include:

- Stalling will get them a better deal. The most obvious example is when the other side knows you have a deadline to meet.

- The other party has no vested interest in negotiating, and is doing so only to see if they can sucker someone into giving them a windfall profit.

- The other side is only negotiating out of necessity, with no intention of concluding an agreement. For instance, country "A" with restrictive trade practices, enters trade negotiations with country "B" only to forestall the implementation of retaliatory measures.

- They are using you as a negotiation pawn. Perhaps simultaneous negotiations are taking place with other parties, and your negotiation is being used as a smoke screen to exact a better deal elsewhere.

- Indecision about reaching agreement. A common example is the family-owned business where an emotional tug of war can occur over whether or not to sell the business, even in the midst of on-going negotiations.

Although the reasons for stalling are varied, you may find yourself in a situation where you have to bring the negotiation to a conclusion—with or without a deal. Of course, if you have other fairly satisfactory alternatives, there's less anxiety involved in biting the bullet. Nevertheless, no matter how bad you want a particular deal, you may reach a point where you have to find out whether or not a deal is going to be made.

When a negotiation gets to the stage where you have to challenge your adversary to conclude an agreement, try to do it in such a way that you give yourself an outlet to pull back from the brink. Be firm and matter-of-fact about it, without getting angry. If you lose your cool in frustration, you will only succeed in killing whatever chance there is—however remote that may be—for saving the deal at the last moment. Say something such as, "Look Ed, we're going round and round, and nothing is being accomplished. Can you give me one good reason why we should continue these negotiations?" If the reply is "No!" simply respond with, "Well, give me a call if you change your mind. If not, perhaps we'll get a chance to work together in the future."

On the other hand, if the other negotiator really wants to do business, the response will probably be encouragement that an agreement can be reached. If that happens, apply some form of pressure to get your counterpart to move beyond the simple reassurance. Otherwise, if the intent is merely to stall, you're only subjecting yourself to prolonging the inevitable. There are several approaches you can take toward getting a commitment. They include:

1. Asking for an offer. "Ed, if you really want to settle, why don't you make me an offer that can wrap the deal up?"

2. Making an offer yourself. "Well, Ed, I'm not convinced that we're getting anywhere, but I want to do business with you so I'm going to take a chance and make one final offer."

3. Setting a deadline to conclude an agreement. "I'll hang in here for two more hours, but if we don't wrap it up by then, I'm catching the 6:30 P.M. flight to Cincinnati."

4. Identifying the reason why the negotiations are deadlocked. "If we're going to get a deal done, Ed, you better clue me in as to what your problem is. Otherwise, we're just spinning our wheels."

5. Getting higher authority involved in a settlement. "Frankly, Ed, I'm not convinced we can get anywhere, since I don't think you have management commitment toward making this deal. However, I'm willing to stay and listen to what Mr. Smythe (Ed's boss) has to say."

Probably the most difficult aspect of bringing a negotiation that's going nowhere to a head, is the emotional hang-up associated with the fear of failure. This is especially true when you appear to have more to gain from an agreement than the other party. Unfortunately, it's this very emotional element that enables the other party to keep stringing you along, even though there is no intent to reach agreement. Therefore, the more you worry about no deal being made, the longer it will take to either reach agreement, or find out that a deal isn't in the works.

Finally, as hard as it may be to do, if there is a failure to reach agreement after you bring the matter to the brink, always leave without rancor. You never know what the future may bring, and two hours after you leave, a phone call may be received advising you that the other party has accepted your offer. Even if that doesn't happen, other opportunities may arise to do business in the future. Therefore, ending a fruitless negotiation by telling the other side to "stuff it" will accomplish nothing other than perhaps a moment of self satisfaction.

11.6 HOW TO MOVE AHEAD BY STANDING STILL

You may recall the discussion on dealing with an opponent who uses stonewalling tactics in sections 6.2 and 6.3. The flip side of the coin is knowing how and when to do a little stonewalling yourself. Naturally, the better you're able to do this without being blatant about it, the more effective it can be.

For starters, the better prepared you are to defend your negotiation position, the easier it is to remain firm and refuse to budge from your negotiation stance. And the harder it is for your adversary to punch holes in your arguments, the less likely the chance of you being accused of stonewalling.

As a companion tactic, keep the pressure on your opponent by honing in on the weaknesses in his negotiation position. This combined offensive and defensive strength will allow you to repeatedly resist attempts to move you from your initial position. It also serves to stave off any implications that you're simply stonewalling to force the other party to accept your position—or at least move in that direction.

The longer you're able to sustain a justifiable defense of your own position, accompanied by corresponding attacks on your opponent's negotiating position, the greater the chances of your opponent caving in to your demands. Successful stonewalling depends upon playing your opponent's patience to the limit. It's akin to coaxing someone to the edge of a cliff, and then hoping they keep teetering without falling off. In other words, it's ok to get your opponent frustrated, but not enough so they get fed up and call it quits.

Stonewalling feeds on people's impatience, so if you manage to hold a "steady as she goes" course long enough, even if you can't get your opponent to totally agree with what you're proposing, you may at least frustrate him into making substantial concessions. On the other hand, stonewalling entails a very real risk that the other side may conclude that bucking their heads against a brick wall isn't in their best interests. And once someone forms a notion that the party they're bargaining with is just being unreasonable, it can be next to impossible to get the negotiation back on track. Therefore, anytime you decide to employ stonewalling tactics, be sure to have other options available if the negotiations fall apart.

11.7 GAINING GROUND BY GETTING GROUCHY

A necessary part of any negotiator's arsenal of weapons is the ability to keep composed under pressure. Remaining calm, even when provoked, allows you to make rational decisions, rather than emotional ones. All things considered, keeping your composure is as essential as anything for negotiation success.

Nevertheless, on occasion, it may be appropriate to display a little anger of your own. For instance, you might be the victim of a belligerent negotiator who refuses to calm down despite repeated pleas for some form of civility. At other times you may encounter recalcitrant negotiators intent on stalling, and otherwise preventing any progress from being made. Therefore, the only available remedy may be a demonstration of controlled anger on your part.

All you want to do is send a strong signal to the other side that, (1) their behavior is intolerable and, (2) you no longer intend to put up with it. This shouldn't be done by simply blowing your top and unloading your frustrations on the culprit. This will only result in two negotiators operating out-of-control, with nothing constructive to be gained. Instead, you want to feign anger, meanwhile maintaining complete control of your emotions.

It may seem childish to do a little amateur acting using anger as your prop. However, meeting fire with fire—or at least pretending to—may be necessary. First of all, some people operate on the misguided assumption that bullying tactics are part and parcel of the negotiation process. This sort of mind-set conditions them to be hostile with the deliberate intent of browbeating you into submission. Meanwhile, other folks are just hostile by nature.

Whatever the reason for the hostility, when attempts to reason with these people show no results, you are forced to choose between continuing to tolerate the behavior, or taking some form of action to rein it in. You could, of course, threaten to break off negotiations unless and until the bully calms down. However, this isn't always feasible. For one thing, your negotiation position may be such that a threat to take a hike could spell disaster, especially if the offending party is hostile by nature, rather than by design. Irrational people do irrational things, and a threat to leave may be accepted with little regard for the consequences.

Furthermore, threatening to break off negotiations may only serve to gain assurance that the aberrant behavior will improve, with the bully quickly reverting to form as the negotiations continue. As a result, at times it may be appropriate to feign anger to bring a bully back to reality. The intent is to send a strong signal that you won't be bullied, and have no intention of putting up with their nonsense. Let's look at how this can be done.

Background

John Adams, a sales representative, is negotiating with Joe D., a buyer for a large chain of stores. For over an hour John has been subjected to all sorts of hostility, despite his attempts to keep the discussions civil. Finally, John decides it's time to pull Joe up short.

> *Joe D.:* Slamming his papers on the table, loudly says, "Adams, you've got to be stupid. I'm tired of wasting my time trying to explain things to you. Either you want the @#$%¢&* deal or you don't. What's it going to be?"

John: Standing up and leaning across the table says, "I've had about enough of your bull—! If you can't conduct this negotiation in a civilized manner without getting personal, just say so, and we'll end this negotiation right here and now."

Joe D.: Taken aback by the sudden outburst by John, who up until now has been dignified and restrained, pauses a moment, then smiles and says, "Hey, don't get uptight. Let's see if we can resolve this thing." (The negotiations then continue to a satisfactory conclusion with no further belligerent behavior on the part of Joe D.)

Frequently, as in this example, bad behavior stops the moment you challenge it. This is particularly true where someone is just using bullying tactics as a negotiating ploy. However, if you challenge someone and it only serves to exacerbate the situation, don't get drawn into a prolonged shouting match. Call a temporary halt to the negotiations, to allow things to cool down. Then, before negotiations resume, inform the other party that you don't intend to continue the discussions unless they are conducted in a dignified manner. If your counterpart continues to be obnoxious, walk out again, and if feasible, let the culprit's superiors know that negotiations are on hold because of the individual's behavior.

TIP: Someone out of control is prone to make careless mistakes. If you see this happening, it may be worth your while to suffer in silence for the sake of the negotiation benefits that are accruing as a direct or indirect result of the behavior. However, that's a judgment only you can make.

11.8 ASKING FOR THE MOON TO GET WHAT YOU WANT

As has been mentioned several times before, you should always leave a cushion in any initial offer to give yourself room to maneuver toward an agreement. Nevertheless, for the most part, your offer shouldn't be so extreme that it won't even be considered credible by your adversary. A completely unrealistic initial offer might cause a negotiation breakdown right at the start, resulting in the other party walking away before any bargaining has even begun. Alternatively, it might encourage an equally far-fetched counter-offer, making it that much more difficult to reach a final agreement.

However, there are instances when you should at least consider starting-off negotiations with what could be viewed as pie-in-the-sky demands. These circumstances include:

1. *When the other side makes an initial offer that is unreasonable.* If this happens you have a choice of (a) refusing to negotiate until they give you a reasonable offer, (b) making a credible counter-offer, and negotiating hard to close the gap—which means they have to move a lot further than you do, or (c) responding with an offer that's equally out of touch with reality.

   Simply refusing to negotiate has the potential for causing an immediate crisis, which could possibly break-up the bargaining before it has even begun in earnest. Alternatively, if you respond to an outrageous offer with a reasonable proposal, you may be putting yourself in unnecessary difficulty. This can happen if the other negotiator wants equivalent concessions made along the way to close the gap between his unrealistic offer, and your credible response. Naturally, this is a negotiation nightmare, since you're trying to move the other position the proverbial mile, while the other side only has to move you a few yards. This can put you with your back to the wall in terms of an ability to make any further concessions. This isn't an insurmountable obstacle if the opposing offer was merely a negotiating ploy, but it may mean a long and arduous negotiating session. As a result of the inherent difficulties involved in choosing alternatives (a) or (b) as the method for responding to an outrageous offer, simple expediency dictates giving consideration to counterattacking by making an equally outrageous initial offer of your own.

2. *When you are making an initial offer where you are uncertain as to the real value of the item.* The subject matter under negotiation may be such that you aren't really sure of its reasonable worth. Although this isn't likely to happen in most business transactions, in some instances it's not beyond the realm of probability, especially if the topic of negotiation is some type of intangible. When you're faced with this kind of dilemma, it pays to make a ridiculously low offer initially, which you can later raise if circumstances justify it.

3. *When the other side doesn't perceive the true worth of the item being negotiated.* This can happen when the other party is ill-informed, merely naive, or you have information—unknown to your opponent—that the true value is far different than surface appearances indicate.

4. *When your negotiating position is so strong that you're justified in asking for considerably more than would ordinarily be justified.* This

can happen when a buyer has a unique need for something you're selling. Therefore, by virtue of being in the driver's seat, you may be able to ask for—and get—a premium price. Conversely, if you're the buyer in a situation where the seller has an urgent need to make the sale, you may be successful in offering significantly less than would otherwise be reasonable.

CAUTION: Be prudent about making unrealistic offers and demands when the subject matter of the negotiation has a readily recognizable value. It's great to anticipate a windfall profit, and there is always a temptation to give yourself plenty of maneuvering room for making concessions. However, extreme demands can at best lead to a difficult negotiation, and at worst can lead the other party to walk away, leaving you with no deal at all. Furthermore, in agreements that require some form of continuing performance by the other party, if you stick it to them at the bargaining table, they may make life difficult for you during the period of performance. The most fruitful negotiations are generally those in which both parties are reasonably satisfied with the final agreement.

11.9 WHEN YOU SHOULD LOWBALL YOUR DEMANDS

Although as a general principle, the ultimate goal of every negotiation is to get the best deal you possibly can, there are instances when it's advisable to sacrifice a short-term advantage for long-term gains. A prime example is where you want to get your foot in the door as a new supplier, in the hope of obtaining substantial future business. One way this is sometimes accomplished is by low-balling, which is nothing more than offering a price near— or even below—cost to be sure of getting the sought after business. If everything goes according to plan, then prices can be raised on future work, and/or a marginally profitable price will be offset by increased volume.

There are, of course, reasons other than attempting to secure future business that can force you to be conservative in terms of the deal you hope to get. Perhaps you're limited by having a number of competitors, or maybe the subject matter of the negotiation is something that's price sensitive. Whatever the reason, it pays to be careful in terms of how you go about negotiating an agreement when you are considering offering very favorable terms as an incentive to conclude a deal.

First of all, just because you offer someone a bargain doesn't mean they will necessarily see it as such. For one thing, a favorable first offer might just encourage the other party to push for an even better deal. This is in line with the tendency to believe that unless there is some haggling, along with the resultant concessions, then all evidence to the contrary, the bargain isn't a bargain at all. As silly as it seems, folks aren't always happy if they don't have to battle a little bit for their bargain.

Another little recognized aspect of any deal that looks too good to be true is the suspicion that there is a catch to the offer. Prudent business people want to feel confident about getting what they pay for. And although they certainly would like the lowest price they can get, they don't necessarily want to risk subpar performance for a bargain basement price. Thus, a bargain basement offer may spur the other party to thoughts about poor quality, potential bankruptcy, and all kinds of imaginary ills that would seemingly justify why the offer is so advantageous.

From your own vantage point, you have to carefully consider whether or not your objective in making a lowball offer is worth the risk. For instance, are there other alternatives that could be explored? Can you negotiate an option provision for additional quantities, rather than just buying in with the hope that future business will result? After all, who's to say that the other side doesn't recognize what you're trying to do? Furthermore, maybe their game plan is to take advantage of a lowball offer with no intention of providing any follow-on business.

Another possible consideration for making a lowball offer is with the hope of knocking competitors out of the box when more than one party is being negotiated with. However, when someone holds multiple party negotiations, they usually do so with the intent of getting a better deal by playing one competitor against another. Unfortunately, those competing sometimes become so enmeshed in seeking to be the victor, that they throw caution—and money—to the winds, and end up as a victor transformed into a victim. That is to say, they win the competition, but lose their shirt in the process.

Safeguarding against this type of predicament requires a thoughtful assessment of the advantages and disadvantages of any offer you might make—not from the vantage point of beating out the competition, but solely as to whether or not it's a good deal for you.

NOTE: Competitive negotiations can operate, not only to the detriment of sellers trying to lowball their way to victory, but also for buyers who find themselves caught up in the competitive furor of bidding against one another. Here, as opposed to lowballing or buying-in, the problem is the possibility of paying too much, rather than receiving too little. This is particularly true in the entertainment industry, where the hunt for talent sometimes finds euphoria overwhelming logic.

Given all of the possible scenarios for disaster that lowballing presents, the ultimate question to ask is whether or not the risks of making little or no money on the present deal are worth the potential long-term rewards. In most cases, the answer will be probably not, unless you have a high level of certainty that the future benefits will be forthcoming.

11.10 USING THE OLD "DIVIDE AND CONQUER" SAW

You can do extremely well during negotiations by exploiting any competing aims and objectives that exist within your opponent's organization. How you go about obtaining this information will vary. Sometimes, differences of opinion among members of the opposing negotiation team will come to light during the negotiations themselves. More often than not, these differences will be difficult to detect, since it's basic practice to present a united front during negotiations. Therefore, unless the opposing negotiation team leader doesn't have control of his troops, you will have to be on the alert to detect any internal disagreement.

One way to do this is to carefully observe members of the other negotiation team for subtle signs that indicate disagreement with something said by other members of their team. It may be as unobtrusive as a frown, raised eyebrow, or sullen silence. And if you're lucky, it may be as obvious as openly correcting or rebutting something said by their own team member.

Another method for obtaining information about differing opinions within your opponent's camp is through meetings that occur prior to negotiations. These contacts may be made by your marketing or technical people, and may not even involve the subject matter of the negotiation. Therefore, any employee who meets with customers, clients, suppliers, or any other party with potential for future negotiations, should be schooled to pick-up this sort of business intelligence.

One of the most fertile areas for differences to exist is between technical and non-technical personnel. Engineering and scientific types are more likely to look favorably upon suggestions that improve technical performance, than those folks with a bottom-line cost orientation. For this reason, you can have more success in promoting expensive bells and whistles with engineers, than with administrative people who are lobbying for a bare bones project. Knowing this can serve you well if the subject matter of the negotiation is such that you can use technical quality as an argument during negotiations.

In these situations, gear your presentation toward technical personnel on the other team who are apt to be your logical supporters. Even though they aren't likely to openly support what you espouse during bargaining sessions, they may well lobby for your position in behind-the-scenes meetings of their own negotiation team.

Actually, there are many variations of a "divide and conquer" strategy that you can use. In all cases, the ultimate objective is to single out those people in the opposing negotiation party who, for one reason or another, are apt to sympathize with the position you're advocating. To be successful in this sort of endeavor, you have to enlist this tacit support within the enemy camp without being obvious about what you're doing. A handy method of doing this is to simply argue your case in terms of the issues that you recognize as important to these people. By doing this, as a minimum you neutralize these people from being critical about your assertions. In addition, if they have sufficient clout within their own organization, they may well act as vocal supporters of your negotiation position at the other team's strategy sessions. And there's no better way to attain your negotiation objective than by having an ally in the enemy camp.

TIP: When you're up against a good negotiator, one way to overcome this handicap is to try and get the negotiator's boss involved in the act. Once the boss enters the picture, placate the boss, while playing tough with the lead negotiator. Once the other side perceives that you're more amenable to dealing with the boss, he may increasingly become the decision maker on their negotiation team.

11.11 HOW TO TRADE OFF SLUSH FOR SILVER

A sure-fire guarantee of getting a good deal is to give up little or nothing for what you're getting. At first glance, this seems pretty improbable, and realistically you will have to give value to get value. Nevertheless, sometimes there's a tendency to concede a lot more than is necessary to reach agreement. You may know, or have heard about, someone who paid an excessively high price for a company, a building, or some product or service. There are, of course, many varied reasons why this happens. And, in fact, what initially is regarded as a high price, may sometimes turn out to be a bargain.

Nevertheless, often more is given away during negotiations than is necessary to reach agreement. The causes are many, but one of the most predominant is a failure to recognize the value of the item to the other party. Your negotiating opposites may place a higher value on something because it has more worth to them than it does to you. This can apply to either a concession in your negotiation position, or to the subject matter of the negotiation.

Therefore, to gain the maximum value for anything you negotiate, don't get caught in the trap of merely looking at the item from your own point of view. Think about its potential value to the other side. This is particularly true when it comes to making concessions. If the other side is particularly adamant about pressing you to make a concession in a certain area, you can be reasonably assured that it's of some importance to them even if the reason for their interest isn't obvious.

In fact, their desires may have no substantive basis at all, and instead, be purely emotional. Everything from luxury goods for the consumer to elaborate corporate headquarters buildings are sold on emotional appeal. Therefore, if you happen to be negotiating an agreement to sell anything that you can attach an emotional appeal to, the odds are that you can improve your bargaining position on that basis alone.

You may even be able to trade-off a relatively useless concession for a very valuable one even though there's no logical basis for your counterpart to make such a deal. Let's look at such an example.

Slush for silver

"A" is negotiating with "B" for a quantity of 1,000 electric motors. "A" is arguing that by substituting a cheaper component, the unit cost can be reduced by $1. "B" adamantly insists that the more expensive component is essential to meet quality standards. "B" further argues that additional costs would be necessary for increased inspection and sampling if the substitute part was used. Unknown to "A," "B" knows that the cheaper part will perform just as well, but he refuses to concede the point. Finally, "A" offers to share the savings 50/50 if the substitute part is used. "B," after arguing a little more, finally concedes. "B," who has given up nothing, essentially makes a windfall profit of $500, (50 cents × 1,000 units) by trading a concession of no value to him for pure profit.

It's neither logical or rational that someone will concede something for nothing. However, this overlooks the part that ego plays at the negotiation table. The more emphasis you can place on the purported value of something, the greater the odds of getting a substantive concession in return. And if you are equally persuasive in arguing the impossibility of making a trade-off, the greater the value you're likely to be offered.

There's nothing mysterious about this concept at all. The simple fact is that there are a lot of big egos who position themselves at the negotiating table. They will take great pride in besting you—and probably bragging about it later. The truth is that the best deals are generally made by those who don't trumpet their success to others. Self-promoters are often the biggest fools when it comes down to bottom-line negotiating.

You can take advantage of this ego-driven desire to best you at the bargaining table by making your opponents think they have succeeded in winning a concession you didn't want to make. In essence, the harder you make an opponent work for a concession, the greater the perceived value they place on it. In short, if you work at it, you can turn the other person's pride into your profit.

Chapter 12

COUNTERING NEGATIVE NEGOTIATION TACTICS

On one occasion or another, you will likely encounter negotiators who use every possible tactic to gain what they conceive to be an edge at the bargaining table. In fact, you may do business with negotiators who seemingly expend their energies on scheming, rather than justifying the merits of what they're advocating.

As you will likely discover, everyone doesn't enter a negotiation session thoroughly prepared. Some negotiators give little credence to proper preparation, but instead rely on their own basic bag of bargaining tricks to carry the day. Actually, they may spend so little time prepping themselves on the issues involved, that they have little idea—other than a few preconceived notions—as to what a favorable deal should consist of.

Remarkably enough, these negotiators always walk away after reaching agreement, confident in their own minds that they just finished fleecing another flock of sheep. However, if they have been negotiating with a properly prepared opponent, they will never realize that they ended up with the short end of the stick. All of which goes to prove that ignorance is indeed bliss—at least for those who commence negotiations with more confidence than knowledge.

Yet, not every negotiator you deal with will specialize in short cuts. The best of the bunch, and particularly those who make a living at it, will combine thorough preparation with their negotiation expertise, making themselves formidable foes for anyone. So, even though solid preparation is the bulwark upon which negotiation success is built, you still have to know how to counter negative tactics when they're used against you.

12.1 WHAT EVASION SHOULD BE TELLING YOU

During the course of negotiations, you may detect signs that indicate your adversary is being evasive, either in general, or on some individual aspect of the negotiations. There are many indicators that can signal this. A few tell-tale signs are:

- Failing to furnish documentary support when it is requested.
- Don't have readily available answers for your questions.
- Make vague promises such as, "We can try to do that," or, "That may be possible."
- Won't make definite commitments.
- Make false claims about what they can and can't do.
- Reverse their position on issues.
- Respond to questions with generalities, rather than specifics.
- Profess lack of knowledge about fundamental aspects of the subject matter of the negotiation.

Of course, any of the actions listed above aren't necessarily indicative of a level of evasion that would justify not doing business with the perpetrator. Negotiations are by their nature played pretty close to the vest. As a result, isolated instances indicating evasion shouldn't be taken as conclusive evidence of deceit. Instead, what you want to look for is an overall pattern of conduct indicating a level of deception that would give you reason to pause before you conclude any binding agreement.

When you do detect what you consider to be evasive behavior, try to probe to find out what the other side is concealing from you. Zero in on the questionable conduct, and press forward to get the answers you seek. Otherwise, your suspicions will be left to fester, without ever being proved or disproved.

One handy way to test your opponent's truthfulness is to ask questions for which you already know the answer. Do this in a casual manner, and don't rebut incorrect or misleading answers—at least not initially. Remember, you're testing the veracity of the other party, and to do this successfully, you need to establish a pattern of conduct. If you immediately challenge an erroneous response, your opponent will become wary and defensive, making it much more difficult to detect any deception.

With this caveat in mind, it is still wise to ask follow-up questions to be certain the question and answer are clear to both yourself and your adversary. Doing this removes the opportunity for the other party to later assert that the question and/or answer were not understood or are being misinterpreted.

Once you are reasonably convinced that the other side is being deliberately evasive in a substantive way, you have some hard choices to make. In a few instances, circumstances may be such that you deem it inappropriate to bring your suspicions to the attention of the other party. But for the most part, you should voice your suspicions in a direct confrontation. Obviously, you want to be as diplomatic as possible, but the overriding consideration is to see if satisfactory explanations are forthcoming in answer to your concerns.

You then have to decide whether the actions constitute a misguided concept of how negotiations are conducted, or instead represent the cover-up of facts that could have a significant bearing on performance of any negotiated agreement. If it's the latter, and you decide to go ahead despite misgivings, it behooves you to take measures to protect yourself by placing appropriate safeguards in any written agreement.

12.2 SURE-FIRE WAYS TO BRING MOVING TARGET OFFERS TO A HALT

Moving target offers are the negotiation equivalent of a magic act—now you see it, now you don't. What they are in substance is nothing more than an attempt to extract further advantages at your expense. They are a tactic for revising existing offers, purportedly on the basis of changed conditions of some sort. However, to preclude the negative aspects of an offer withdrawal, including the possibility of ending negotiations, moving target offers are designed to rationalize the basis for changing an offer. Let's look at how a moving target offer works:

Background

Harry Huff, a purchasing agent for a manufacturer, is negotiating with Peter Push, who represents a supplier of customized computer systems. They are engaged in negotiating an agreement whereby Push's company will install and maintain a complex computer system for Huff's employer. Back and forth bargaining has brought the negotiations to the point where Push has just made an offer of $5,000,000 to do the job. Let's pick the discussion up at this point.

The moving target

Huff: "Peter, I think we can wrap this up for $5,000,000. Let me take fifteen minutes to clear this with our VP of Purchasing."

Push: "Hold it a second Harry. Five million doesn't include maintaining the system for the first year. That's another $750,000."

Huff: Looking and sounding pretty perturbed replies, "What do you mean? We both agreed from the start that we were negotiating on a total package basis. What are you trying to pull?"

Push: "Wait a minute. We are talking a total package for the installation of the system. How could we talk about maintaining the system if we never agreed on a time frame for maintenance support?"

Huff: "Your proposal discussed one year's support as part of the package."

Push: "That's correct, but pricing wasn't discussed."

Huff: "Look, I'll kick this around with my superiors. Let's get back together in the morning."

Push: "Sounds good to me."

Huff: As the meeting gets down to business the following morning, Huff says, "Let's tie things down. Am I correct that your offer is the total package for installation and maintenance support for one year?"

Push: "It sure is Harry. That's what I said yesterday. Incidentally, what about training and documentation? Do you want to contract for those now, or do you want to negotiate a separate agreement?"

Huff: "You mean to tell me that documentation and training aren't included in the $5,750,000? What in heck do you call a total package? You give me a figure, I accept it, and then you add something else? You're just playing games with me."

Push: "Look, for $5,750,000, you get the system installed and a year of maintenance support. That's a package deal. I'm not telling you to buy documentation and training, but if you want it you have to pay for it.

> On the other hand, I'd suggest you consider a minimal documentation and training package which runs about $250,000. Here's a breakdown of what you get."

Huff: "What if we just skip the training and documentation?"

Push: "To be perfectly honest with you Harry, I don't see how you could operate without the basic training option. The system's new, so your people would be flying by the seat of their pants. As for the documentation, I'm not saying you have to have it, but you'll find yourself buying it later anyway. Don't get me wrong. You can skip either option, but it doesn't make sense to buy an expensive system, and not be able to operate it right."

Huff: "Needless to say, I'll have to take this whole deal up with Perkins (the VP of Purchasing), but it ticks me off that what we thought we were getting for $5,000,000, will now cost us $6,000,000."

Push: "It's the cheapest package around Harry, and don't forget you're buying state-of-the-art."

The example given is one of the more common forms of a moving target offer, where it's alleged that some component wasn't included in the price previously given. A frequent reason this tactic succeeds is that one party to the negotiations isn't exactly sure of what they want. This can be avoided by (1) pinning down your requirements precisely, and (2) specifically identifying what every offer is based upon. It's also wise, whenever possible, to insist on all-inclusive offers to prevent being hit with a "that's not included" argument.

Another common excuse for a moving target offer is that higher authority won't agree to the deal. However, moving target offers are based on as many kinds of justification as the creative abilities of negotiators permit. And brazen negotiators, who think they can get away with it, will keep changing their offer without even looking for an excuse. Preventing someone from unjustifiably revising an offer on you isn't difficult. There are two avenues you can take, depending upon the strength of your negotiating position, as well as your personal inclination.

The first method is to simply stand your ground and insist that the original offer remain on the table or you will not negotiate any further. The more circuitous route is to change your own offer to make it less desirable, using as the rationale, the revision to the other side's offer. Say something such as,

"Well, since you're revising your offer, I'll have to take another look at my own figures." Then, come back with an offer much less satisfactory than your previous one. Try this once, and you'll see how fast moving target offers can be shot full of holes.

12.3 TACTICS FOR COUNTERING INTERRUPTIONS

As was discussed in Section 9.10, planned interruptions during a negotiation session can be a useful tool in furthering your cause. Which, of course, means they can be an equally effective tactic when used by your opponent. Furthermore, even unintended interruptions are at best a nuisance, and at worst can be distracting enough to hinder your effectiveness. Consequently, it's important to minimize the potential for any distraction, except for those that you intentionally initiate.

The probability of interruptions interfering with the negotiation process can be greatly reduced by a little pre-planning before negotiations begin. Agreements to limit the number of participants, and holding meetings at off-site locations, are ingredients of the interruption prevention process. However, beyond these fundamentals, you have to learn to counter interruptions initiated by the other negotiator once negotiations commence. And that isn't always as easy as it seems.

For one thing, you may have the misfortune to be negotiating with someone who seemingly doesn't ever stop talking. This type of person just keeps rambling on oblivious to the circumstances. These folks are also prone to interject their comments whenever anyone else is speaking. Frankly, it can be a little unsettling to discover that this sort of person is seated across from you at a conference table and is about to make you a captive audience for the duration of the negotiations.

Whenever you find yourself with the misfortune of having to deal with someone who refuses to let you get a word in edgewise, there is little you can do other than assert yourself and insist on being heard. If you're interrupted as you speak, first try to keep the initiative with remarks such as:

- "We'll get to that in a moment."
- "Let me finish this point."
- "Hear me out on this."

If this sort of subtlety doesn't work, then turn your message up a notch with a long pause and a cold stare, followed by saying, "May I finish?" Hopefully, this will embarrass the person into silence. However, a few hard-core motormouths may still not get the message. If that happens, you have little choice, but to insist quite bluntly that you be given the opportunity to speak without being interrupted.

Fortunately, there's a positive side to all of this, which is that uncontrollable verbalizers aren't good negotiators, simply because effective two-way communication is required. Therefore, it should be a relative rarity to encounter such people at negotiation sessions. And if you do, their overall negotiating effectiveness is likely to be so limited as to give you a decided advantage during negotiations—assuming you can suffer through the session without losing your composure.

More serious forms of interruption to contend with are those deliberately perpetrated by your counterpart to throw your game plan out of whack. A common irritant is when the other negotiator deliberately interrupts your presentation to immediately try to counter every point you raise. This can be short-circuited simply by pointing out that you are willing to listen to the opposing viewpoint, and expect the same courtesy in return. Incidentally, this sort of constant rebuttal may be a sign of disorganization on the part of your adversary. The interruptions may be geared not so much toward disrupting your thoughts, but rather to defend a weak negotiating position.

Another ploy, as mentioned in section 9.10, is the "power play" visit by someone higher-up in the other organization, aimed at coercing you into moving more quickly toward agreement. Often, this sort of visit is a subtle hint that your superiors will be contacted if an agreement isn't finalized in short order. It's generally accompanied by some form of generic sales pitch emphasizing the importance of the project, and how much the other company is interested in seeing it brought to fruition. The unstated implication is that you're being an unreasonable bottleneck.

A visit by the other negotiator's boss may also signal an attempt to double-team you at the negotiating table. Don't get caught in the trap of letting the second person try to squeeze additional concessions out of you. This is generally attempted by the second person playing the part of the "good cop" (see section 7.1) and appealing to your reasonableness. The plea will be some variation of, "You certainly can move just a little to get this deal done." Of course, this is after the initial negotiator has squeezed you down to your last concession.

The practical approach to dealing with a "power play" interruption is to stand firm. Once it's recognized that you aren't going to be maneuvered, the other side will be more realistic about accepting an agreement that's more to your liking. You can also do a little counter-attacking of your own by announcing that you have a pre-planned departure time, and suggesting that the negotiations can be resumed later at your place of business. Incidentally, the opportunity for power plays is more limited when negotiating sessions are conducted at your home base, which is one more reason to seek a "home court" advantage when you negotiate.

12.4 HOW TO CONTEND WITH BULLYING TACTICS

You may find bullying tactics being employed against you by an opposing negotiator. If it's of a continuing nature from the opening bell of a negotiation meeting, and involves outright hostility, you may have to respond with feigned anger, or a refusal to negotiate unless the behavior ceases. This was covered in section 11.7. However, for the most part, the type of bullying you face will be sporadic, and deliberately pursued by a perfectly rational person in an attempt to gain a negotiating edge.

It helps to counteract attempts to bully you by trying to pinpoint the other negotiator's purpose, and then responding accordingly. Some fairly common reasons for the use of bullying tactics, along with appropriate ways to respond, are as follows:

1. It may be an attempt to steer you away from an area that the other negotiator doesn't want to discuss. This is often the case when you zero in on a weak point in the other side's negotiating position. A sure-fire signal this is happening is when you ask a valid question and, instead of an answer, get an angry and/or sarcastic retort. When this happens, ignore the non-reply and ask your question again. As an alternative, say something such as, "Perhaps my question wasn't clear enough. What I want to know is . . . " If you don't get a satisfactory response the second time around, be emphatic about getting an answer before going on to discuss anything else.

2. Bullying tactics may be employed at the beginning of a negotiation session to test your tenacity. What the other negotiator is looking for is your reaction. If you act submissive in the face of bullying at the outset, you can expect this sort of behavior to continue throughout the course of the negotiations. Therefore, draw your line in the sand right away to let your counterpart know that you won't be shoved around. You might say, "Look, we've got a lot to accomplish here, and it's not going to get done unless we both cooperate. If that's not going to be the case, then we might as well not even get started."

3. Under certain limited conditions, bullying may be used in a deliberate attempt to get you to break off negotiations. This can happen when your opponent doesn't want to continue the negotiations at the present

time, but prefers that the onus for ending the talks be placed upon you. For instance, when a labor negotiation is in the public spotlight, neither side wants to be viewed as the party responsible for breaking off the talks. In situations such as this, when you are forewarned that the other side is attempting to gain some sort of advantage by coercing you into ending negotiations, it pays to hang in there, and force them to play their hand. It may not be pleasant to do so, but then again, the alternatives may be even less desirable.

4. Bullying may be employed near the close of negotiations in an attempt to gain last minute concessions. It pays to be extra cautious when you're nearing agreement after a difficult negotiation. You may not only be tired, but also frustrated at the difficulties encountered along the way. This can leave you particularly vulnerable to the use of anger by the other side. So don't let your guard down until an agreement is reached. Otherwise, you may give away in minutes what you fought long and hard for over the course of the negotiations.

12.5 COUNTERATTACKING INTIMIDATING BEHAVIOR

Aside from bullying tactics, other kinds of intimidating behavior may be directed toward you during the negotiation process. As a general rule, you should ignore intimidating behavior, if that's at all possible. However, always analyze the threat in terms of the probability it will be carried out, as well as the implications for you if it is. Let's look at a few forms of intimidation and the means of neutralizing such threats.

1. Deadlines may be used in a variety of ways as a means of intimidation. One of the most hackneyed customs is to spring some sort of deadline requirement when there is an apparent deadlock in resolving differences in the respective negotiating positions. The scheme is to force you to be the one to make the final concession. This type of gambit usually takes the form of an ultimatum such as, "If we don't wrap this up today, then the deal is dead."

When confronted with such an ultimatum, anyone who resists the urge to panic and give the other side what they're looking for will win this challenge hands down. In the first place, these deadlines are usually shallow to begin with. Who, in their right mind, is going to throw away a deal they want by walking away at the last minute? Furthermore, if there were genuine reasons for a deadline, you would have heard about them before the negotiations even began.

Therefore, the best approach for coping with this tactic is to play right along with it. In fact, if you use a little bit of finesse, you might have your opponent wishing the subject hadn't been raised. To do this, when the deadline ultimatum is issued, give a response that's as close to glee as you can get without looking foolish. By doing this, you're sending a message that you're not that anxious to do business, which is just the opposite of the panicky plea that your adversary is looking for.

This kind of response signals that your last offer was it, and therefore, the other side had better move toward your position if they want a deal. To be extra convincing, take some action that indicates you are leaving. For instance, ask your counterpart if someone can make plane reservations for you. Here, as with other forms of intimidation, the one who generally wins is the one who cares the least—or at least is able to convey that impression to the other side. There's no room for timidity when it comes to countering intimidation attempts. In fact, the minute the other negotiating party sees that you won't be stampeded is the point when intimidation attempts will cease.

2. A garden-variety intimidation gimmick is for a negotiator to threaten to do business with the competition. This is frequently used to coerce someone into agreeing with what would otherwise be unacceptable terms. A variation of this theme is to threaten to perform the work in-house. Here again is what generally constitutes an oversold threat. If they were going to do business with the competition, or do the work themselves, they wouldn't be wasting time and money negotiating with you.

For the most part, these are idle threats made to squeeze a better deal out of you. The best response is a simple, "Suit yourself." If you express any indication of concern, you're inviting the other negotiator to press you harder for concessions. Having the confidence to resist these threats is part of the process of getting the deal you want—not the deal the other side wants you to accept.

3. A somewhat trickier type of intimidation to deal with is the assertion by your counterpart that some people within his organization are opposed to the deal being negotiated. This problem takes the form of statements such as, "Our product engineering people are working against this deal." It's by no means uncommon for factions within an organization to have opposing viewpoints. However, if a project has gone as far as the negotiation stage, it's obvious that the opposing faction lost the power struggle. Hence, it's highly unlikely that the deal would be canceled at the last moment. So this sort of claim is

merely useful fodder for negotiators to use in trying to secure better terms at the bargaining table. Therefore, don't be panicked into cutting a bad deal, because of a fear of the project being scuttled. Actually, if there is an internal power struggle, the proponents of the project will be anxious to see the deal go through, which works to strengthen—not weaken—your negotiating position.

Besides the more common intimidation practices typically associated with business transactions, are those utilized in specialized negotiation situations. These can range from strike threats during labor negotiations, to saber-rattling on the international negotiation front. In fact, the possibilities for intimidation are limited only by the imagination of negotiators intent on finding ways to intimidate the opposition. Nevertheless, whatever the subject matter may be, the best protection against these practices is simply a steadfast refusal to be intimidated.

12.6 KNOWING WHEN TO POUNCE ON AN OPPONENT

When your opponent engages in intimidation and other negative tactics, it's important to cut this behavior short early on in the negotiation process. Otherwise, it becomes more difficult to control. In fact, any type of ploy should be challenged promptly, since even if you don't fully succeed in halting such practices, your adversary will know you're not an easy mark.

Nevertheless, you shouldn't overreact to every tactic that doesn't meet with your approval. If you tactfully suggest that your counterpart's actions aren't likely to lead to an early and amicable agreement, and the response is simply denial, along with a continuation of the objectionable practices, don't provoke further confrontation. That is, unless the behavior is outrageous and irresponsible to the extent that it can't be tolerated.

First of all, what you're seeing may represent the personality traits and/or standard negotiating style of your opponent. Consequently, your objections—no matter how vehement—may have little or no impact. Furthermore, as long as you recognize the tactics being employed for what they are, you can successfully work around them. In addition, persistently admonishing your opponent about a negotiation table tactic you consider to be unreasonable, may have unforeseen results. For instance, the objectionable practice may cease, but your adversary may then resort to one or more retaliatory practices such as:

- Nitpicking everything you say or do.
- Reverting to other undesirable tactics which aren't as easy to recognize.

- Being vague or reticent about answering your questions.
- Accusing you of using unfair tactics.
- Becoming generally more difficult to deal with.

Therefore, in dealing with objectionable negotiation tactics, although it's useful to register your displeasure, it's equally important to refrain from transforming them into the dominant issue under discussion. You can't choose your negotiating foes, so although you may find certain practices distasteful, don't let your objections deter you from reaching your negotiation objectives.

12.7 TURNING THREATS TO YOUR ADVANTAGE

You may encounter threats of one sort or another during the negotiation process. They can range from the relatively insignificant, to the ultimate scare tactic, which is breaking off negotiations without any deal being struck. However, despite the menacing posture that threats pose, they aren't always as intimidating as they seem.

To begin with, it's a quantum leap from making a threat to carrying it out. For example, following through with a threat and ending negotiations involves a lost deal for both parties—not just the party being threatened. That is, of course, unless the negotiation is so one-sided that the threatening party never had anything much to lose. And if that's the case, the recipient of the threat shouldn't have been negotiating in the first place.

Furthermore, the possibility of unsuccessful negotiations should have been factored into your pre-negotiation planning. Therefore, although they may be less desirable, you should have other alternatives available if the negotiation is unsuccessful. As a result, a threat of "no deal" shouldn't propel you into pushing the panic button, and accepting unreasonable terms and conditions.

In fact, the best method for disarming such a threat is to be cavalier about it. An obvious lack of concern about a threat to break off negotiations forces the other party to either back off, or follow through with the threat and end negotiations. Since the latter entails far greater risks than continuing to negotiate, in most instances it's not likely to happen. Instead, the other negotiator will just keep on negotiating, perhaps still huffing and puffing about ending discussions right down to the satisfactory conclusion of an agreement. However, once the initial threat hasn't been carried out, the tactical advantage switches to you, since the other side has tacitly acknowledged its reluctance to let the deal go down the drain.

As far as the specifics of dealing with a threat when it's first made, you can either (1) ignore it, and continue the discussions, (2) respond by acknowledging it as the other negotiator's prerogative, or (3) counterattack with a veiled threat of your own. Let's look at each of these possibilities individually.

1. When someone threatens to break off negotiations, you can simply continue on with the discussions as if the threat wasn't even made. This forces your opponent to repeat the threat, but this may not happen. The reason is that by ignoring the threat you're sending a signal that you either don't take it seriously, and/or don't care whether or not the negotiations come to an end. This may give the other negotiator pause about repeating the threat if it's just a ploy that's not intended to be carried out. Your nonchalance shows the threat isn't likely to work, while continuing the discussions lets your counterpart avoid the embarrassment of having to back off if the threat is repeated and rebuffed.

2. You can choose to force the other negotiator to bite the bullet by responding with resignation when the threat is made. For instance, say something such as, "Look Ms. Marple, if you want to call it quits, that's your choice. I have no intention of accepting unreasonable terms just to complete this deal." Your opponents then have the option of ending the negotiation, or continuing the discussions, but in any event, if they were bluffing, they now know you have called them on it.

3. Yet another alternative for coping with a negotiation-ending threat is to reply with a little intimidation of your own. The specific course it takes will be based upon the facts of the negotiation you're participating in. However, from a general standpoint, it's useful to respond with escalating demands related to the alleged reason why the other negotiator is threatening to walk out. For instance, if your counterpart is threatening to scuttle everything because you won't agree to accept certain delivery dates, offer to do so, but increase your costs to a level that would either compensate you accordingly, or make it impractical for your opponent to accept.

Any threat made at the negotiation table is usually designed to exact some form of concession from you. It essentially is a last resort ploy to win with intimidation what couldn't be won with reasoned arguments. The ability to overcome this tactic is commensurate with your willingness to run the risk that the threat will be carried out. Of course, your opponent is banking upon your inability to resist the pressure.

In point of fact, people don't always stand their ground, and instead capitulate to the demands of a negotiating opponent. Depending upon the circumstances, this "less may be more" approach to negotiating can't be arbitrarily condemned. In the final analysis, if you can live with the end result, and it's the best available alternative, then that may be the appropriate way to go.

That decision can only be made by the negotiator—not by armchair critics who delight in telling you how they could have gotten a better deal.

12.8 HOW TO ENJOY PLAYING A BROKEN RECORD

No matter what sort of tactics your negotiation opponents employ, one of the keys to holding your own is to be persistent. If you keep playing the same refrain long enough, the opposing negotiator will eventually conclude that you're not going to give in on certain points. As a result, you will get the concessions you want or at least force the other side to propose alternatives you can live with.

Naturally, you just can't persist in playing a broken record on everything that's in dispute. Therefore, be selective about doing it, otherwise the opposing negotiator will justifiably conclude that you're being unreasonable. Nevertheless, always stand your ground when an adversary is trying to poke holes in your position. If you start to waffle by responding with comments such as "maybe," or "possibly," you are just encouraging a continuing assault on the issues you're trying to defend.

You should strive to be persistent without giving the appearance of being stubborn. Use factual arguments to defend your position whenever possible. However, there will come a time when you will exhaust your supply of fresh facts, and then have to resort to reiterating the key points over and over. The trick is to keep emphasizing the same point from differing angles. Although every fact situation will differ, let's look at a sample of how this can be done.

Background

Alicia M. is negotiating a lease for retail space with Alan B. She wants certain alterations to be made, which he is resisting.

Discussion

Alan: "For what you're going to be paying, it's just not economical for me to make any changes to the property."

Alicia: "I'm going to be paying you a percentage of gross profits, so anything you do to improve the store will increase the returns to you."

Alan: "There's no guarantee that will happen."

Alicia: "It's common sense that the design of a store impacts sales."

Alan: "I'd be taking all the risk. If your business doesn't succeed, I'd be out the cost of renovations, and would have to make further changes to lease the space again."

Alicia: "My clientele will follow me from my present location. That benefits you from increased customer traffic throughout the mall."

Alan: "Look, why don't we put it in the contract as a leasehold improvement. You can foot the bill yourself for the renovations."

Alicia: "For what I'm paying you should do it. Besides, if I stay where I am, the owner promises to make the renovations I want."

Alan: "Yeah, but what kind of foot traffic do you get where you are now? Besides, the mall adds prestige."

Alicia: "Speaking of prestige, look at what you're getting. Everyone in the city thinks of Alicia's Fashions as the premiere trend-setter."

Alan: "It's just too expensive. I can lease to someone else without the added expense."

Alicia: "You can't find anyone else who will upgrade the mall's image like I can."

Alan: "It's just not doable for the terms I'm giving you."

Alicia: "Well, I have to have the improvements. If not, I'll just have to stay put a year until the new mall is ready down the avenue. Incidentally, those folks told me I could have my space set up just like I want."

Alan: "Alright already. You wore me down. Let's get this agreement signed off."

The way to persist is to continuously counter every objection from a new angle as in the example. However, when that well has been run dry just steadfastly refuse to budge. The end result may be an opposing negotiator silently classifying you as a "stubborn @#$%¢," but that's a small price to pay for getting your way.

12.9 WHY BOOZE AND BARGAINS DON'T MIX

Any prudent person knows that alcohol inhibits the ability to make sound judgments. Nevertheless, socializing—apart from drinking—can have a sensible side within a negotiation context. On many occasions, lunch or dinner can provide the forum for quietly settling major sticking points that couldn't be resolved within a formal negotiation setting.

A negotiation meeting brings together people with both divergent viewpoints and differing personalities. There is also a good deal of posturing done by negotiators on both sides of the table. The causes can be varied, but a frequent contributor to this is a perceived need to assure team members, as well as behind-the-scenes power brokers, that the negotiator is in command of the situation. There may even be different viewpoints represented at the bargaining table by members of the same team. Finally, the sheer number of people in attendance at some negotiation meetings can make reaching agreement a difficult task at best.

As a consequence, key points are often better discussed and resolved by the two negotiation team leaders in a quiet atmosphere away from the crowd. Therefore, it's generally advantageous to either extend and/or accept a luncheon or dinner invitation with your negotiating counterpart. The one thing to beware of is letting your guard down by the consumption of one drink too many. Whenever you're associating with any member of the other negotiating team, or for that matter anyone else within their organization, it's wise to play your cards close to your vest. If your opposite number decides to toss the drinks down, there's no purpose to be served by you doing likewise. And if your opposite number does get drunk, there's little point in discussing anything of substance, since it's not likely to be remembered anyway.

Incidentally, along with the careful consumption of alcohol, it makes sense to be well rested in general during negotiations. You may run into an opponent who concentrates on simply wearing you down as a means of achieving negotiation objectives. So get plenty of rest the day or two preceding an important negotiation, and try to avoid marathon bargaining sessions if it's at all possible to do so.

Chapter 13

NEGOTIATION POINTERS FOR SPECIAL SITUATIONS

Many specialized areas have additional negotiation requirements beyond those in routine business transactions. These include everything from the formality under which negotiations take place to the goals of the parties involved. Of course, with the wide scope of negotiation activity that occurs, it's impossible to address every field in depth. On the other hand, certain nuances common to specialized areas in which negotiations take place can't be ignored.

For example, it's necessary to know the proper techniques to use when negotiating with banks, hiring consultants, or bargaining with agents and other third parties. And it's impossible to ignore the many aspects of negotiating with employees, either directly, or with their union representatives. The increasing importance of international negotiations, the relative formality of dealing with government agencies, and the specialized nature of real estate negotiations also need to be addressed.

Then, there are other business-related areas of negotiation which sometimes get overlooked. If you have ever struggled over justifying a budget request, you know how significant this seemingly routine function can be. Finally, whenever you negotiate with suppliers and/or customers there are factors far beyond getting the best deal that shouldn't be forgotten. This chapter discusses many of the special considerations that are fundamental to negotiating successfully in these areas.

13.1 BARGAINING WITH BANKS—IT'S NOT AS HARD AS YOU THINK

Business executives like to grumble and growl about bankers. After all, when a hot deal is seemingly bogged-down by paperwork, and an endless string of loan restrictions, who else is to blame? Surprisingly, more often than not, the problem doesn't originate with the bank, but rather with the attitude of business people toward their banking relationship.

When it comes to negotiating with banks, you have to look beyond the current deal, and assess the potential for a mutually rewarding relationship over the long haul. All too often, picking a bank to do business with receives less thought than what kind of seasoning to have with a salad. Initial bank selection may result from convenience, today's low rate on a loan, or cousin Clara's recommendation—which is the bank she works for. Naturally, any of these items can be valid considerations, but the process isn't quite that simple if you're seeking long-term success.

There are a number of details that should be explored if you're searching for the "right" bank for your business. These include investigating the financial status of any bank before you start doing business with them. A good banking relationship goes both ways. So just as a banker is rightly interested in your financial status, you too should familiarize yourself with the bank's condition.

Although the faint of heart may be reluctant to ask a banker, "How sound is your bank?," the advantages justify summoning up the courage to do just that. In the first place, it demonstrates some degree of financial sophistication on your part, which may well impress a banker. Furthermore, if a banker isn't too anxious to address the question, then you shouldn't be in a hurry to do business with that particular bank.

In addition, it's important to work with a bank that's a good fit for your business. All things considered, you're better off with a bank where you'll be a major customer, rather than a "small fish in a big pond." This doesn't necessarily mean avoiding larger banks if you run a small business, particularly if the bank encourages and works closely with smaller commercial accounts.

It's also useful to acquaint yourself with everyone you can at a bank, particularly senior people who may sit on loan committees. Of course, personalities won't—or at least shouldn't—get a loan approved if the facts and figures aren't there, but they can certainly help tip the scales in borderline cases.

Getting to know as much as possible about a bank before you start doing business with them is only part of the equation for a successful merging of interests. Your obligations include, not only familiarizing the bank with the nuts and bolts of your own business at the start, but also keeping them appraised as part of an on-going process.

As you work with your bank, make sure that required financial reports are furnished promptly. But don't stop there. Meet with bank officials on a regular basis, and keep them advised on the current state of the business—both good news and bad. This improves your credibility which can help if your business hits a snag.

The flip side of the coin is that if a bank has to hound you for information, or is led to believe that you're less than forthright, the suspicion may arise that the business isn't doing well. And that's not the type of framework to operate in. In this regard, if a problem does crop-up in meeting loan payments, it's easier to work out if the bank has been on board from the beginning.

Keeping your banker well-informed has other advantages. Loans are made based on risk assessment, which has led to the overworked cliche about bankers only wanting to lend money to folks who don't need it. However, although the financial status of your business is the primary factor in assessing risk when you need a loan, your credibility in dealing with the bank also comes into play. So being diligent about on-going communication with your banker provides the foundation for the bank to move fast when you need a loan approved in a hurry. And that alone is reason enough to expend the extra effort in working closely with your bank.

NOTE: Whether you're negotiating with a bank, labor union, supplier, customer, or any other individual or organization, it's important to carefully consider all aspects of the relationship. All too often, too much emphasis is placed on short-term deal-making, to the exclusion of long-term interests. Success in the long run doesn't result from any one deal, but from a process of establishing and sustaining successful business partnerships across a broad spectrum.

This is a lesson that's sometimes lost in the urge to secure the best deal possible at the negotiating table. What's forgotten is that the best deal over the long haul may mean accepting less than you could get on any one agreement. This is particularly true when one party is in the position of being able to virtually dictate the terms of the agreement. Bankers are particularly vulnerable to the charge of using a position of strength to impose unrealistic terms on business borrowers. However, even if such perceptions are valid—and there are enough bad loans afloat to dispute it—bankers are by no means the only culprits.

13.2 SIMPLE STRATEGIES FOR NEGOTIATING A LOAN

If you wanted to identify one area of negotiations where one party thought they were at a decided disadvantage from the start, the role of borrower might fit the bill. Most borrowers feel they have little or no leverage when it comes to applying for a bank loan. Nevertheless, despite the seemingly one-sided nature of such transactions, the handicap isn't as great as it appears to be. And by adopting the proper negotiating strategy, you can come away with a better deal than you anticipated going in.

For starters, you should follow the prescription in the preceding section for learning as much as possible about a bank before you attempt to do any business with them. On a more specific level, when it comes down to obtaining a loan, the most significant person you will deal with at the bank is your loan officer. This is the person who matters most in developing a good working relationship with your bank. Actually, getting to know something about the loan officer's method of operations is best done before you commit to doing business with a bank. The type of information that can prove helpful includes:

- Do you think your personalities will mesh? You'll be dealing with this person on a regular basis, so this isn't just a trivial nicety.

- Does the loan officer have experience in making loans to your type of business? If so, your performance is likely to be compared with that of comparable companies within your industry. If not, you will have a lot more educating to do in regard to the specifics of your business operation.

- What is the extent of the loan officer's authority? If you're working with a relatively junior person, the ability to make loan commitments may be pretty limited. If that's the case, then it's wise to assess how competent the individual will be in presenting your application to a loan committee.

- Is the loan officer sincerely interested in learning about your business? The more knowledge the banker has, the better the chances for getting the loan approved.

TIP: Incidentally, if you have a loan officer who moves on to another job, don't idly assume that the new officer has been thoroughly briefed on the intricacies of your business. Even if that's true, seeing is believing, so take the time to make sure the replacement is up to speed about how your business operates.

Educating the bank about your business operation is a key to obtaining favorable terms on a loan. The nature of your business, as well as the industry you're in, are indicators of the business risk the bank will be taking. In terms of preparing your loan proposal, also be specific about (1) the purpose of the loan, (2) the amount of funds needed, and (3) how you intend to repay the loan.

The banker will ask for various supporting documents to assist in evaluating your proposal. Be both cooperative and prompt in complying with these requests. Otherwise, it may be assumed you're either hiding something, or not particularly organized. The biggest handicap a loan brings—other than finding a way to repay it—are the restrictions contained in the loan agreement. Fortunately, this is also the area where you have some latitude to negotiate.

Rank all of the restrictions the bank wants in terms of your priorities. Then, agree to those that you can most readily live with, and try to trade off acceptance of those for other proposed restrictions that you find to be less desirable. In addition, look for areas where you can suggest even tighter restrictions than the bank asked for, in exchange for deleting some other provision you don't want. However, don't do this haphazardly, since you don't want to make things more difficult than they already are.

Obviously, the better the prospects of the loan being repaid, the less stringent the restrictions should be. However, that won't necessarily be true if you're not prepared to argue your case. So don't be bashful about making your position clear. Dealing with banks, as with any other negotiation, shouldn't be done with your hat in your hand. Incidentally, it doesn't hurt to let the bank think they have competition for your business when you get down to the nitty-gritty of negotiating loan terms. That may not get you everything you want, but it may well get you better terms than you could otherwise expect.

13.3 LABOR UNION NEGOTIATIONS—SEEKING THE MIDDLE GROUND

Labor-management contract negotiation is a highly specialized area requiring in-depth knowledge of labor law in general, and NLRB (National Labor Relations Board) procedures in particular. Therefore, advice and counsel of experts should be sought in these matters. However, from a general standpoint, there are several unique aspects of labor negotiations that influence bargaining strategy, and therefore can't be ignored. These are:

1. First and foremost is the fact that careless actions on the part of management can influence the stance of unions at the bargaining table. These negatives that can do nothing other than stiffen the position of union negotiators cover the spectrum from the executive suite to first-line supervision. For instance, fat bonuses and pay raises at the executive level run contra to a contract bargaining strategy that pleads union wages have to be held down because of poor profits. And first-line supervisors who adopt a hard-line adversarial stance

with union workers only serve to encourage "us versus them" attitudes by the union rank and file. These and similar practices tend to make the bargaining at contract renewal time more difficult. Therefore, management policy and practices should always be viewed in light of their potential impact on labor negotiations.

2. Managers should recognize that union leadership and rank and file goals may not be synonymous. Furthermore, there may even be sharp differences of opinion within the rank and file itself. For example, those members with seniority may place a priority on pay raises, while newer members may be more concerned with job security. These diverse viewpoints can present both opportunity, as well as problems, during contract negotiations.

3. Trade-offs can be used effectively to obtain long-term goals at the expense of short-term concessions. For instance, to obtain productivity gains, it may be beneficial to trade increased economic benefits in exchange for the removal of contract provisions that restrict management flexibility.

4. Although in the typical business negotiation, it's prudent to be as specific as possible in setting forth the agreed-upon terms in the contract, this isn't necessarily so with labor contracts. For instance, loosely written language covering factors such as job assignments and so forth, can provide supervisors with greater flexibility in managing their units. Nevertheless, the down side is that ambiguous language may lead to more difficulty in contract administration, and a greater number of grievances.

From a general point of view, it behooves both unions and management to seek common ground in their negotiations. With worldwide competition prevalent, bitterly adversarial union/management relations can no longer prevail if companies are to compete successfully, and also provide the job security that workers cherish. Labor relations is a field where done deals are only good until the next time around. Therefore, the necessity for working together is far more acute than the typical business transaction. Unfortunately, labor negotiations in the past have generally been far more adversarial than win/win in their philosophy.

13.4 PARRYING SALARY DEMANDS AND OTHER PERSONNEL ISSUES

An unenlightened manager might conclude that negotiating with employees simply consists of learning twenty different ways to say "No." However, that sort of attitude certainly isn't conducive to recruiting and retaining a productive work force. So, although a boss/subordinate relationship may be the ultimate position of strength in terms of negotiating power, it's sensible not to take advantage of this fact.

Probably the most common and perplexing negotiating issue with employees is the subject of salary. There are two broad categories of potential problems in this area. The first consists of employees who because of job performance and/or special expertise deserve the pay raise they are seeking—or at least more than they're being offered. Nevertheless, the requests can't be granted due to salary limitation restraints, or any of a number of other factors. The second category is represented by employees who have an inflated view of their value—a not uncommon phenomenon, which you may have had the misfortune to encounter on more than one occasion.

Naturally, your primary concern will be those people who have what constitutes a reasonable request, even though for one reason or another you're unable to grant it. These are often seat-squirming encounters, since you're dealing with people you don't want to lose. Unfortunately for you, especially if the circumstances are such that the employee can readily command more money elsewhere, you may have your back to the wall because of an inability to meet the employee's salary demands.

Many managers approach this sort of situation with a feeling of resignation, and resort to responding to such requests with some form of platitude such as, "I'd like to help you out Jane, but my hands are tied." Alternatively, vague promises are made for the future, which may or may not pan out. The first approach is tacitly accepting defeat, while imprecise promises may only be postponing the inevitable, since the employee will either leave or become unproductive if the raise doesn't come through in the future. Therefore, it's a cardinal rule to refrain from making promises that can't be kept.

The only practical way to resolve this sort of problem is to use a little creativity in coming up with satisfactory alternatives to granting the pay raise. Employees, even though they would obviously prefer the money, can accept valid reasons why it can't be granted if you level with them. If you then are able to offer them some form of non-monetary benefit, the odds are that you may well be able to retain a highly prized employee.

All kinds of incentives are possible, ranging from a new office, or more flexible working hours, to greater job responsibilities and/or a new job title. Incidentally, if you're faced with salary policy problems which are preventing you from giving a worker a pay raise, creating a new job with added duties may be the solution. This sort of dilemma is common when you have someone who has reached the ceiling of the salary range for the position.

A less crucial—but possibly more perplexing problem to deal with—concerns employees who are asking for pay raises that aren't warranted based on their job performance and/or comparable salaries for the position in question. But even when you're not dealing with a star performer, adequate replacements aren't always easy to find. Furthermore, an employee with any length of time on the job can represent a substantial investment to an employer. In addition, there are the costs involved in hiring and training replacements. Consequently, other than an outright dud, it's beneficial to retain these people.

Negotiating these folks out of their salary demands starts with pinpointing why they think a pay raise is justified. The responses given typically center around (1) similar jobs elsewhere pay more, (2) seniority, (3) comparisons with other people, or, (4) job performance. Let's look at these one-by-one:

1. Shooting down pay requests based on comparisons with other companies requires getting at the facts. In many cases, the employee has erroneous information, or isn't comparing similar jobs and duties. Frequently, indirect compensation in the form of fringe benefits isn't taken into account. In short, use factual comparisons to show the employee why the pay raise request isn't justified.

2. When employees give you a seniority argument, point out that pay is primarily based on performance, and the salary they are presently getting is based on, not only their present performance, but also their performance over time. Prove this by pointing out what the starting salary for the position they occupy is, in comparison to what the employee is earning. Obviously, someone coming to you with a seniority-based pay raise argument is probably substantially above the base for that position.

3. When workers confront you with pay raise requests, allegedly justified by making comparisons with other people, either inside or outside the company, don't get drawn into a comparison debate. Some of these requests are grounded on nothing more solid than cocktail party conversations. In any event, promptly let the employee know that the discussion will center on the employee's salary and performance; not some unknown phenom working someplace else, or a co-worker who the employee thinks is being overcompensated.

4. Many pay raise requests simply result from workers' inflated opinions of their performance. Although, you should be positive in setting the record straight, don't hesitate to point out where improvement is needed.

In general, when pay raise or promotion requests must be turned down, always try to be specific in telling employees what they have to do, to improve their chances in the future. Often you will find, that if you tell an employee certain training is required, the employee will never follow through and pursue this requirement. In fact, this lack of motivation may be a primary reason why you are turning them down in the first place.

The advantage of outlining specifics is two-fold. It gives those people with potential the motivation to pursue what needs to be done to improve their skills. On the other hand, those not so motivated won't follow your suggestions, and you will have a ready reply the next time they make a pay raise and/or job promotion pitch.

TIP: You will typically run into a few ladder climbers who bounce from job to job for an increase in pay, never really staying in one spot long enough to justify their worth. Don't waste a lot of time in explaining to these people why another pay raise isn't in order. If they aren't getting the raise, they will move on somewhere else anyway, since they're interested only in the money, not in any other form of non-monetary compensation you might give them. Instead, concentrate your efforts on rewarding those who will reciprocate with loyalty and teamwork any efforts you make on their behalf.

13.5 NEGOTIATING WITH FEDERAL, STATE, AND LOCAL GOVERNMENTS

Negotiating with agencies at any level of government can be a frustrating experience for the uninitiated. First and foremost, it requires a mastery of a complex maze of laws, rules, and regulations. Furthermore, even though government requirements for goods and services constitute a seemingly endless source of potential business, the competition is both intense and unpredictable.

For example, it's not unknown for a government agency to cancel a procurement during the bidding process. Procurements can be halted for any number of reasons, including changed requirements, protests by potential bidders, or simply lack of funding. That's not a pleasant prospect if you have spent thousands of dollars working on a proposal that may wind-up in the waste basket.

Then, of course, there are the wider implications of the politics of doing business with government agencies. For instance, the impact of world events, and/or legislative opposition to a project can realign or eliminate even the largest of programs. And on the local level, concerted efforts by only a handful of opponents can scuttle even the most basic and seemingly noncontroversial project. Consequently, doing business with government at any level isn't the highway to heaven that some people envision. In fact, for those who plunge ahead in pursuit of government business without first assessing the potential risks and rewards, it can seem more like a pothole filled journey on the road to ruin.

Another important element to consider before you pursue government business is what happens after you are successful in winning a contract. Compliance with the detailed requirements of government contracts can be both burdensome and costly. Every bureaucracy has auditors, inspectors, and contracting personnel to ensure that government requirements are complied with. In fact, a company performing on its first government contract might easily conclude that all of these people are assigned to monitor that one particular project.

You may also discover that your operating systems and procedures run afoul of government regulations. Non-conformance can range from accounting systems to security procedures to quality assurance methods. All of these issues pinpoint the potential problems that can differentiate government business from commercial sales. So, before you seek a piece of the government pie, you better be sure that it's easily digestible by your business.

No matter what level of government you hope to do business with, there are several fundamentals to follow once you have more than a passing interest in a particular project. These are:

1. Identify the key government people involved in the decision-making process. The best source for specific details about a project are the program managers and technical specialists who establish the requirements for a procurement. Getting to know these people will give you a clearer picture of what's needed to compete effectively. This isn't always easy, and it requires legwork, but if you're successful any bid/ no-bid decision will be a lot easier.

2. Learn the technical and administrative requirements that apply. Both the technical specifications, and the administrative details should be clearly understood before you decide to participate in the bidding process. Otherwise, you may later discover that complying with all of the boilerplate provisions in your contract can be costly.

3. Pinpoint the nuances of the government agency you're dealing with— both procedural and political. Every government office operates differently—even within the same level of government, and when subject to the same rules and regulations governing contract awards. Knowing these subtleties can save a lot of headaches caused by assuming that Branch "A" operates the same as Branch "B" just because they are both divisions of Agency "C."

4. Evaluate your chances of winning the award. For instance, is there real competition, or is the project essentially wired for one company, with competitive proposals being solicited merely to comply with legal and/or administrative requirements?

5. Assess the prospects for future business. You might have intentions of bidding on a project, even though it's essentially unprofitable, with the intent of positioning yourself to receive more lucrative business in the future. Be careful though since, for example, the contract you're getting may be a one-shot deal that's being awarded with the purpose of extracting more favorable terms from an existing contractor when future awards are forthcoming.

CAUTION: Even if you aren't directly involved in the government marketplace, you may be a first or lower tier subcontractor under a government contract. As a result, the government requirements imposed on the prime may be passed on to you in the subcontract. Therefore, don't assume that life will be easier because you're dealing with a commercial customer, rather than directly with a government agency.

13.6 THE NUANCES OF INTERNATIONAL NEGOTIATIONS

Doing business in the international marketplace has never been easy, and every change in the political landscape only complicates matters further. Nevertheless, those who take the time to prepare themselves beforehand can be as successful in Munich as they are on Main Street. However, the importance of negotiation preparations take on an added dimension when bargaining is to be done on an international level. Not only will you have to contend with cultural differences, but bargaining styles themselves can reflect these variances. What it all boils down to is expending the necessary effort to overcome any barriers that exist.

Among the factors to consider when negotiations will be conducted with companies and/or individuals in other countries are:

- Plan where negotiations will be held. Even if negotiations are held at home, it's worthwhile to visit the other parties' location for familiarization purposes.
- Overcome language barriers. Even if you know the other party speaks English, others may be at negotiation meetings who do not. Therefore, it's generally prudent to have someone on your negotiation team who can serve as a translator.
- Acquaint yourself with the country's customs. You don't have to become an expert, but you should know enough to avoid offending someone.

- Know the cultural differences, particularly as they relate to negotiation practices. This isn't a minor matter, since factors such as the degree of formality/informality at meetings, authority of the negotiator, and the extent of socializing, are among the many elements that vary from culture to culture.
- Research the company you're dealing with. This takes on even greater importance in international negotiations than it does domestically. For one thing, you want to be doubly sure of the ethics of the other party since it's difficult at best to pursue legal remedies in foreign courts.
- Whenever possible, have agreements interpreted according to United States law.
- Be courteous and accept local business protocol. When socializing, refrain from discussing business, unless the other party initiates the discussions.

TIP: When negotiating with nationals of non-English speaking countries, even though the other party speaks English, it can be advantageous to suggest the meeting be conducted in that person's native tongue. This appears to be imposing an unnecessary handicap on yourself, but there are several advantages to be gained in doing this. First of all, it serves as a solid trust-building gesture. It also prevents the other party from later alleging misunderstandings because the negotiations were conducted in English. Finally, it gives you more time to think during discussions as you wait for translations to take place.

13.7 SPECIAL ASPECTS OF REAL ESTATE NEGOTIATIONS

There are certain facets of negotiating real estate transactions that differ somewhat from other fields. First of all, real estate negotiations are greatly influenced by local issues. The location of the property determines such issues as local taxes, ordinances, as well as the very value of the property, which, of course, will fluctuate in accordance with local market conditions.

As a result, a business considering the purchase of property in an unfamiliar geographic area should have a local real estate expert on the negotiation team in a consulting capacity. Not only can this person furnish the fundamental details pertaining to the local area, but he or she can also be invaluable as a general information resource.

For instance, a company being offered a package of relocation incentives usually has little or no knowledge of local politics. Yet, if the incentives being offered require any form of governmental action, it's prudent to have a sound assessment of whether or not governmental approval will be forthcoming. In short, the details of relocation incentive packages offered by communities should be carefully nailed down beforehand.

Incidentally, a company considering relocation should carefully analyze all aspects of the move, and avoid being overwhelmed by an attractive property and tax package. A relocation is a long-term proposition, and today's hot location may be tomorrow's depressed area. Furthermore, such factors as low property taxes are subject to change. This is especially true in rapidly growing areas where current low tax rates may have to be raised in the future to pay for infrastructure needs such as new roads, schools, and so forth.

Another important aspect of real estate negotiations is that every property is different. As a result, emotion often plays an important role which manifests itself in the form of statements such as, "I've got to have that piece of property." In real estate, probably more than any other field, sellers play to that sentiment. It's a rare real estate transaction that doesn't have the seller and/or the seller's agent implying that another buyer is waiting in the wings.

Consequently, sound negotiation strategy dictates that you don't appear to be too anxious. Let it be known, that the property under consideration is only one of several alternatives being considered. In addition, for many business purposes, such as building new facilities, plant expansions, and the like, there generally isn't the degree of urgency attached that requires immediate action. This is especially true if your company has adequate long-term strategic plans. Therefore, it's prudent to plan your moves around the fluctuations in local real estate conditions.

13.8 HIRING EXPERTS—AGREEMENTS THAT SHOULD BE PINNED DOWN

There are two main considerations in hiring consultants and other experts. The first is finding the right consultant for the task at hand, and the second is setting up an agreement to specifically identify the terms and conditions of the assignment. The fact is, that just like any other profession, consultants come in all shapes, sizes, and degrees of expertise. And since outside experts are hired and entrusted with assignments that can have far reaching consequences, it makes sense to exercise care when you're seeking guidance for your company.

How do you go about finding the right expert? The best way is a referral from trusted business associates. Other alternatives include recommendations from trade associations or industry groups that you belong to. Actually, finding a consultant is the easy part. It's finding the best one for you that requires a little bit of digging.

Incidentally, the best use of outside experts is to prevent future difficulties, not to solve existing problems. Folks often like to see how deep a hole they can dig for themselves before looking for advice. But remember, consultants are experts in their field—not miracle workers.

When interviewing consultants, avoid "formula fixers" who have a standard solution that's recommended to solve every problem. In addition, safeguard against the "recommend a solution and run" approach by establishing in advance that the consultant will assist in implementing any recommendations that are made.

Always take the time to investigate the credibility and expertise of consultants before you hire them. Remember, you want a problem solver—not a report writer. It's also important that your personalities mesh, so ask yourself if you can work with a particular individual.

Most important of all, always draw up a detailed agreement specifying what the consultant will do, what resources you will furnish, and who will work on the job. The last point shouldn't be treated casually, especially if you're dealing with a large consulting firm. This is one area that can cause unnecessary conflict and dissatisfaction with consultants.

For instance, you may assume that "Eric Erudite," a leading expert in his field, will be doing the work. Later, it's discovered that newly minted MBAs are actually assigned to solve the problems. That, in fact, may be a reasonable approach, if they are working under the guidance of an expert. However, to be certain of whom you're getting—and paying for—list the key personnel who will be doing the work in your agreement.

In addition, try to establish a specific time frame for finishing any assignment. Open-ended time frames mean on-going expenses, as well as less incentive to solve the problem. Nevertheless, be sure to allow enough time to do the job right, since switching consultants in midstream is like trying to change a tire on a moving car.

The following questions should be adequately answered whenever you're considering hiring consultants:

- Why do you need an expert?
- Do you have in-house expertise that could do the job?
- Will hiring outside experts create internal conflict?
- Has the consultant under consideration completed this type of project before?
- Have you checked the consultant's performance with prior clients?

- Can you agree on a set fee for the work? If not, and the fee is open-ended, can milestones be established for periodic review?
- Will the consultant provide implementation support and follow-up?
- How much authority will the consultant have?

Finally, don't neglect the subject of fees whenever you're hiring outside expertise. There's a lot of competition out there, so negotiate as good a deal as you can. But equally important is to recognize that consulting cost containment is an on-going proposition.

As a minimum, any billing should show what the billing is for, the number of hours billed, and the level of the people who performed the work. Beyond that, your employees should be instructed to work closely with outside experts to minimize downtime. It is, after all, a little unfair to gripe about the size of consulting fees when the consultant's time—and your money—are being eaten up by internal bottlenecks.

13.9 BARGAINING WITH AGENTS AND OTHER THIRD PARTIES

Another wrinkle is added to the negotiation process when you are dealing with an agent or some other third party who is representing a client. From a general standpoint, there are positive and negative aspects to this form of bargaining. On the bright side, it's usually more efficient to deal with agents, since they are experienced negotiators, and have a working knowledge of the particular field they specialize in. On the other hand, this very expertise enables agents to cut better deals than the client would otherwise obtain—which you end up paying for. So to the extent that agents can make your life easier, they also serve to make it more expensive.

There's also the argument that some agents tend to place their own interests above the interests of the clients they serve. For instance, it could conceivably be better over the long-term for an athlete, author, or television personality, to remain with their present team, publisher, or television station, rather than moving on for the sake of immediate financial gain. In addition, agents can conceivably favor higher up-front compensation payments for their own interest, when deferred compensation might be the better route for their client.

Frankly, these arguments cut both ways, and they have a rather shallow ring to them when made by employers unhappy over the sums they pay for the services of the talent they employ. Furthermore, how good or bad an agent is in representing the interests of a client, is the client's decision. It's hard to argue that an employer—whose financial self-interest dictates securing the services of talent at the lowest possible cost—will better serve a client than an agent whose livelihood is enhanced by obtaining the most money possible for clients.

Given these aspects of the employer/agent/client relationship, let's look at how best to bargain with agents. The foremost requirement for success is no more complicated than the courage to say "No" to exorbitant demands. This isn't easy to do when faced with the possibility of a competitor picking up a tab that you're unwilling to pay. However, the long and the short of avoiding getting caught up in a competitive bidding frenzy is to set your limits before you start bargaining. Pre-planning the upper limit you will pay, and refusing to exceed it, will remove the euphoria and/or hysteria associated with competitively bidding for talent.

Another important element in bargaining with agents is to strive for incentive-based compensation arrangements. Last year's home runs, touchdowns, or box office smash hits, are history, and there's no guarantee that the performance will be repeated. Yet, lucrative contracts are doled out with that expectation in mind. If you don't want to be stuck with paying for high priced talent that isn't performing, then you should insist that the risks of mediocrity be shared. Negotiate for lower levels of base compensation, with higher amounts to be paid in the form of bonuses and incentives if the performance expectations become reality.

When contracts are being negotiated, it's important to meet with the agent's client. Agents may resist this, since they (1) don't want their client to muddy the waters by saying the wrong thing, and (2) don't want you convincing the client that your way is best. However, insisting on a three-way meeting before the heavy duty bargaining begins is appropriate. This will give you an opportunity to emphasize both the long and short-term advantages of signing with your organization.

Incidentally, don't hesitate to point out how well you treat talent. It's often the little things that can win over an agent's client, especially when you're in the same financial ballpark as everyone else.

In fact, the treatment of talent when they are under contract can help keep them in the fold when it comes time to negotiate a new agreement. It's easy to say, "Hey, with the money we're paying, we shouldn't have to pamper people." That overlooks the fact that a little pampering is something anyone can appreciate, no matter what their level of compensation is. Naturally, this won't keep everyone from deserting the fold in search of bigger bucks elsewhere. However, it may help keep some talent home on the range. Meanwhile, others may return in the future, after unhappy experiences elsewhere convince them that money shouldn't be the sole consideration in determining who gets their services.

13.10 NEGOTIATING WITH SUPPLIERS FOR LONG-TERM SUCCESS

Success in improving product quality and reducing inventory levels is dependent upon working closely with your vendors. Therefore, it's necessary to take a long-term view when negotiating supplier contracts. This can't be accomplished by focusing on a negotiating strategy that emphasizes making awards to the low bidder. In the first place, it's impossible to expect that stringent quality control and JIT (Just-in-time) inventory requirements can be arbitrarily passed down to vendors. For these measures to succeed, a close working relationship is required. Therefore, simply looking for the low cost supplier won't suffice. Furthermore, a low price, in and of itself, may signal the potential for missed deliveries, poor quality, vendor bankruptcy, and any other number of ills.

As a result, although cost is always an important part of supplier negotiations, it shouldn't predominate to the extent that it overwhelms other elements that are conducive to a close working relationship. The fact is that a good supplier will be as concerned about controlling costs as you are. Factors to consider in forging supplier relationships for the long-term include:

1. Don't impose unrealistic contract provisions. The more difficult it is for the vendor to comply, the less flexibility there will be to adjust to changing conditions.

2. Make certain that your suppliers understand the terms of the contract. Boilerplate clauses are often ignored by smaller vendors who may not fully understand their significance.

3. Be specific about requirements. The more precise you are about spelling out what you want, the more likely it is that suppliers will be able to comply.

4. Be considerate of supplier requests during contract negotiations. Try to look at supplier needs from the supplier's side of the table.

5. To foster a continuing relationship, try to negotiate longer term contracts. Suppliers will be more amenable to meeting your needs if they know that any investments made to meet your requirements will be recouped.

6. Encourage suppliers to work closely with you on design and development efforts.

7. Establish realistic delivery schedules that allow suppliers to properly plan their own manufacturing schedules.

13.11 HOW TO OFFSET BEING VIEWED AS A "SMALL POTATOES" SUPPLIER

When smaller companies do business with larger firms, there may be a tendency for the bigger company to project a "take it or leave it" attitude. That, of course, as pointed out in the preceding section, doesn't bode well for establishing long range relationships that benefit both parties. Nevertheless, it can and does happen. Consequently, if you find yourself in such a situation, it pays to show your bigger brethren the advantages you possess. There are many ways to do this including:

- Demonstrate your emphasis on providing quality products and/or services.
- Document your record of on-time deliveries.
- Present evidence of your ability to control costs, while maintaining high quality standards.
- Don't make promises you can't keep.
- Be cooperative in working toward an agreement that meets the customer's requirements, while still adhering to your own negotiation objectives.
- Emphasize that your small size gives you the flexibility to quickly adjust to changing conditions.
- Don't hide existing problems in meeting a requirement in the hope that a solution can be found later.
- Don't be subservient. Expect to be treated as an equal partner and you will be.

The most difficult hurdle to overcome when you are a smaller company negotiating with a larger enterprise is the fear of having the other side walk away if you don't accede to their demands. This is especially true if the potential deal represents a significant portion of your future business. Nevertheless, if you don't assert yourself, the deal you get will likely be one that presents problems down the road. So it's better to fight for something you can live with, than tacitly accepting something you can't.

13.12 DEALING WITH CUSTOMERS SO THEY'LL RETURN

Building a base of repeat customers requires an approach that goes beyond the terms and conditions of any one deal. One aspect of this is the negotiated agreement itself. If you squeeze a customer to nick them for every cent you can get, you may make a sale, but lose a repeat customer. How you conduct the negotiations is also a factor. A customer who views you as hard to deal with is unlikely to return for a second dose of the same medicine.

Always try to be relaxed when you're dealing with sales prospects—or for that matter, in any negotiation setting. If you're uptight, it can make a potential customer uneasy. On the other hand, if you appear to be laid back, that in itself can encourage high strung customers to loosen up both their personalities and their purse strings.

When negotiating with customers, it's helpful to use an individual approach rather than a "one size fits all" strategy. To do this, try to evaluate potential customers in terms of their likes and dislikes. That way, you can vary your tactics to cope with both the perceived needs and personality of the buyer.

However, negotiating the sale is only the starting point for bringing back repeat customers. Performance of the agreement is what will ultimately determine whether you have a one-shot deal, or a long-term satisfied customer. Naturally, performance parameters will differ widely according to the product and/or service being sold. Yet, there is one aspect of performance that is crucial to repeat business, and that's customer service.

When businesses seek ways to expand their sales base, customer service is seldom viewed as a viable tool to maintain or gain market share. Instead, service is more likely to be condemned as a drain on profitability. Frankly, it takes foresight and courage to make a long-term financial commitment for customer service when the return on investment isn't easily quantifiable. Yet, one of the most important factors in establishing credibility with customers is good service when it's needed. In short, a good track record with customer service gives you the credibility that brings customers back.

In the long-term, it will become increasingly difficult for businesses who operate on a theory of, "Negotiate the toughest deal you can, and kiss the customer good-bye." With a highly competitive worldwide marketplace, repeat business will be increasingly important, and that means deals can't be negotiated in a vacuum without considering their future impact.

13.13 TOOLS FOR NEGOTIATING BUDGET REQUESTS

One special aspect of negotiating that can leave many people pulling their hair is the process of negotiating budgets. It's understandably aggravating for a manager who is unable to justify a budget request to see a counterpart submit an obviously overloaded budget and get every last cent requested. However, these frustrations can often be remedied if you adopt a couple of "position of strength" techniques when making your budget presentation.

One technique is to show the negative impact of not getting the resources you're requesting. This is the proverbial "the heavens are falling" argument. What you want to do is portray some calamity that will take place if your budget request isn't granted. For instance, production quotas won't be met, deliveries will be late, and so forth. However, to do this successfully, you have to document a convincing case.

An alternative tactic is to show specific benefits that will be derived from granting your budget request. Of course, most requests for increased budgets— other than inflation related adjustments—allege some form of benefit will result. But to be successful, you want to pinpoint benefits that you know are a high priority with the people who have the power to grant your request. In the business world, any requests that can substantiate increased profits and/or productivity gains, are more apt to be approved.

An important element for winning budget approval is to provide specific figures to support your assertions relative to the benefits that will result from granting your request. Quantifying the benefits in terms of dollars and cents adds credibility to your arguments. And even though they are only estimates, carry them out to the lowest possible level. It's amazing how much credibility people will place in numbers such as $101,576.35, even though they know it is only an estimate.

Incidentally, it's always useful to avoid using the word "estimate." So, even when it's obvious that's what it is, just avoid identifying it as such. Naturally, if you're asked why you didn't identify certain numbers as estimates the reply is simply, "It's obvious that it's an estimate, so there isn't any reason to identify it as such."

Preparing your budget requests with extensive justification for your position also lets you avoid the arbitrary budget padding that takes place. Padded budgets tend to destroy credibility to the extent that even justifiable items are often questioned. This isn't to imply that valid contingency amounts shouldn't be included in your budget request. However, by identifying contingencies and their related amounts, you gain a degree of credibility which may be lacking in similar requests.

When you argue your case on budget items, try to establish a fallback position which will allow you to receive at least a partial approval of what you're looking for. For example, if you are unsuccessful in seeking two employees, negotiate for one, or even a full-time or part-time temporary worker. The point is to at least get your foot in the door in working toward your ultimate goal. If you can do that, then it makes it easier at the next budget go-around to get the rest of what you wanted.

Chapter 14

HOW TO KEEP NEGOTIATIONS FROM STALLING

For one reason or another, negotiations often bog down just when you think you're not too far from closing a deal. There's really no mystery to this, since the nearer two parties get to reaching agreement, the less leeway there is in the respective positions. As a result, resistance on both sides of the table starts to stiffen. When this juncture is reached, it's crucial to look for ways to keep the negotiations from stalling out—perhaps never to be resumed.

There are many different methods you can use to keep the talks rolling when they start to stall. Sometimes it involves a bit of creativity in coming up with a different approach to skirt an impasse. On other occasions, you may be forced to take a hard line if your negotiating opponent does some last minute maneuvering in an attempt to extract additional concessions. The following sections discuss a variety of tactics that you can use to overcome some of the more common obstacles that frequently threaten to derail the negotiating process.

14.1 INVENTING OPTIONS WHEN YOU DON'T HAVE ANY

You may participate in negotiations where both you and your opponent use up the slack in your respective negotiation positions, leaving no further room to maneuver. This is frequently the point where most unsuccessful deals go down the drain. However, when this sort of impasse occurs, it's worthwhile to stand back and explore other alternatives that can resolve and/or circumvent the impasse-creating problem.

It's always best if the two parties can work together in coming up with a solution. However, even if your adversary is reluctant to consider such a joint approach, it's worth your while to put your own creativity to the test. On certain occasions, a relatively simple solution may come quickly to mind. At other times, the negotiations may actually break off when the impasse is reached, and will have to be resumed if and when you can come up with a satisfactory alternative.

The biggest drawback in exploring alternatives is often nothing more than the fact that both parties have been proceeding on one course without anticipating that an impasse would be reached. Consequently, neither party has given any thought as to how the conflict can be resolved. This is quite natural, since no matter how carefully you plan before negotiations commence, it's impossible to foresee all of the potential problems that may arise.

More often than not, the final hang-up is a seemingly irreconcilable difference of opinion on price. When this occurs look for compensating factors that would make an otherwise unreasonable price acceptable. For example:

- Stretching out delivery dates.
- Relaxing product and/or packaging specifications.
- Increasing or decreasing the quantity of items bought.
- The inclusion of an option provision for additional quantities.
- The inclusion of performance, cost, and/or delivery incentives.
- More favorable payment terms.

Sometimes the solution to the stalemate may involve a substantial restructuring in terms of the subject matter of the negotiation. In fact, what's finally agreed to may have little or no relationship to what was originally being negotiated. For example, parties unable to agree on the purchase of an office building in Boston may decide they can do business on a tract of land in Tampa.

On other occasions an added incentive that brings about agreement may be of little substantive value to you, but for one reason or another has appeal to your counterpart. Therefore, it's useful to listen carefully for clues as to what's important to the other party while negotiations are taking place. Something said may have little significance at the time, but it may help later if an impasse does take place.

For instance, as negotiations are underway for the sale of a retail outlet, the present owner frequently reminisces about how he managed the business.

When negotiations reach an impasse, the potential buyer, remembering this, offers to hire the owner as the manager of the business. This turns out to be the necessary ingredient that persuades the owner to go through with the transaction. In essence, when you hit an impasse, a solution may be at hand if you can come up with some form of creative compromise.

14.2 MAKING LAST MINUTE CONCESSIONS TO GET AGREEMENT

On occasion, negotiations may proceed to the point where the positions are relatively close, but your opponent still refuses to agree to a deal. More often than not, the other side is just holding out to see what sort of final concessions you will make. As you may recall, in the discussion on piece by piece concessions in section 11.2, it was pointed out that you should always keep a potential concession in reserve, even when negotiations are on a total package basis. The purpose of this is for its use as a last minute deal clincher.

Nevertheless, you shouldn't just toss this concession on the table. You want the other side to think they have squeezed you dry, and have nothing left to concede. By doing that, the concession will appear to be a last ditch give-away in a final attempt to reach agreement. Consequently, when you offer this final deal sweetener, emphasize that there will be no further concessions.

In fact, to add an air of finality, you may not want to make this final concession until after the negotiations have broken off because of a failure to reach agreement. This has the added advantage of the possibility the other side will contact you in the interim and accept your last offer, making the final concession unnecessary. However, you don't want to wait too long before contacting the other party, since they may reconcile themselves to the fact that the deal is dead and proceed with other alternatives. Whether or not you choose to let the talks be suspended temporarily is an evaluation you have to make based on your assessment of the risks involved.

In any event, when you do make a last minute concession, combine it with an appeal to the ego of your counterpart. No one likes failure, and therefore if it's possible to reach agreement, most people will do so, rather than walk away with nothing for their efforts. Let's look at how such a pitch can be made.

Background

Hank, a buyer for a large home improvement outlet, and Herb, a salesman for a building materials wholesaler, are negotiating a purchase order for building materials. After bargaining back and forth, they are $3,000 apart, with Hank at $98,500 and Herb at $101,500. The latter figure, is within Hank's upper limit of $105,000, while Herb will settle for an even $100,000. Of course, neither party knows the other still has room to move, and both negotiators have positioned themselves as having made their best offer.

The last minute concession

Hank: "Well, Herb, I guess that's it. It's too bad we got this close without making a deal."

Herb: "Hank, I've made you the best offer I can. You won't do any better elsewhere."

Hank: "I think we can. It's a pretty competitive market. Frankly, I don't understand how you can walk away from a sale of this size. I'd hate to have to explain that to my boss." (Hank is playing on Herb's emotions)

Herb: "It's all in a day's work. You win some and lose some." (He's sweating the deal, but projecting an image that he couldn't care less.)

Hank: "I'll tell you what, Herb. I can't do it alone, but I'm willing to call Al (the outlet owner) to see if I can go to $100,000. However, there's no guarantee he'll go along with it, and I need your agreement that we have a deal before I call him."

Herb: "I'd like to, Hank, but I told you that I was stretching my limit when I offered you a price of $101,500."

Hank: "We're down to peanuts now, Herb. You don't want to throw a $100,000 sale down the drain for the sake of a lousy $1,500, do you? Not only that, but what about future business? You know how fast we're growing."

Herb: Grimacing says, "Go ahead and make your call, but I'm telling you right now, if you can't get approval we won't be doing any more business."

Hank: Leaves the room and calls his wife to check what time they are meeting for dinner, returns and says, "We're in luck, Herb. I talked to Al and convinced him to approve the deal for $100,000."

Of course, you never know how these scenarios will play out. The important angle is to make your last minute concession appear as a last resort to salvage the agreement. If you do that, unless the other side truly finds your offer to be unacceptable, the odds are that an agreement can be reached.

14.3 SHIFTING GEARS TO REACH
FINAL AGREEMENT

There are a number of factors that can stall a negotiation, all of which are controllable if you take the necessary action to counteract them. How you go about doing this is primarily determined by the type of bottleneck you face.

Sometimes a negotiation becomes bogged down when the parties are unable to agree on how to resolve a particular topic. When this happens, rather than senselessly arguing over the controversial issue, it helps to completely change the subject and talk about some other aspect of the deal. Frequently, as all of the other issues are ironed out one-by-one, it becomes easier to reconcile the difference on the previously insolvable item.

On other occasions, the problem is one or more members of the other negotiating team who are seemingly opposed to every position you take. When you're faced with this sort of dilemma, take the other negotiation team leader aside, and agree on the critical issues in private meetings. Sometimes this situation arises solely because too many people are participating on both sides of the table. Another alternative, if the circumstances are appropriate, is to break the meeting down into smaller fact-finding groups. Of course, if it's politically feasible simply reduce the number of attendees at future sessions.

Once in a while you may encounter a situation where the other negotiator appears to be stalling for no apparent reason. Once this becomes obvious, diplomatically inquire as to what the holdup is. Actually, the problem may just be indecision on the part of the other person.

This can result from a reluctance to take the terms of the agreement to higher levels for approval. Perhaps the negotiator has a second-guessing boss, or maybe certain provisions are known to be objectionable to one or more people in the approval loop. In any event, if you can't establish the cause, get the negotiator's superiors involved. Whatever the reason, whenever negotiations start to stall, try to find a way to shift the focus toward more productive areas that will keep the discussion moving along toward a conclusion.

14.4 OVERCOMING THE LAST MINUTE
OFFER WITHDRAWAL

A not so pleasant event may sometimes occur as you reach what you think is the satisfactory conclusion of a negotiating session. It may be your misfortune to experience an unexpected withdrawal of an offer. This can take a variety of forms, but most of the time it happens when higher authority must approve an agreement. The buyer comes back to say something such as, "I'm sorry, but I'll have to pull my offer of $500,000 off the table. I couldn't get approval topside."

When this happens, it's easy to get irate, and respond with a, "It's that or nothing," reply. However, that's not always either practical, or reasonable. From a practical standpoint, you may not have very satisfactory alternatives if the deal falls through. Therefore, a "take it or leave it" attitude can be a pretty risky position to avow. In addition, even in the absence of it being expressly stated, some form of review and/or approval is the norm rather than the exception with most agreements of any magnitude. Even where the person negotiating has the authority to make a commitment, this is often tempered by the need for a legal or administrative review of some kind.

Of course, before negotiations begin, the authority of your counterpart should be established. This was covered in section 3.5, while identifying behind-the-scenes decision makers was discussed in section 3.6. It's worthwhile to review those sections, as well as section 9.1 on assessing the other negotiator's clout. Nonetheless, the authority of the negotiator isn't always determined, and even when it is, it doesn't preclude someone from coming up with an argument such as, "We've agreed to a couple of provisions that run counter to our accounting system, so I'm forced to get this reviewed by top management."

In any event, your reaction shouldn't be reflexive anger at being rebuked, but instead should be based upon where your rejected offer was in relation to your negotiation objective. For instance, if you prepared a pre-negotiation position based on a most desirable selling price of $600,000, and a minimum price you would accept of $400,000, the withdrawal of a $500,000 offer by the other side still leaves you with room to maneuver.

Of course, any refusal of an offer should be challenged by insisting that the objecting party advise you directly as to why the offer is unacceptable. If the other negotiator won't comply, then refuse to negotiate further. This forces the other negotiator to get the objecting party involved, to break off negotiations, or to back off and accept your offer. This is, of course, a general rule which will prevent you from being snookered by the old ploy of extracting additional concessions by asserting that some higher level wouldn't approve the agreement. In fact, if the turned down offer was the maximum you would make, you usually have little recourse but to follow this approach.

However, there may be extenuating circumstances which don't justify forcing the issue to the point where negotiations break off. For instance, perhaps the objecting officials are at too high a level to expect their appearance at a working level negotiating session. Alternatively, perhaps you didn't really expect your offer to pass scrutiny at higher levels, and since you have plenty of room left to maneuver, don't want to push things too far.

In any event, whether you force the issue to the extreme of threatening to walk away, or merely register mild disapproval, insist that the other negotiator make the next move. Generally, it will be some form of counteroffer and negotiations can continue from there. However, make it clear that whatever is finally agreed to will be subject to approval of higher authority on your side of the table, after—and only after—your counterpart has secured approval on his end. This gives you an advantage which can't logically be objected to, since it's only doing what the other side has already done.

14.5 HOW TO FEND OFF NON-NEGOTIABLE DEMANDS

Anything that you consider to be non-negotiable should be identified when you prepare your negotiation position. This was discussed at length in section 1.10. As stated there, the general rule is not to tell your opponent that something isn't negotiable. The reasoning is simple enough. First of all, it encourages the other side to manufacture their own list of non-negotiables for bargaining purposes. Therefore, as mentioned in section 1.10, try to fend off attempts to target these issues with one sort of excuse or another.

On the other hand, developments during negotiations may make what was previously thought to be non-negotiable, a potential bargaining chip. As a result, there's little purpose to be served by insisting that the items aren't on the table for discussion. So, for all practical purposes be low key during negotiations about anything you consider to be non-negotiable.

Nevertheless, as negotiations near their conclusion, it may become apparent to your adversary that you have one or more items that you refuse to make concessions on. Assuming the other side decides to make an issue of this— and if they know what they're doing they will—you have to take measures to defend your position. If this happens, you might want to try one of the following techniques:

1. Offer to set off your non-negotiable items against issues which they refuse to concede on. Even if you haven't been told directly by the other party that certain terms aren't negotiable, the discussions have undoubtedly pinpointed items that your counterpart won't budge on.

    EXAMPLE: "Ted, instead of haggling about both items, why don't we agree to use my payment terms, and your delivery dates? That way we each get a provision we want."

2. Justify your non-negotiables by asserting that you have made concessions elsewhere that more than compensate for the items that are off-limits.

EXAMPLE: "Heck Fred, I've conceded three points, and now you're telling me that my packaging requirements aren't acceptable. Unless, you want to reopen the discussion on those three points, then you have to accept the packaging specs. Even with that, you still owe me. This isn't a question of packaging being non-negotiable. It's a question of fair trade-offs."

3. Assert that your non-negotiable items are in fact negotiable, but make the trade-off possibilities so unreasonable that they won't be accepted.

EXAMPLE: "I never said my quality control specs weren't negotiable. That's crazy! Look, I'll tell you what I'll do. I offered $49 a unit for 5,000 units. That's $245,000. If you want to use your QC specs that's ok with me. However, I can only pay $35 a unit, and I only want 500 units. That comes to $17,500. I'm not buying more than that until I see if the quality meets our requirements."

14.6 SIX APPROACHES FOR GETTING THROUGH TO THE DECISION MAKER

Occasionally, you may find yourself facing a negotiator who isn't being very cooperative in moving the negotiations along. The reasons for this can vary from a deliberate attempt to slow things down, as when your counterpart knows you're facing a deadline, to the simple misfortune of dealing with an indecisive person. Whatever the cause, you may inevitably have to take some form of action to keep things moving along. If so, one or more of the following tactics may be helpful in this regard.

1. The simplest action you can take is to tactfully suggest that since the discussions appear to be going nowhere, perhaps they should be moved to a higher level for resolution. Naturally, before doing this, make certain that your superiors are thoroughly briefed on the negotiations that have taken place. This tactic will work well when you are dealing with an indecisive individual, who may be more than happy to be taken off the decision making hook.

2. If you think the other negotiator may not be receptive to a suggestion on getting superiors involved, look for a justifiable reason during negotiations. For example, if the other negotiator insists that a boss won't buy a certain provision you're advocating, at that point insist that the boss be brought into the loop.

3. Bring your own boss into the negotiation meetings. The other negotiator may feel compelled to bring someone at an equivalent level to the talks.

4. Have your boss contact the other negotiator's superiors on an informal basis such as, "Just wanted to let you know how things are going."

5. Force the issue from the very top of your organization to the highest level on the other side. This can be done by expressing a need for urgency such as, "I certainly hope this can be wrapped up tomorrow." This way pressure will immediately flow through the chain of command on the other side. As a result, either your previously indecisive counterpart will start making some fast decisions, or someone who can will appear on the scene.

6. Go over the other negotiator's head yourself. This can create tension, so try to do it in such a way that it doesn't appear to be deliberate. Any form of excuse that will get you talking to the other person's boss will do the trick.

14.7 TACTICS FOR CONTROLLING "EXPERT" INTRUDERS

Section 9.10 pointed out how you can effectively use your own experts to strengthen your negotiating position, while section 13.8 covered techniques for hiring outside expertise. Yet, one of the biggest hurdles you may encounter during negotiations is when experts are used by the other side. When experts are arrayed against you, they not only strengthen the opposition's position, but they can also prolong the negotiations because of a need to counter their arguments.

The best way to control the use of experts is to keep them out of the conference room in the first place. One method is to have an agreement limiting the use of experts at the start of negotiations. Of course, the other side may not go along with this, but if they do, it's also restricting your own ability to use outside expertise. Therefore, don't make such a proposal if you in any way anticipate the possibility of calling in experts of your own.

Assuming there is no prior agreement, your next best point of attack is to strenuously object the moment you know an expert is about to be used by the other side. Couch your objection in terms of the quid-pro-quo. That is, you aren't using experts, so the other side shouldn't. How well this approach works depend upon the other side's evaluation of whether or not the expert's testimony will outweigh the negative aspects of incurring your wrath.

Other techniques for controlling the use of experts, and/or minimizing the damage they do include:

• Avoid using your own experts. Doing so is an invitation for the other side to use theirs.

• Attack the expert's credibility.

- Assail the relevance of the expert's area of expertise to the subject matter being negotiated.
- Immediately rebut the expert with your own.
- Listen to them, and then essentially ignore what was said as the discussions proceed.
- Use a "Yea, but . . ." defense to downplay what they're advocating. It goes like this: "Yea, but that isn't what we're talking about here," or, "Yea, but other studies show that's inconclusive."

Of course, before negotiations even begin, you should try to anticipate areas where the other side may contemplate using experts to support their position. If you're fairly certain this will happen, you should arrange to have your own experts available.

CAUTION: In certain limited negotiation situations, third parties are used to influence the negotiation process by external means. The most common use is to bring public pressure on one of the negotiating parties. For instance, media exposure is sought alleging that Company "A" is unwilling to negotiate to settle a strike, or to reach agreement for settlement of some alleged claim of negligence brought by the alleged victims. If you ever encounter an attempt to negotiate in the media, don't respond with your own allegations. In most cases, it only serves to promote even greater publicity. The best approach is to keep the negotiations at the bargaining table and off of the newsstand.

14.8 ESTABLISHING DEADLINES TO MOVE A DEAL ALONG

One obvious way to force the issue when negotiations start to stall out is to impose a deadline for the deal to be concluded. Naturally, if you're just bluffing, and your opponent calls the bluff, you either have to break off negotiations, or telegraph that it was a ploy by continuing to negotiate past your stated deadline. For this reason, there's often some reluctance to use this as a tactic.

Of course, if a deadline passes, and you don't follow through by breaking off negotiations, your credibility is weakened. Therefore, if you throw down this sort of a gauntlet, it's generally preferable to carry out your threat—assuming that's the best available course of action at the time. However, if for one reason or another you continue to negotiate, that doesn't mean you can't carry out your threat at some future point in time.

In fact, if you're involved in a series of deadline threats that pass, when you ultimately carry one out, it can have a significant impact. For example, when a deadline threat is made, the other side will often make some sort of promise to keep you from acting on your threat. Then, once the deadline has passed, they will quickly backtrack from this commitment. This type of maneuvering can happen several times before you find yourself forced to take drastic action.

Whenever you find yourself in a position where carrying out some form of deadline threat is necessary, try to do it in such a way that the door is left ajar for the other side to contact you. For instance, saying, "Call me by nine tonight, if you want to meet tomorrow," is a relatively mild alternative compared with stating, "This deal is dead, if we don't wrap it up today." The former approach also presents an opportunity for you to reestablish contact without losing face if you don't hear from your counterpart.

14.9 WHY DEADLINES HINGE UPON YOUR ALTERNATIVES

It's one thing to contemplate imposing a deadline when your adversary is dragging his feet, and quite another thing to actually make such a threat. The inevitable fear is, of course, that your counterpart couldn't care less, and that if you are forced to walk away, then the deal will be dead and buried. Although this possibility is always real, it often isn't as likely to happen as one might surmise.

First of all, if the other side really wants to reach an agreement, they will work toward that end. Consequently, if they have just been stonewalling, indecisive, or otherwise dragging their feet, a deadline ultimatum may be just the tonic to snap them to their senses. Furthermore, many negotiations ebb and flow, with one side or the other recessing, or otherwise breaking off the talks temporarily. Therefore, there is really nothing to preclude an attempt to resume failed talks, and if an agreement is something that both parties desire, the odds of resumption are high.

Nevertheless, the overriding consideration in how far you choose to go with a deadline threat is the availability of satisfactory alternatives. Whenever other possibilities exist that are relatively as good as the deal you're negotiating, the less risk you run in threatening to walk away. Of course, if the situation is such that your deadline isn't just a bluff to hasten a negotiated agreement, but is, in fact, a necessity imposed by business conditions, then you should be prepared to move on to an alternative course of action before you even sit down to negotiate. Otherwise, especially if your adversary knows you're facing a deadline, the other side may prolong negotiations solely in the hope of extracting favorable last minute concessions from a desperate foe.

TIP: For the most part, it's unwise to let your negotiating counterpart know that you have a deadline to meet which requires negotiations to be concluded by a certain date. This just sets you up for stalling tactics by the other side. However, if they know, or have reason to believe that you have a deadline to meet, don't ignore the issue. Instead, let them know you have time constraints that require negotiations to be concluded by a certain date, but give them a date in advance of the actual deadline. For instance, if you need to conclude an agreement by September 3rd, tell your adversary it's August 10th.

This can give you a real tactical advantage if your opponents try to negotiate you right down to the wire. The minute the deadline passes without you blinking an eye, the better the deal you're likely to get. In fact, when the supposed deadline arrives you might want to make a "this is it" offer. Your opponents might initially refuse on the assumption you're just bluffing. However, once the deadline passes, your opponents may have a quick change of heart if they think there won't be any deal at all. This is especially true if you leave them with the offer and tell them to call you.

14.10 EMPLOYING "POWER PLAYS" TO APPLY PRESSURE

You may encounter conditions where, despite your best efforts, little progress is being made. At times, this may merely result from a genuine impasse, or the need for the negotiations to be brought to a close which is discussed in the next chapter. On other occasions, it may be your best judgment that the hang-up isn't so much the subject matter under negotiation, as the personalities involved on the other side of the table. Sooner or later, if you do enough negotiating, you will deal with people who either don't know what they're doing, or are by nature indecisive. When this happens, it may be in your best interests to get others involved in the discussions.

Employing some type of power play to apply pressure on the negotiator isn't at all unusual. In its most common form, higher level contact is made to bring pressure on the negotiator to move things along. In typical business transactions, this involves executive contact with a counterpart in the other organization. In rarer cases, pressure can be exerted through government officials and/or the media.

Whatever the approach, the key to success is bringing pressure to bear without having it backfire. For instance, going over someone's head isn't very effective if the other side perceives it to be a simple negotiating ploy to force a hasty and ill-conceived agreement. Therefore, whenever this maneuver is attempted, it's important to present a cogent argument justifying why you're taking such action. Of course, the argument doesn't necessarily have to be valid, just so long as it conveys the appearance of legitimacy.

Chapter 15

TECHNIQUES FOR CLOSING NEGOTIATIONS

When negotiations near the stage of wrapping the deal up, there are several elements to consider that can assist in closing negotiations. For one thing, you have to be realistic and know when to quit pushing for better terms. Alternatively, it's smart to look for ways in which you can further your objectives in the future. This can sometimes be done by getting the other side to agree to conditions that will help you accomplish this.

Timing is another factor that's very important in bringing the bargaining to a conclusion. Arguably, there may be no such thing as the right moment to make a closing pitch, but certain times are better than others. Unfortunately, in some instances, getting a deal concluded means perfecting your ability to slice through reams of red tape. Above all else, getting to the end of the road may mean that you have to assert yourself in various ways. This chapter explores a variety of tactics that can help you bring negotiations to a satisfactory close.

15.1 KNOWING WHEN TO QUIT WHILE YOU'RE AHEAD

You may have the good fortune to engage in negotiations where you have a distinct advantage over your adversary. This may be due to a real or perceived position of strength, or from something as basic as a less than skilled negotiating opponent. Whatever the cause, it's generally wise not to exploit this advantage beyond its reasonable limits. Pushing an opponent too far may (1) startle them into suddenly walking away, (2) force them into a bad deal, or (3) leave you holding the bag down the road when they experience difficulty performing an agreement they shouldn't have accepted in the first place.

When people are in a position of strength, there's a tendency to try and squeeze the last dime out of a deal. Such an attitude tends to overlook the long-term consequences. This is especially true where the agreement will result in the other party performing their part of the deal over a protracted period of time.

Every once in awhile, those who for one reason or another have a weak negotiating position, will accept less than palatable terms on the assumption that a bad deal is better than no deal. This can result in quality defects, delinquent deliveries, and most any other unpleasant event imaginable. The bottom line is that the lowest price you can get isn't necessarily the best price over the long haul. Consequently, although your primary focus should always be on protecting your own interests, it's necessary to recognize that not forcing unreasonable terms on your opponent is part of that process.

15.2 NEGOTIATING TERMS TO GET LATER WHAT YOU CAN'T GET NOW

Negotiations often get stalemated by impasses linked to a failure to reach agreement on an item that is of extreme significance to one of the parties, and equally objectionable to the opposition. One technique for overcoming this obstacle is to search for some way to make the undesirable item more acceptable to the other side. However, frequently even this approach is doomed to failure, especially if it's a deal breaking provision from the viewpoint of the objecting party.

When this happens, it's worthwhile to regroup and assess precisely what it is you want to accomplish. It may well be that rather than scuttle the deal, your long-term goals are better served by looking for ways to get what you want later rather than sooner. This can sometimes be done by negotiating terms that will achieve your aims at some future date. There are all sorts of provisions you can negotiate that will serve your long-term interests when you're unable to reach agreement on what you want at the present time. Let's look at a few typical examples:

1. "A" wants certain performance specifications written into the contract, but "B" won't accept them. "A" in an attempt to close the deal

suggests putting an incentive provision in the contract that will re-
ward "B" for meeting "A's" performance specs. The use of various
performance incentives as discussed in section 11.4, can be a handy
substitute for the inability to negotiate more stringent performance
provisions into a contract.

2. "C" wants a higher unit price than "D" is willing to pay. Rather than
   negate the deal, they agree to a price escalation factor that will increase the price if agreed-upon inflation indicators exceed certain
   limits.

3. "L" is reluctant to accept an agreement based on the quantities that
   "M" wants to buy. They resolve the dispute by putting an option provision in the contract.

4. "X" wants to buy two buildings from "Y," who is willing to sell only
   one. They agree instead to include a provision giving "X" a right of
   first refusal if "Y" decides to sell the other building at a later date.

The range of possibilities for negotiating provisions that can overcome an
immediate deadlock is endless. It may not always give you everything you
want, but often half-a-loaf is better than none, particularly when the alternative is no deal at all. Quite often, the major impediment is nothing more than
a failure to look beyond the focus of the current agreement. So, anytime you
find yourself essentially stuck over an inability to get the terms you want,
look for ways to accomplish this by some other means.

15.3 WHY NEGOTIATORS SOMETIMES GO
BEYOND THEIR LIMITS

Despite the use of all of your negotiation skills, there may come a time when
you have made every concession you can, without reaching agreement with
the other party. In short, you have made an offer which corresponds with the
minimum acceptable position you prepared during your pre-negotiation planning. This has, of course, been amended during bargaining sessions to take
into account any unexpected and/or unknown factors that were brought to
your attention which would justify changing your position. All of this has been
to no avail, and you have apparently reached the end of the road in terms of
what you're willing to offer to reach agreement.

Yet, despite the fact that it flies in the face of the facts and figures you have
worked so diligently to prepare, you don't want to give up the deal. There's
something inside you that says, "Even if I don't get the minimum deal I wanted,
I would rather have less of a deal than no deal at all."

Should you avoid logic, and give the other party what they want—or at least make another offer which is beyond what you had planned? The simple answer is "No," however, very little is very simple when emotions come into play. On a personal basis, people day in and day out deviate from their predetermined goals at the last minute to get something they want. Perhaps you, or a family member, has at one time or another set out to purchase an automobile, solemnly swearing not to spend more than a certain amount of money. Nevertheless, not too long thereafter, a car costing considerably more is lovingly maneuvered into your driveway.

Of course, business deals are somewhat different—and generally have a lot more riding on them—than a love affair with a new automobile. Yet, here too, emotions can enter into the process. Likewise, deals can be made for sums that far exceed their value when viewed from a detached standpoint. For example, it's not uncommon to read in the business press about a company paying substantially more to buy another business than financial analysts view the acquisition to be worth. On a different level, many a real estate developer has spent more for land or buildings than is deemed appropriate by the experts.

Sometimes these gambles pay off, and other times they don't. When they do, the one-time foolish buyers suddenly become geniuses. Is it luck, intuition, or a little of both? Obviously, critics will deem it to be luck, while the fortunate buyer will modestly call it business acumen. What's important is that people can and do negotiate deals that on paper look lousy, but sometimes turn out to be astute buys.

Does that mean you should always throw caution to the wind and offer whatever is necessary to get the deal you want? Of course not, but there are occasions when you may consider making an offer that on paper appears to be a tad unreasonable. For instance, a plant site may have attractions for a company that outweigh the relatively high price being asked for the land. Or perhaps it's worth paying a premium for a competing business for no better reason than to eliminate a bothersome competitor.

So, all in all, there may be a time or two when you opt to offer more to get an agreement than might appear to be justified. It's certainly not wise to make a habit of it, but if the circumstances are such, there may be occasions when you can't be faulted for going ahead anyway.

15.4 HOW SOLVING SOMEONE'S PROBLEM CAN SAVE THE DAY

Sometimes when a negotiation hang-up occurs, there's no apparent reason for it. You may have offered very favorable terms, but find yourself unable to bring the bargaining to a conclusion. This dilemma is sometimes the result of a reluctance of the other party to close the deal for reasons that aren't apparent on the surface. In fact, they may have nothing at all to do with the terms and conditions of the proposed agreement.

When you're confronted with such a quandary—and the possibilities are endless—it's impossible to solve the problem until you know what it is. On occasion, the other negotiator may be willing to level with you. This is especially true if you have established good rapport during the bargaining sessions.

At other times, you may be left to fend for yourself in trying to figure out what the problem is. About all you can do is look for any clues that may have surfaced during the negotiation meetings. Of course, there's nothing to prevent you from asking what the problem is, and hopefully your counterpart will level with you. If that happens then it isn't always that difficult to come up with some creative way of resolving the difficulty. A few examples of such problems and how they can be resolved include:

- A difficult boss who is making it hard for the negotiator to close the deal. (Get your boss to carry the ball to his counterpart.)
- A business owner reluctant to sell because of a long-term attachment to the business. (Keep her on to manage the business.)
- A supplier worried about cash flow. (Include a provision for progress payments in the contract.)
- A buyer concerned about financing. (Arrange to help out with the financing.)

The bottom line in closing any deal is the ability to pinpoint any problems your adversary may have and then provide the solution. Admittedly, it's not always easy to do, but it certainly is worth the effort to bring a deal to a close.

15.5 THE IMPORTANCE OF TIMING IN REACHING AGREEMENT

An awareness of the importance of timing is essential throughout the negotiation process. All the way from knowing when the timing isn't right to begin negotiations to the most opportune moment to make your closing pitch, proper timing can't be ignored. For instance, there are numerous circumstances where it's wise to postpone opening negotiations such as:

- With suppliers who have large backlogs. (If they don't need the business, they may be hard to deal with.)

- When the local real estate market is overheated.
- When you're in the wrong end of a supply and demand cycle. (For instance, a commodity you buy has escalated in price due to temporary market conditions.)

Actually, the number of factors that can influence the proper timing to initiate a business transaction are endless. On the other hand, you can't always put off negotiations until conditions are conducive to getting a bargain. The best you can do in this regard is to be aware of any timing influences that can impact upon negotiations and plan accordingly. Of course, the flip side of the coin is to attempt to schedule negotiations when conditions are most favorable for you, such as when your counterpart has compelling reasons to be cooperative.

Apart from considerations in initiating negotiations, proper timing is equally important in bringing the bargaining to an end. It helps in this regard if you plan for it as negotiations proceed. One good approach is to hold in reserve the resolution of a particular issue which is of obvious importance to your counterpart. Even though you know you can reach agreement on the matter during negotiations, keep your suggestions to yourself. Then, when negotiations wind down toward the nitty-gritty, this item will remain as the major unresolved matter.

At an opportune moment, when everything else is settled and it appears that the open item will be the stumbling block that kills the deal, make your closing pitch. Say something such as, "Carl, here's how we can get the deal done." Then, go on to offer your resolution of the issue. Generally, your suggestion for resolving the matter will provide the momentum for wrapping things up. More often than not, the sheer relief of your counterpart in settling an issue that was thought to be a deal breaker will propel the other side toward agreement.

Beyond anything else proper timing requires a keen sense of just where the negotiations stand. This isn't always as easy to discern as it would appear to be, especially if you're dealing with an experienced negotiator who knows how to play a negotiation table version of poker. Yet, even here it pays to look for subtle signals that indicate the other side may be susceptible to a pitch to close the deal.

15.6 USING TIME AS LEVERAGE

As the saying goes, "time is money," and nowhere more so than when your opponent has a self-imposed deadline to complete negotiations by a certain date. There's no quicker way to close negotiations—other than giving the store away—as watching the time roll toward what you know is a deadline staring your counterpart in the face.

Once you know for a fact, or can pretty well assume, that your opponent is under deadline pressure, you have an obvious advantage as negotiations near the wire. However, before you go about playing this ploy for all it's worth, a few precautions are in order. First of all, how useful the deadline is to you, depends upon what sort of alternatives the other side has if negotiations can't be completed. Furthermore, it's smart to be cautious about not forcing the issue too far, since your opponent isn't likely to accept unreasonable terms under any circumstances.

Finally, absent knowledge that confirms the fact, the alleged deadline may be merely a tactic being used by the other side to speed things up. Why would someone do this? Perhaps they don't want you probing too deeply into the details of their offer, and are using a deadline as an excuse to keep you from doing so. A clue to look for in this regard is if the other negotiator lets you know right from the beginning that there are time constraints imposed for completing negotiations.

In terms of getting the best results when your opponent has a deadline to meet, the following guidelines are helpful:

1. Avoid mentioning your knowledge of the other side's deadline pressures. Telegraphing your awareness of the fact alerts them to the possibility that you will use this knowledge to push for last minute concessions.

2. If your opponent lets you know there is a deadline to be met, don't signal that you attach any particular significance to it.

3. Actively negotiate right down to the wire so as not to raise suspicions that you're deliberately dragging things out.

4. Let your opponent make the last offer which should come shortly before the deadline arrives.

5. Take some time to give the offer due consideration. Even though you know you won't accept it, you don't want your adversary to know that.

6. Reject the offer and make a counter-offer that's more beneficial to you. If it's accepted, you have a deal.

7. If your adversary refuses your counter-offer, just keep on talking. Let them make the next move, since they are the ones with deadline pressures. They will either finally concede, make another counter-offer, or break-off the negotiations. At what point a deal is reached will depend upon your best judgment as to when to call it quits.

8. Always keep in mind that the other side may have a built-in time lag as to when the actual deadline is. Therefore, even after the supposed deadline has passed, they may continue to negotiate.

9. Don't overdue it in trying to squeeze last minute concessions when the other party has a deadline to meet. After all, if you kill the goose, it won't be around to lay other golden eggs in the future.

15.7 HOW TO SLICE THROUGH RED TAPE BOTTLENECKS

Negotiating a satisfactory agreement is troublesome enough in itself, but your headaches don't always end there. In trying to get a deal wrapped up, you can encounter obstacles on both sides of the fence. When the bottleneck rests with the other party, you have to get through to someone who can make a decision on the agreement as discussed in section 14.6.

Even more irksome than circumventing roadblocks erected in the opposition camp, is having to work your way around stumbling blocks on your side of the aisle. These can take a variety of forms ranging from indecision within the approval loop, to outright resistance by people who oppose the agreement. First, let's look at how to address the problem of getting around those individuals within your organization who openly oppose approval of an agreement you have negotiated.

In a perfect world, corporate infighting and internal politics would be passé. However, even the most optimistic crystal ball gazer would hesitate to include that prediction in any forecast for the future. As a consequence, it's inevitable that internal conflicts will arise over negotiated agreements. These differences of opinion can range from petty politics generated by power struggles and bickering, to sincere disagreement over the viability of the subject matter of the negotiation.

Most of the time, the battles are fought before the go-ahead decision is made that results in the negotiation taking place. However, some wounds heal faster than others, and on occasion, those opposed to a project will carry their fight right down to the point where a negotiated agreement goes through the approval cycle. As a result, you may find yourself fighting a rearguard action as you seek internal approval. When this happens, it shouldn't be taken lightly, since if the opposition succeeds in shooting enough holes in the deal, you will find yourself right back at the bargaining table. Therefore, let's look at some measures you can take to overcome this difficulty. They include:

1. Pinpointing potential supporters and detractors in the approval loop.

2. Building a power base of supporters before you formally present the agreement for approval.

3. Trying to co-opt the opposition by gaining their support. If possible, show them how their ideas and/or objectives have either been included in the negotiated agreement, or will be furthered by its approval.

4. Assessing potential objections to the agreement. When you seek approval, raise these objections yourself, and then proceed to show why they are not valid. Doing this is akin to blowing up the enemies' ammunition dump.

5. Making a solid presentation. You obviously worked long and hard to negotiate the deal, so labor just as hard to get it approved.

6. If it appears that you are being cut out of the approval process, take whatever measures are necessary to get through to the decision maker. After all, you negotiated the deal, and are therefore the proper person to explain and defend it. When someone wants to shoot down an agreement, it's a lot easier to do so if the negotiator isn't present at the meeting to defend it.

Aside from any organized resistance to a negotiated agreement, you may also have to overcome a wide variety of run-of-the-mill hurdles that are common to any organizational environment. These include indecisive people, (work around them) restrictive policies, (interpret them in your favor) and a myriad of details (handle them after the fact). It isn't a rewarding experience to have to overcome a bevy of bottlenecks to get a negotiated agreement approved. However, it's part of the process, and shouldn't be ignored, since bottlenecks in your own camp can unravel a deal a lot faster than the time it took to get it negotiated.

15.8 LETTING THE OTHER PARTY KNOW YOUR LIMIT IS REACHED

Sooner or later, it's necessary to bring matters to a head, and either close the deal, or recognize that an agreement just isn't in the cards. Sometimes, negotiations drag on endlessly simply because neither party is willing to take the initiative to conclude matters. Part of the problem lies in the natural reluctance of either party to be the one that makes the last offer. There's an inevitable feeling that it won't be accepted, and/or the other side will come back with yet another less desirable offer.

Overcoming this hurdle requires the fortitude to exercise a bit of brinkmanship as discussed in section 11.5. However, once you have exhausted every possible means of reaching agreement, you have to not only make a decision that your limit has been reached, but also convey this to your counterpart. So, sooner or later, when you make your last concession or offer, it's necessary to emphasize the fact that you are at your limit.

Don't be hesitant about calling it quits. More often than not, the other side will play out the string as far as it will go—which includes rejecting your final offer. They, quite understandably, won't accept it as the best they can get until you prove it is. Therefore, there will come a time when you simply have to get up and walk away.

Experienced negotiators know this, and don't have any hesitancy to do so at the proper moment. Complex negotiations can have the parties breaking off negotiations, and subsequently resuming talks several times over a period of weeks and months. The key is the ability to walk away after giving the other side the impression that you have had enough, while at the same time leaving leeway for them to initiate further contact.

On the one hand, conveying finality is necessary to convince the other side that you are at your limit. The flip side of the coin is that this be done in such a way that your counterpart won't be discouraged from contacting you later and accepting your last offer. Furthermore, you never know when an unexpected, but satisfactory, alternative may be proposed if and when the other side does contact you. Does all of this sound like it requires a little bit of acting ability? As they say, it isn't necessary, but it sure helps.

15.9 USING ULTIMATUMS AS A LAST RESORT

As just mentioned, when you have reached your negotiation limit, you want to let your adversary know that fact in no uncertain terms. Yet, as a rule, you want to leave the door slightly ajar—at least to the extent that the other side may be willing to call and accept your last offer. Aside from that, you never know what future negotiation opportunities may arise with the same people.

Consequently, no matter how frustrating an apparent failure to reach agreement may be, it doesn't pay to end everything with an emotional outburst. You certainly can use some form of ultimatum such as a deadline to force the hand of your counterpart, but going beyond that isn't good business sense. Ultimatums are to a large extent overplayed, since no one takes kindly to being threatened. Therefore, no matter how bitter you may feel, take your frustrations out on a golf ball or some similar form of tension reliever.

NOTE: In certain limited situations, a dead deal can be resurrected time and time again. Examples include repeated attempts to buy a business, or purchase a piece of real estate. Although such cases aren't the norm, when there is no particular urgency to reach agreement you can keep trying. It's not only that persistence may pay off, but also the fact that conditions change as time passes. The economy, personal and/or business circumstances, and individual motivations, are all subject to fluctuation. In fact, something as simple as establishing a good relationship with the other party over a period of time may bring success. As a result, if you ever confront such a situation, don't just give up, and most important, don't issue any ultimatums, since you have nothing to gain and everything to lose by doing so.

Part IV

POST-NEGOTIATION STRATEGY

Chapter 16

WHAT TO DO AFTER
YOU REACH AGREEMENT

Shaking hands after an arduous negotiation session may signal that at least a tentative agreement has been reached, but it's by no means the end of your worries. More often than not, when people get careless, the written agreement can cause further conflict and may even result in yet another round of negotiations. This chapter covers the essentials of preparing written agreements that will adequately protect your interests.

Even then, your job hasn't ended. In some instances, as soon as the negotiations appear to be concluded, the second-guessers within your own organization will crawl out of the woodwork. As a result, it pays to be prepared to cope with these nay-sayers. Beyond that, agreements that require an extended period of performance will require careful monitoring to make certain that negotiation table commitments are carried out.

Unfortunately, everything doesn't always work out as planned. This may mean that events may occur at a later date that justify renegotiation of the agreement. This may be even more trying than the original negotiation. However, if it does become necessary, it pays to know how to go about reworking an agreement the right way. All of these aspects of the negotiation process are covered in the following sections.

16.1 AFTER THE HANDSHAKE: IMPLEMENTING DONE DEALS

When the parties to a negotiation finally succeed in hammering out a deal, it's time to turn to implementing what has been agreed upon. Although reaching agreement is certainly cause for heaving a sigh of relief, it's definitely not the time to get careless. It's of no value to spend days, weeks, or even months, both preparing for and conducting negotiations, to have it all crumble because of a failure to properly implement what has been agreed upon.

The general steps to take in properly implementing a deal include:

- Recapping what has been agreed upon.
- Securing any necessary reviews and approvals.
- Writing up the agreement.
- Following up periodically to be sure the agreement is being fulfilled. (This is only relevant when there is work to be performed over a period of time.)

These topics are discussed further in the following sections. However, one aspect of agreements that warrants emphasis is the need for some form of legal review for anything other than the most routine transaction. It's relatively easy to say, "I'll get the lawyers involved later if anything goes wrong," or alternatively, "This deal is cut and dried, so there's no need for a legal review." There are a couple of problems with this type of cavalier attitude.

In the first place, if a deal goes sour and lawyers have to be called in, it's sometimes a question of curing an ill that could have been prevented in the first place. You may also find that the expense of remedial action far outweighs any costs and/or inconvenience associated with having your lawyer look at an agreement before it's signed. Furthermore, negotiations require a high level of personal interaction, to the extent that being so close to the situation can cause even seemingly simple pitfalls to be overlooked. Therefore, apart from legal technicalities, your legal counsel may pinpoint potential problems that you hadn't thought of. As a result, you are well advised to make sure your agreement passes legal muster before you plunge ahead.

16.2 HOW TO CONVERT PROMISES INTO COMMITMENTS

Before you even verbally commit to a negotiated agreement, it's important to be sure that both parties are singing from the same sheet of music. This is especially true where a negotiation has involved a number of complex issues, and there have been offers, counter-offers, and a great deal of shifting of positions before reaching tentative agreement.

In this type of situation, it's not unusual to have one party assume that an issue was settled one way, while the other negotiator thinks otherwise. Unfortunately, when this isn't discovered until later—most often when the written agreement is reviewed—a great deal of friction can be created. At the least, one or both of the negotiators end up with egg on their face, while at the worst, the deal can collapse because of the disagreement over what was negotiated.

This sort of predicament is easily preventable if at the conclusion of negotiations, time is taken to summarize the agreed upon terms of the settlement. Therefore, take the initiative in insisting that the negotiation results be reviewed, even when the other side sees no need for this to be done. In terms of procedure, you may want to take a short recess to go over your notes and recap what was agreed upon.

It's not uncommon for the agreed terms to be gone over after the negotiation session has adjourned, but before the written agreement is prepared. This is frequently done by telephone as a matter of convenience, particularly if the two parties aren't located close to one another. However, unless the circumstances are compelling, it's preferable to do the summarizing at the conclusion of the meeting. That way, if there is a major disagreement, it can be ironed out then and there. Nevertheless, irrespective of how it's handled procedurally, it should be done before the written agreement is drawn up.

16.3 WHY YOU SHOULD OFFER TO WRITE-UP THE AGREEMENT

There's only one reason why you should be the one to prepare the written agreement, and that quite simply is to be sure that you, rather than the other party, controls what goes into it. It's easy to conclude that since you were careful enough to summarize the essential terms of the agreement, that it then becomes immaterial who actually prepares the written agreement.

What gets overlooked is that many of the minor details that will be in the agreement won't even be thought about—much less discussed—until the written document is reviewed. As a consequence, what the document says is to a great degree controlled by the person who prepares it. Moreover, a lot of the little nitty-gritty details of who does what in terms of performing the agreement can be significant.

Of additional importance is the fact that if something is in a formal document, there's a greater reluctance to take exception to it. As a result, even though the other party might have preferred that a particular provision be written up differently, they are less likely to object to it when they see it in writing. After all, by the time you get to the point in the negotiation process where all that remains is to sign the agreement, there's a natural reluctance to prolong matters any further.

The bottom line is that what gets put on paper and signed is what counts—not what someone thought they agreed to at the bargaining table. If you're the one who writes the agreement up, then it's your interpretation of what was agreed to that goes into the agreement. Naturally, that doesn't mean you can change the essence of the agreement, but it certainly gives you latitude in interpreting how the negotiation results are finalized. For this reason alone, it pays to be the one who does the paperwork.

16.4 PITFALLS OF POORLY WRITTEN AGREEMENTS

In a worst case scenario, a poorly written agreement may result in a costly lawsuit. At the least, it can lead to heated disagreements over the interpretation of provisions in the document. This is not only time consuming, but also detrimental to a good working relationship between the parties. Therefore, it makes sense to take the time to be sure the contract is properly prepared. Some typical failures of carelessly written agreements include:

- Terms left out of the agreement.
- Poorly worded provisions that result in arguments over interpretation.
- Loosely written provisions that allow too much leeway in performing the requirements.
- The inclusion of standard boilerplate provisions that have no relevance to the agreement.
- The inclusion of documents by reference without carefully checking the contents beforehand. (This is common when lengthy specifications or statements of work are incorporated by reference.)
- Contradictory provisions with no language stating which is the controlling provision in the event of conflict.

The complexity of the subject matter of the agreement will to some extent impact the length of the written document. And of course, the longer the document, the greater the likelihood of errors creeping into the process. However, the solution isn't simply to write a shorter document, since the primary focus should be on including everything required to fully implement the agreement of the negotiating parties. Therefore, brevity for the sake of brevity should be avoided.

On the other hand, agreements shouldn't be written up to be more confusing than they have to be. This is a common problem owing to the use of arcane language and jargon that sometimes seem to render documents unintelligible—at least to the inhabitants of planet earth. As a result, every effort should be made to make agreements readable, in addition to being as brief as possible within the constraints of including everything that should be included.

CAUTION: Although it's in your best interests to be the one who prepares the agreement, if it is written by the other side, review it carefully before it is signed. Beyond that, don't be hesitant about asking questions if there's something in the document you don't understand. Pay particular attention to boilerplate provisions that may be included. These may be either out-of-date, or irrelevant to your agreement. There is a tendency for these to be included in all documents originating with the same organization, whether or not they apply. In fact, if you do question boilerplate provisions, you may receive a shorthand reply that they are standard in every agreement. Don't be put off by this sort of response. If they don't apply, have them taken out, and if they are relevant, make sure you understand them.

16.5 TWELVE TERMS EVERY AGREEMENT SHOULD HAVE

In addition to provisions required from a legal and administrative perspective, you should make sure that everything necessary to adequately reflect what you negotiated is included in the written document. Some basic, and other not so obvious, provisions that should be included are:

1. The specifics of performance requirements for both parties to the agreement. This includes detailed specifications and statements of work where relevant.

2. Detailed payment provisions, including any condition under which payment can be delayed or withheld. For example, late delivery and/ or items that don't meet the contract performance requirements.

3. Delivery provisions that reflect the intent of the parties, including any agreed upon method for adjusting the delivery schedule during the period of performance. For instance, a buyer may want a provision that allows deliveries to be accelerated or stretched out during the performance period.

4. How and under what conditions the agreement can be modified.

5. Any agreed upon procedure for dispute resolution.

6. Any option provision, including when and by what means it can be exercised.

7. The specifics of any performance incentives, including the procedures for determining if they have been met.

8. Qualifying language relative to any issue that is excluded from the agreement, but in the absence of a statement to that effect, would reasonably be construed as having been omitted by error.

9. Necessary administrative procedures to implement the agreement.

10. All legal requirements as determined to be necessary by your legal counsel.

11. Any provision that you or your advisors feel should be included in the contract, which the other side insists isn't necessary. Work hard for inclusion of such provisions, since they are the very ones that will likely lead to future problems if they are left out of the document.

12. Definitive starting and completion dates, unless the nature of the work dictates that some form of flexibility should be built in.

Obviously, this list could be expanded or reduced, and much depends upon the subject matter of the negotiation. The important point is to be sure that every agreement includes all of the necessary provisions to prevent a later dispute. It's often the very issue that one or both parties say, "That's not necessary. Let's leave it out," that later comes back to haunt you.

16.6 COPING WITH SECOND-GUESSERS ON THE HOME FRONT

Of all of the truisms associated with the negotiation process, one that you're certain to encounter if you do any extensive negotiating is being second-guessed. Long after an agreement has been signed, you will likely have critics telling you either what you did wrong, or how they, in similar circumstances, got a better deal elsewhere. The truth is that many critics think they're negotiators, when they're actually just Monday morning quarterbacks.

Of course, before a contract is signed, you face the task of coping with people trying to kill the deal—or at least scattering roadblocks in your path. How to work around this sort of problem was discussed in section 15.7. Although second-guessing after the fact ordinarily doesn't have any impact on what was negotiated, there are a couple of possibilities to be aware of .

One is that critics will go so far as to attempt to force cancellation of a contract before it's completed. This is especially true if performance is subpar, at least from the viewpoint of the critics. Needless to say, this is one reason why you should stay on top of agreements as they are being performed.

Alternatively, opponents may try to force the renegotiation of an agreement to incorporate those issues which they favor. Because of the inherent difficulties in contract cancellation and/or renegotiation, it's not something you should have any difficulty in shooting down if an attempt is made. However, you should at least be aware of the potential for problems if there is organized resistance internally to what was negotiated.

Not so crucial, but particularly aggravating, is the sort of penny-ante criticism from those who persist in reminding you—subtly or otherwise—that they could have done a better job. Frankly, this is the sort of thing you have to learn to live with as a negotiator. It definitely doesn't pay to be thin-skinned at the bargaining table, and this trait is equally useful in fending off or ignoring armchair critics.

For the most part, little is to be gained by trying to justify what you did when negotiating the agreement, to anyone and everyone that wants to pick something apart. The fact is that you're the one most familiar with the terms and conditions, and critics seldom recognize the nuances and necessities of the trade-offs and concessions that were made to get a deal.

Of course, you may encounter conditions under which you have to defend what you did. This is most likely when provisions of the agreement are openly challenged at meetings, or questioned by superiors. For this reason alone, you should always keep a negotiation file containing the notes and backup substantiating how the negotiation was conducted. This will serve you well if a question arises as to why a particular issue was handled one way rather than another. There usually is a justifiable reason, but relying on your memory won't suffice, particularly as time passes, and you move on to other matters. Having your notes handy to refresh your memory may at least spare you some embarrassment.

A negotiation file can take on even greater significance if a dispute erupts over the meaning of some provision of the contract. This shouldn't happen if the agreement is drafted properly, but the fact is that no matter how carefully a document is drafted, something may arise that wasn't anticipated at the time. As a result, being able to refer to your notes may not only resolve the problem, but also prevent the issue from escalating into something more serious such as a lawsuit.

16.7 HOW TO FOLLOW-UP PERIODICALLY TO AVOID PROBLEMS

When a negotiated agreement requires the performance of work by the other party over an extended period of time, it's crucial to monitor the project to make certain it's being performed according to the contract terms. Who does the actual follow-up will vary according to the subject matter, as well as the structure of your organization. If you, as the negotiator, are responsible for the follow-up effort—either directly, or in a supervisory capacity—there are several factors you have to consider.

First of all, the extent of follow-up action will to a large measure be dictated by the nature of the work. Obviously, routine purchase orders only require minimal monitoring, and can be primarily handled by clerical personnel. On the other hand, a complex research contract, or a sizable construction project will require on-going follow-up.

Another factor that influences the degree of follow-up is the past performance of your contractor on similar projects. If you're dealing with a supplier who has worked with you in the past, and has always performed satisfactorily, then only a minimum of follow-up effort is necessary. In addition, to a lesser degree, the progress reporting requirements in the contract itself can reduce the amount of personal involvement that's needed.

A smorgasbord of reasons can be cited justifying the importance of methodically monitoring the performance of contractual agreements. Of them all, possibly the most compelling is that most projects don't suddenly go sour. There's a gradual build-up of minor matters going wrong, until finally everything boils over into a major crisis.

Even a business that on the surface is booming, can encounter difficulties that impact upon the performance of an agreement. For example, a company may take on so much business that everyone's delivery dates can't be met on time. And when that happens, human nature being what it is, the delivery dates that get slipped will be those belonging to buyers who aren't following-up closely.

Thus, there's little doubt that effective follow-up can catch minor problems before they escalate into major ones. And if they are handled properly, follow-up practices, rather than being intrusive, can serve to enhance the working relationship with the other party to the agreement. Therefore, although monitoring an on-going project may involve more grunt work than glamour, it's solid insurance that the end result will conform to what you worked so hard to negotiate.

16.8 FIVE FOLLOW-UP TECHNIQUES THAT PROMOTE PERFORMANCE

The follow-up procedures you adopt will, of course, be dictated by your relationship with the other party, the subject matter of the agreement, the internal structure of your company, as well as your own personal preferences.

Taking that into consideration, one or more of the general techniques below will work most comfortably with your individual circumstances.

1. *Informal procedures*—You may decide that informal follow-up techniques such as random phone calls, correspondence, and perhaps social contact if it's practical, best fit your needs.

2. *Contract procedures*—Reporting requirements in the contract may be the primary basis for monitoring performance. This is essentially a management by exception technique, and whenever the reports indicate any form of deviation, more extensive monitoring can be undertaken. It should be noted that relying on this method alone places a great deal of emphasis on the quality and timeliness of the reporting procedures, as well as the integrity of the contractor.

3. *Periodic on-site visits*—There's no better way to find out what's going on than by personally visiting the company you're doing business with. However, the expense, both in time and money, renders this approach impractical in many instances.

4. *Through intermediaries*—Your situation may be such that technical and administrative people who deal with the contracting party may be in a position to provide you with direct follow-up assistance, and/or more general business intelligence on the company you're working with.

5. *Third party contacts*—A number of different third party sources can be tapped for information of value in assessing the on-going financial and business status of your contractor. Bankers, credit bureaus, and business associates, are just a few of the sources you can use to keep your ear to the ground.

TIP: Always try to be as unobtrusive as possible when following-up on the performance of an agreement. Above all, don't try to interfere and/or dictate how other parties should run their business. Nevertheless, on occasion, no matter how diplomatic you may be, you may encounter a lack of cooperation in fulfilling your need to monitor an agreement. When this happens, insist on your rights if need be. Anytime you're not being overbearing in your requests, but are being met with resistance, it's at least a poor business relationship.

Beyond that, it may signal that information is being withheld because performance isn't going as well as planned. That's not always the case, since many companies—particularly those which are privately held—are very sensitive about releasing any sort of information. Whatever the cause, it should be an attention grabber whenever you can't get data you feel is necessary to monitor contract performance.

16.9 HOW TO RENEGOTIATE A DEAL
THAT GOES SOUR

It's always a great relief to sit down and sign a business agreement after what seems like—and sometimes is—hours of squinting at fine print by the pound. And usually, both parties end up satisfied with the deal over the life of the agreement. However, conditions can and do change over time, and situations do arise where an agreement is no longer in your best interest. It's under these circumstances that you should consider attempting to renegotiate the agreement. Unfortunately, this option is usually neglected unless a business is in dire financial straits.

Reasons for changing an existing agreement are numerous. For example, a change in financial condition may justify seeking the revision of loan terms. Changes beyond your control can also make a prior deal less desirable at the present time. This can result from either overall economic conditions, or something specific to your industry and/or business. Whatever the reason, outside influences, as well as internal factors, can quickly turn prior business agreements upside down.

There are many factors to consider whenever you're thinking about renegotiating any agreement. One of the most crucial is your state of mind. Most people are reluctant to even suggest that contract terms be renegotiated. And, of course, this isn't something that should be done frivolously. Nevertheless, even when it's clear that an agreement needs revision, people hesitate in approaching the other party to the agreement. As a consequence, they often wait until things are so bad that no other option exists.

Whenever you find it necessary to renegotiate, always be positive in your approach. Even if you want the terms of a loan changed because of financial difficulties, the other party doesn't have a lot to gain by forcing you to stick to the terms of an agreement you can no longer meet. So, given valid reasons, creditors will probably be willing to make adjustments.

After all, they may have an enforceable agreement, but if all they can get out of it is a lawsuit, they will probably prefer to work out a reasonable compromise. Speaking of lawsuits, if you have a contractual problem which can't be resolved informally, seek legal advice promptly. Don't wait until things get so bad that you need a magician to find an amicable resolution—unless your attorney pulls rabbits out of hats as a sideline.

Above all else, remember that business agreements aren't cast in concrete. If circumstances justify it, these agreements can be changed. Actually, often the greatest obstacle to getting an agreement renegotiated is simply a reluctance to approach the other party for fear of hearing "No."

Many times, a lot of persuasion isn't necessary to get an agreement modified. For instance, suppose you are supplying goods under a purchase order and can't meet the delivery schedule. Perhaps, unknown to you, the other company doesn't need all of the goods on the delivery dates specified in the contract. For this reason, they might be more than happy to adjust the delivery schedule. In fact, they might have been reluctant to approach you on the subject, and if no one takes the initiative, you are both living with a bad deal.

16.10 SEVERAL STEPS THAT WILL JUSTIFY REDOING DONE DEALS

Renegotiating can save you money, or even prevent financial disaster. Furthermore, there's no mystique involved in how to go about it. The most important ingredient for success, as in any other negotiation, is adequate preparation. Where most people fail is by starting to bargain without laying the groundwork.

The first step in any renegotiation strategy is to establish goals. What specifically do you want to accomplish? It's worthwhile to set everything that's important down on paper. This will include factors such as renegotiating price, delivery, and any other terms and conditions of a written agreement that are giving you difficulty. Then, gather all of the facts you can to show the advantages of negotiating new terms. Obviously, these elements will vary from case to case.

The next step is to outline what you think the position of the other party will be. It's also useful to know as much as possible about the temperament of the person you will be dealing with. Even though in many renegotiation situations, the other party has an obvious edge, solid preparation pays off. For example, when trying to revise a bank loan, a business is generally in a weak bargaining position. But even here, you can improve your chances of getting better terms and conditions by doing some planning beforehand.

Lenders know they have a commanding position and can impose restrictions to protect their interests. To counteract this, try to anticipate the bank's objections beforehand. In other words, think like the banker. By doing this, you will have answers ready for the inevitable questions. Just showing your awareness of the bank's position can improve your chances of getting the loan rewritten as well as avoiding some of the more burdensome restrictions.

Finally, no matter what you are renegotiating, always perform a before "what if" analysis of your alternatives before you make your renegotiation pitch. That way, even if you are unsuccessful, you will be ready with your next best option, which may be nothing more than completing the deal as originally negotiated.

Chapter 17

PROCEDURES FOR WHEN YOU CAN'T REACH AGREEMENT

Despite the fond expectations that precede many a negotiation, and the degree of negotiation skills that you employ, an agreement may not be in the cards. Just as it takes two to tango, it takes two—or more—to conclude a deal. And for any number of reasons, your negotiating opposite may be unwilling to go that last yard.

However, there's little to be gained by pointing fingers, so it pays to leave your future opportunities open by parting with both your dignity and options intact. This chapter discusses this, as well as how to reopen negotiations if conditions are ripe for such a move. In addition, it's worthwhile to briefly touch upon the subjects of arbitration and mediation which are often useful alternatives to negotiation. Finally, no matter what course any particular negotiation takes, there are some general rules that are useful to remember.

17.1 HOW TO LEAVE YOUR OPTIONS OPEN WHEN THERE'S AN IMPASSE

Whenever you hit the wall at the negotiating table in terms of a deal being dead, it's time to move on to your next best alternative. However, as mentioned previously, try to leave with the option of further contact being possible—even if it isn't probable. Naturally, if you are contacted again by your counterpart, the deal may still be alive.

Assuming you haven't proceeded with some other alternative, the resurrection of the negotiations can be nothing other than good news. That is, of course, unless it turns out to be a false alarm, and you ultimately find out that nothing has really changed in your opponent's position. However, everything isn't quite as cut and dried if your alternative was to start negotiating with another source for a similar or substitute product or service, and you have already commenced doing that.

Naturally, if nothing much beyond an initial inquiry has been made to another source, you can readily postpone starting negotiations. However, if enough time has elapsed, and you have already started to negotiate with the alternative source, you have a decision to make. You can (1) tell the initial source you're no longer interested, (2) break off negotiations with the alternative source, or (3) keep the ball rolling on both fronts.

Unless the original negotiations broke up in such a distasteful fashion that you have no desire to do further business with that party, it isn't worthwhile to kiss them off at this late stage. On the other hand, since an impasse was reached, there's no guarantee that going back to the negotiating table will bring favorable results.

Consequently, if you can pull it off, your best bet is to keep both negotiations moving along in tandem. Who knows, if things work out well, you may end up with two sources competing with one another. This can be a pleasant scenario, especially since it results from an impasse where after expending a great deal of effort, no agreement appeared to be likely.

To be successful at this, your best bet is to speed up negotiations with your second source to get them quickly to the point of a final offer. At the same time, you want to stall the initial source as much as possible to give you time to do that. There's an obvious question here as to whether and when you should let the respective parties know they have a competitor.

If you continue to negotiate with the second source, it certainly isn't being very fair-minded to blithely come to terms with the original source, and leave your alternative source holding the bag. The flip side of the coin is that if you immediately advise the alternative source that your initial negotiating partner wants back in the ball game, the second party may immediately withdraw. That will leave you right back in the saddle with someone whom you're still not sure a deal can be worked out with.

The best approach therefore is to try and get an offer from both parties. Then, let the second source know that you have finally received an offer from your initial negotiating partner—assuming that you resume negotiations and do receive such an offer. To be fair, since the second source was brought on board only after reaching an impasse, give that party the opportunity to make the last offer. In the meantime, let your original source know that you have another offer. At this point, give both parties a chance to bid against one another, until one drops out and you're left with the best offer. Of course, if one party balks at doing this, simply accept the best deal being offered at the time.

17.2 TACTICS FOR REOPENING NEGOTIATIONS WITHOUT LOSING FACE

When negotiations break off, and all you subsequently hear from the other party is deafening silence, that doesn't have to be the end of the road for the deal. It's certainly preferable to have the other party contact you, since it not only tells you they are seriously interested in reaching agreement, but it also gives you a tactical edge.

After all, the contact was made by them, so at least in theory, they're more anxious to deal than you are. It also gives you a better opportunity to choose the time and place of renewed negotiations. For instance, when you receive the call suggesting further talks, you can respond by saying something such as, "Sure, can you be here Friday morning at ten?" Since your counterpart isn't that sure about how anxious you are to resume talks, it's highly unlikely that you will get an argument over where the discussions should be held.

On the other hand, if you still want to pursue the potential for reaching an agreement, and a week or two has gone by without hearing anything, it certainly makes sense to pick up the phone and call your counterpart. It may well be that you will be told the other side doesn't want to negotiate any further. If so, at least you have established that the deal is definitely dead.

However, more than likely the other party will be willing to listen to what you have to say. So don't be shy about taking the initiative if you have to. Assuming negotiations do resume, one good way to get some movement toward reaching agreement is to throw something new into the deal. What it is, will be dictated by the subject matter of your proposed deal. Incidentally, the magnitude of the revision to your last offer, isn't as important as the fact that you have made some movement. This indicates good faith on your part in terms of trying to reach agreement.

Hopefully, this tactic will get the negotiation process moving again. However, if the other side refuses to budge from their previous position, you will have to force some movement. You can do this by saying something such as, "I was under the impression that when we resumed negotiations, we would go beyond where we left off. In good faith I revised my offer, so it's up to you to reciprocate if we're going to get this deal done."

This should compel the other side to make a counter-offer, if they seriously intend to move from the position which caused the talks to break off in the first place. If so, the negotiations are back on track, and an agreement may ultimately result. However, if they steadfastly stick to their original position, it's unlikely that an agreement will be reached, unless it's on their terms. Once this happens, you know with some degree of certainty that a deal can't be made. Nevertheless, the effort involved in reopening the talks wasn't entirely wasted. At least you know that the failure to reach agreement wasn't because you didn't make an earnest effort to succeed.

17.3 WHEN TO WALK AWAY AND BE GLAD YOU DID

Apart from bringing negotiations to a conclusion when your limit has been reached, (see section 15.8) there are other reasons that justify calling it quits. Let's look at a few of the most common causes of a failure to reach an agreement. These are:

1. The other side doesn't want a deal. It may stretch your imagination to think that someone would waste their time at the negotiation table if they had no intention from the start of reaching agreement. Although this admittedly isn't the norm, it isn't as unusual as you might think. In the first place, a party may enter into negotiations without really considering the consequences of reaching agreement. This is particularly true where the individual has a strong emotional attachment to the subject matter of the negotiation. Someone who built a business from the ground up is a prime example.

    Another type of situation is where pressure is being exerted from an outside source to negotiate. For instance, media exposure may compel negotiations for public relations purposes where there is no intent to reach agreement, but going through the motion of negotiating will allow the individual or organization to say, "I (we) tried valiantly, but were unsuccessful in reaching agreement."

2. The other side is willing to make a deal, but only on an unreasonable basis. Occasionally, negotiations are initiated where one party has no particular interest in reaching an agreement, but will do so if they are offered a deal that is too good to pass up. Otherwise, they will simply stonewall with an out-of-line negotiation position until the opponent walks away in frustration.

    An offshoot of this tactic occurs where a party negotiates to test the market to see what the product, property, and/or service is worth in terms of market value. In this case, there is no intent to reach an agreement, and negotiations will end once the party has accomplished their objective.

3. Where what's being offered by the other side isn't what you contemplated going into the negotiations. This is a variation of a "bait and switch" technique, where once negotiations get underway the other side offers you a deal completely different than the one you anticipated negotiating. This takes some form such as, "Item 'A' is no longer in production, but Item 'B' is a better quality substitute." Of course, the replacement is much more expensive, and may not even suit your purposes.

4. When facts come to your attention, either within the context of the negotiations, or externally, which make concluding an agreement unattractive for you. This can range from changing economic conditions, to something fundamental to the operation of a particular business.

Whatever the reason, once you determine that no purpose is served in continuing a negotiation, break off negotiations diplomatically. There's nothing to be gained by angry accusations, which, in any event, will only be denied. Of course, if the reason for ending negotiations is a business decision on your part, rather than due to the actions of the other party, give a plausible explanation as to why you don't want to go through with the deal. After all, just as circumstances change to make concluding a deal impractical, they can just as quickly shift the other way. If that happens, you want to be in a position to reopen negotiations with the other party. A friendly parting of the ways will leave that possibility in place for the future.

17.4 NEGOTIATION ALTERNATIVES: ARBITRATION AND MEDIATION

The inability to reach a negotiated agreement may be frustrating, but it pales by comparison with the problems that can arise when an attempt is made to negotiate a dispute on an existing agreement. And no matter how carefully agreements are drawn up, disputes do crop up that require resolution. When negotiations are undertaken to resolve a contract dispute, the action can get pretty hot and heavy. Moreover, if the dispute can't be resolved at the bargaining table, lawsuits may result. Even when things don't go that far, disagreements can cause irreparable harm to the business relationship.

As a result, some form of alternative dispute resolution might be the answer when two parties can't resolve their differences through the negotiation process. The two predominant alternatives are arbitration and mediation. In arbitration, the arbitrator (a third-party expert) issues a decision that is binding on both parties. By contrast, a mediator assists the parties in resolving the dispute themselves, and makes no decisions that are binding on either side.

Arbitration and mediation, not only are an alternative to a lawsuit, but they also tend to be quicker and less expensive. They also have some distinct advantages from a business perspective. First of all, they avoid the need to launder the linen in a public courtroom. Of even greater importance, they help preserve the working relationship, since they are less adversarial in nature. As a result, using either arbitration or mediation procedures are more likely to leave the business relationship intact after the dispute is resolved.

17.5 WHAT TO DO WHEN AGREEMENT CAN'T BE REACHED

Not every attempt at negotiating an agreement will end successfully. Nevertheless, that doesn't mean that the effort expended has to be a total failure. For one thing, if you manage to end a failed attempt at negotiations on a friendly note, more positive results may be achieved in future negotiations with the same party.

But beyond that possibility—no matter how remote it may be—there are lessons you can learn from failed negotiations that you can use in the future. For example, always try to learn from any mistakes you made this time around. Ask yourself if there was anything you failed to do that could have brought about a different result.

On the other hand, don't "what if" yourself to death. It's easy to sit back after the fact and second-guess yourself, which you will probably get enough of from other people anyway. The fact is that you seldom know whether or not a different approach would have worked. The best you can hope for from a self-analysis of the proceedings are better ways to be prepared for future negotiations, as well as identifying any areas in which you might need improvement.

In fact, no matter how you fare in a given negotiation, self-improvement can always help hone your negotiation skills. Therefore, it's always useful to read everything you can on the subject, as well as attend negotiation-related courses and seminars. It's also important not to neglect related areas, such as communication skills, which are extremely vital for negotiation excellence.

Above all else, don't feel you have failed because a single negotiation was unsuccessful. The fact that you avoided accepting a bad deal is a success in itself. In addition, for any number of reasons, an agreement just may not have been in the cards.

17.6 TWENTY-FIVE GENERAL RULES FOR NEGOTIATION SUCCESS

There is, of course, no "one size fits all" solution that can be applied to every negotiation. The spectrum that negotiations cover, as well as the individuality of people, render that to be impossible. In addition, every general rule has its exceptions. Keeping those qualifications in mind, the following general rules are offered as overall guidelines to assist you in the negotiation process.

1. The less you care about making a deal, the better the deal you'll be able to make.
2. Never lose control of your emotions if you want to control the negotiations.
3. Always be confident during negotiations, since people have confidence in confident people.
4. Remember that if a deal looks too good to be true, it probably is.
5. Keep in mind that a price is only too high, if the buyer thinks it's too high.
6. A home court advantage is as good as home cooking.
7. To counter negotiation tactics, you first have to recognize them.
8. Ignorance is bliss if you negotiate with more confidence than knowledge.
9. People aren't happy unless they have to work hard to get a good deal.
10. A bluff is only as good as your ability to convince someone that it's not a bluff.
11. If the other negotiator loses control of his or her emotions, mistakes may soon follow.
12. Never let the other party know that your alternatives to a negotiated agreement are weak.
13. Avoid making assumptions about anything during negotiations.
14. If you're up against a deadline, keep it to yourself.
15. Negotiations require the ability to sell—not to assail—the other side.
16. Resisting threats helps you get the deal you want—not the deal the other side wants to give you.
17. The best approach for handling ultimatums is to ignore them.
18. The credibility of your first offer can set the tone for the negotiations.

19. Don't tell the party you're negotiating with that something is non-negotiable.
20. Using odd dollar and cent amounts gives credibility to your numbers.
21. Treat every concession you make as a major one.
22. When it comes to making concessions, give ground grudgingly.
23. Anyone who shoots their mouth off in negotiation meetings, will put a bullet in their own foot.
24. Negotiation success is 80% preparation, and 20% tactics.
25. If you can live with the end result—take the deal. If not, take a walk.

Appendix

A STEP-BY-STEP NEGOTIATION CHECKLIST

INTRODUCTION

Given the differences in subject matter, formality, and complexity of each and every negotiation, the steps you have to take from start to finish will vary. Furthermore, even similar tasks will not always be done in the same sequential order. Negotiations are fluid in nature, and therefore require a large degree of flexibility as the process moves from the initial planning stage to the ultimate objective of a negotiated agreement.

Nevertheless, given the sometimes frenetic pace of the bargaining process, and the many factors that have to be considered, it can be helpful to have a representative listing of functions that have to be performed as the negotiations move from start to finish. The following checklist is a memory jogger to assist you in this regard. Many of the steps listed are common to most negotiations, but for relatively routine transactions there are items that can be ignored. Conversely, complex negotiations in specialized fields may require that you add requirements of your own that aren't covered in the list.

In terms of content, the list moves along roughly parallel to the sequence that a typical—if indeed, any negotiation can be classified as typical—business negotiation will take. In addition to routine tasks, the list also includes considerations that may have to be addressed based on the strategy that your negotiating counterpart employs. Finally, the checklist is designed to be complete without being overwhelming, and concise without being shallow.

NEGOTIATION PLANNING STAGE

1. Formulate your negotiation objective. Are the requirements of the subject matter of the negotiation clearly established?
2. Determine your alternatives if negotiations are unsuccessful.
3. Identify any alternative approaches that can be offered during negotiations if agreement can't be reached on the primary objective of the negotiation.
4. Assess the other side's alternatives if agreement isn't reached.
5. Establish maximum and minimum negotiation positions. The first is the best deal you can hope to get, while the latter is the minimum you will accept.
6. Pinpoint your tentative negotiation strategy. What tactics will you use to achieve your goals?
7. Decide what aspects of your negotiation position are non-negotiable.
8. Assess the long-term potential of any agreement. Are there prospects for follow-on work, or is this essentially a one-shot deal?
9. Prioritize any concessions you will make to reach agreement.
10. Decide if options and/or performance incentives are to be used.
11. Prepare any written proposals that may be required.
12. Consider timing in terms of when and whether to negotiate.
13. Organize your negotiation team.
14. Appoint a negotiation team leader, if you aren't handling that function yourself, and assign responsibilities of team members.
15. Determine which negotiation team members will participate in negotiation sessions, and brief them on their functions.
16. Start a negotiation file and update it throughout the negotiation process.
17. Prepare a negotiation meeting agenda in conjunction with your negotiation team.
18. Assess the negotiation strengths, weaknesses, and business reputation of the party you will be negotiating with.
19. Evaluate any written proposals that may have been received from any party or parties you plan to negotiate with.
20. Secure the services of any outside experts you will use.
21. Be sure you have the necessary documentation and/or experts to support your negotiation position.

22. Pinpoint arguments to support your price and/or other aspects of your negotiation position.

23. Decide what your first offer will be.

24. Build-in flexibility to revise your offer if it becomes necessary to do so.

25. Determine whether negotiations should be held at home, your opponent's location, or a neutral site.

26. Contact your negotiating counterpart and establish a date and time for negotiations to begin, as well as agreement on where they will be held.

27. Make all necessary travel arrangements if negotiations will be held out-of-town.

CONDUCTING NEGOTIATIONS

28. Before the first negotiation session starts, go over the logistics of the negotiation site.

29. At the beginning of negotiations, determine the negotiation authority of your counterpart.

30. Identify any behind-the-scenes decision makers.

31. Assess your counterpart's negotiating style.

32. During the negotiations determine if your opponent is using any of the following tactics, and if so, take action to counter them.

_____ Attempts to stonewall.

_____ Has a take-it-or-leave-it attitude.

_____ Wants to split the difference between the positions.

_____ Tries to make piece-by-piece concessions.

_____ Makes a total package offer.

_____ Employs position of strength techniques.

_____ Uses a good cop/bad cop ploy.

_____ Adopts surprise tactics.

_____ Uses hardball tactics in an attempt to intimidate you.

_____ Tries a "pity me" approach.

_____ Attempts to bluff.

_____ Offers mirage concessions.

_____ Adopts stalling tactics.

_____ Undertakes divide and conquer tactics.

_____ Is evasive.

_____ Makes moving target offers.

_____ Disrupts the negotiations with interruptions.

_____ Tries to use power plays.

33. Maintain control of your emotions under all circumstances.

34. Steer the negotiations toward the issues you want to talk about.

35. Clearly communicate your position.

36. Make sure you fully understand the position the other side is advocating.

37. Call a recess, or use some other form of interruption, if you need to reassess your position.

38. Strive to make progress in closing the gap in the respective positions.

39. Make any necessary adjustments in your original negotiation objective based on information that comes to light during the negotiations.

CLOSING THE DEAL

40. Attempt to bring the negotiations to a close at the proper moment.

41. If necessary, explore the use of trade-offs, or some other alternative solution to the problem.

42. Decide when you should make your final concession and/or offer.

43. Consider if you should circumvent the negotiator and get higher levels involved in an attempt to reach agreement.

44. Decide if the passage of time can be used as leverage to complete the deal. If not, think about imposing a deadline for acceptance of your offer.

45. Counter any opposition to the deal on your side of the fence.

46. Recap the agreed upon terms with the other negotiator.

47. Offer to write up the agreement.

48. Secure necessary legal and administrative reviews.

49. Enact follow-up procedures where necessary to ensure that the agreement is being performed as negotiated.

50. Leave the door open for the other side to contact you if an agreement can't be reached.

51. Be prepared to take the initiative to reopen negotiations if it makes sense to do so.

52. Prepare to move on to another alternative if agreement can't be reached.

INDEX

Q

R

S